YOUR HOME OFFICE

YOUR HOME OFFICE

Norman Schreiber

Harper & Row, Publishers, New York
Grand Rapids, Philadelphia, St. Louis, San Francisco
London, Singapore, Sydney, Tokyo, Toronto

FIRST EDITION

Designed by Janet Tingey

Library of Congress Cataloging-in-Publication Data
Schreiber, Norman.
  Your home office / Norman Schreiber.—1st Perennial Library ed.
    p. cm.
  ISBN 0-06-096427-8
  1. Home-based businesses—Equipment and supplies. 2. Office practice. I. Title.
HD2333.S35 1990
658'.041—dc20   89-46114

90 91 92 93 94 CG/MPC 10 9 8 7 6 5 4 3 2 1

How do I discipline myself?
How can I become motivated?

To my parents,
Ben and Emily Schreiber

CONTENTS

FOREWORD

People might tell you that the home office is a trend, a fad, a revolutionary phase, and, if they're really drunk, a paradigm for small-business enterprise. Let me tell you the truth. It's fun. It's a hoot. It's a totally addictive life-style.

You get to do the two things you do best: First, there's whatever occupation you were born to do. Then, there's the strategic knack of just being yourself. In a home office, you can attend to those two challenges all by your lonesome.

When I began working on this book, I thought I knew why I was writing it. I even had talk-show-caliber answers for the friend who asked, "Why do you want to write a book about paper clips?"

Then, my research put me in touch with people all over the country who worked at home. Regardless of professions, social standings, cultural backgrounds, and aspirations they seemed to radiate a similar type of self-respect. They sounded like free people. This revealed the true motive lurking deep in my mind. I wanted to celebrate and maybe even instigate a little freedom.

And perhaps there's another reason why this book now exists. In the course of my interviewing I would explain how the book was going to work so the interviewees would know how their knowledge might fit in. Many people with whom I spoke said the same thing: "I think I could use a book like that."

My response never varied: "So can I."

My second incentive was to learn more about how to do better in this life I love. Consequently, I blush to say, this is not a "do as I do" book. Rather, it is a "do as I've learned" book.

*   *   *

I adhere to simple guidelines. You already do or plan to do business at home. Naturally, you want ideas about how to set up or improve your existing home office. (I know I do.) We don't set up for the purpose of having an office. We set up so that we can carry out the various tasks of business. The book is divided into the different functions of a business (e.g., mail-handling, marketing, computers).

This setup is not just a neat way of making categories. Often people who are very good and smart at what they do set up a home office and discover a nasty little secret. They have to learn stuff about things that they've never bothered with before. It may take you three days to learn that you'll have to make coffee, and three weeks to learn that if you want pens you'll have to order them yourself. But how long can you wait to learn about marketing or good record-keeping systems or better ways to communicate or . . .

No doubt, some sections will be of immediate interest. Some may be perennial faves. Some even could be incredibly boring—that is, until you desperately need to know something about the topic being covered.

Let me pass on specific thoughts about the computer chapter (Chapter 6: Management Information Services). I feel you will be helped by the somewhat unorthodox views and friendly information presented. If you do have a computer, you probably can skip all that stuff about what to really know when you buy one. (You don't have to think about the fact that I worked extra hard on this section and probably risked my health. I'll be all right.) I think you'll be interested in the array of products and software I have included.

Also, Apple Computer advocates probably will complain that I've skimped on coverage of their favorite machines. Most of what is said in that chapter is applicable to both the Macintosh and IBM-compatible worlds. But I am guilty of practicing a subtle form of DOSism. When I talk about specific products, mostly software, you can assume I'm referring to MS-DOS versions. I don't indicate whether there's a Mac version. And I don't include any software that's exclusively for the Macintosh. This attitude made it easier for me to convey the ideas that most interested me.

In addition to all the ''how-to'' information in the various chapters, I've included:

• *Resources*—names and addresses of businesses and organizations you can learn and buy from; books with solid information that help you further explore strategies; videotapes that show you how; and audiotapes that tell you how.

• *Products*—a selection of about 150 useful items (e.g., file folders, business machines, fax paper, furniture) that help us do our jobs better and more effectively. You won't need, want, or have room for everything described in *Your Home Office*. Not all products were selected through the process of personal experience. I consulted reviews and other home officers, and I also scrutinized sales literature. I suggest you view these listings as a representation of what's available, as well as a guide to help you make decisions.

Whenever possible, I've included a price and a contact address and/or telephone number. The cited prices are intended only as a guide. Regardless of what manufacturers might suggest, dealers are free to charge what they will. Also it is likely that prices have changed since the writing of this book.

I include the contact information so that you can, if you like, have a chance to learn more about the product and company and also find out if a dealer is near you. Unless specifically indicated, there is no mail or phone order information. Manufacturers prefer that you buy from retailers. It makes for smoother relationships in their lives.

It is my hope that *Your Home Office* provides tips, strategies, and even some useful information about the various aspects of running a business at home. The material herein is presented as options and opportunities for you to pick through and consider. Everybody line up—it's mind-jogging time.

ACKNOWLEDGMENTS

I thank all the people who in their very special ways made the writing of this book possible. First of all I must thank the hundreds of people whom I interviewed and with whom I corresponded. Their gracious sharing of experience and expertise has contributed greatly to whatever value this book may have. A thank-you to Simon DeGroot and the National Office Products Association for making my task easier. I am very grateful to HeadStart for lending me a HeadStart computer so that I could better explain MS-DOS computers and software. I thank my editors, Hugh Van Dusen and Lisa Miles, who treated me and the project with respect. On a personal level, I thank my wife Jane and my son Jason; the rest of my family—parents, Ben and Emily; brothers, Alan Schreiber and David Elrich; sisters, Marge Schreiber and Maureen Sullivan; extended family—Tom Atkins, Myron Berger, Robert and Emily Brenner, Grady Jefferson, Debbi Kempton-Smith, Phillip and Edith Leonian, Barry Lopez, Eugene McDaniels, Robert and Dian Rattner, Lisa Rosenthal, Mila Rosenthal, Dani Roth, Margaret Stix and Glenn von Nostitz, Witold and Elaine Urbanowicz; and my teachers—Harry Wedeck, Samson Raphaelson, Wendell K. Phillips, Ray Toepfer, and Everett Meyers.

Your Home Office is intended to be a book of ideas, suggestions, and possibilities that might be of help to the reader. The author and the publisher are not engaged in rendering legal, accounting, or other professional advice. Because of the general nature of the information contained herein, the author and publisher remind you that the book in no way is intended to be a substitute for the individualized advice the reader might receive from a qualified professional. The reader is encouraged to seek the services of a qualified professional for such advice as it applies to each reader's individual circumstances.

TRADEMARKS

It is customary for manufacturers and other businesses to register as trademarks brand names (e.g., Rolodex), product names (e.g., Framed), and certain coined phrases (e.g., Conversational Soft Sell). The sheer volume of products and businesses noted in this book makes it cumbersome to note individual trademarks. However, the absence of such designation should not be regarded as affecting the legal status of any trademark or tradename.

CHAPTER 1

Welcome to the Home Office

By opening this book, you have demonstrated that you really care about your future and the quality of your life. You already have or are seriously thinking about creating a home office.

People who display the drive to work at home shimmer with other wonderful characteristics: independence, creativity, panache. Some people have home offices because they run businesses from home. There are both full-time and part-time home-based businesses. Some people are card-carrying employees who have learned the key to doing their jobs best. Get away from the company office and spend some time in your own home office. Then there are the telecommuters. They too are salaried, but they do all their work at home, thanks to a computer and telephone.

Probably we now are talking about home offices because of changes bubbling through American life. All sorts of statistics, some of them even accurate, support the finding that Americans have a profoundly different view of the role work plays in their lives than they did twenty-five years ago.

We want our work to mean something. We want it to be personally rewarding. We want our work to be part of our lives. We want it to be good for us and our families. The notion of working full- or part-time at home responds to these aspirations. And it's fun.

This might be a good time to distinguish between *home office* and *home-based business*. It's a distinction that, later on, we will willfully blur, but we should keep it in mind.

A *home-based business* is exactly what the term implies—a business that is run from the home. A *home office* is the area set aside in the home for working at one's business or managing one's affairs. A home-based businessperson may not have set up an office. Someone in a home office may be doing work for a business located elsewhere.

The experiences of textile broker Gary DePersia neatly illustrate the distinction. For the past twelve years DePersia moved his firm Aegis Associates back and forth between his home and various offices he rented. At home he worked on the kitchen table. At home he, in effect, established his office each day and disassembled his office each night. Periodically he got disenchanted and rented office space downtown.

One day, he realized there was some basement space he could use specifically for his work. He designed and built an airy, well-lit, comfortable home office. That's where he is now, and he doesn't anticipate working from downtown ever again. Gary DePersia needed a home office to make his home-based business feel right.

Wes Thomas, a public relations consultant in the high-tech area, opened his home office for the most charming of reasons—absolute necessity. "I used to have a three-thousand-square-foot office on Fifth Avenue in Manhattan, and I was paying a fortune for it," says Thomas. "I had illusions of having a big PR agency and I lost a lot of money, doing it that way. Finally I got smart and said, 'stop trying to pretend I'm a big massive agency, and let me just do what I do best.' "

One day, Wes Thomas edged a giant moving van onto Fifth Avenue, stashed the contents of his office into the vehicle, and moved everything—lock, stock, and Rolodex—into his home. It was a bit awkward at first what with the sudden infestation of cardboard cartons. But the result is just fine.

"The bottom line," says Thomas, "was that I slashed almost all of my overhead. Moreover, I discovered that I was getting an enormous amount of work done because I had flexible hours. I found myself working to three or four in the morning. If I got tired I could sleep when I wanted. I realized I was having fun. I never had fun in offices before. Now, when I walk into an office in New York I get deeply depressed for hours."

Or, look at Egil and Karen Juliussen. They run two Dallas-based businesses from their home, which happens to be in Nevada. They don't do it with mirrors. They do it with telephones and facsimile machines.

Certainly, this book wades right into home-based business issues, but the focus always is on how to enjoy and thrive in your home office. When I first started writing professionally, I worked at a typewriter on a small table in a corner of our bedroom. I didn't know it was a home office. I just thought it was an otherwise useless space. My old high-school friend Joe introduced me to the term *home office*. His explanation led me to believe that *home office* was a technical accounting term for "Hey, here's a chance for a deduction."

I guess accountants are like Californians, in terms of creating trends and buzz words. When the personal computer was taking hold in the early 1980s, people talked about their home offices openly and shamelessly. Even so, when I started tackling this subject, I found some interesting anomalies. To really research *home office* in *Books in Print,* you have to consult the topic labeled *cottage industries*. You can also check out *home-based businesses*. When I used my computer to tap into distant data bases, I found lots of interesting stuff under *home office*. Most of it had to do with the British Home Office and its immigration policies, particularly toward Pakistanis. Another good portion had to do with neat woodworking projects you can do in your spare time. There also are abundant citations about corporations (particularly those in the insurance industry) where the concept of a home office has a totally opposite meaning.

All that is starting to change. The home office—as an option for living and working—is getting into print. What demographers have noted, electronic manufacturers have adored. With home offices, there is a whole new locale for consumers to stuff things that plug in and light up and make noise. Thus, we were treated to the specter of garish stereo discount chains that lowered the decibel level of their commercials to announce their new home office centers.

Electronic products do play a useful role in the home office. Computers, copiers, and fax machines have brought the resources of grown-up business to our homes. Still, let's get our priorities straight. The home office doesn't exist so that 100,000 units of this or that electronic product can be shipped from the manufacturer to your front door. It would be a nice gesture on your part, but don't bother. The electronics manufacturers, however, should be thanked for spotlighting this trend.

The real story of the home office is that people have decided to bring fulfillment, direction, and control to their lives by working at home. The statistics supporting this fact come from all over the place. Venture Development Corporation, a market research/consulting firm, had its Electronic Home Office Planning Service do an extensive study on working at home. Venture's report estimated that 15 million people work at home full- or part-time. By 1993, Venture expects this number to reach 29 million. These numbers *do not* include the many dedicated souls who bring work home from the office.

Various commentators feel compelled to explain the home office movement, and have come up with some pretty logical reasons. The personal computer's impact has to be high on the list. For a relatively low price, individuals get the power of a full organization, embodied in a machine that fits on a desk. Of course, certain home businesses directly result from computer power. These include word processing, typesetting, mailing list vendors, and researchers. Many other businesses benefit from the number-crunching, list-making, and word-processing niceties of the computer.

The so-called new entrepreneurial spirit contributes to the trend. People are a little bolder these days about starting their own businesses. As long as you're going to be unemployed, why not have a card that says "consultant"? The 1980s saw the launching of many excellent, innovative businesses fueled by kitchen coffeemakers.

Similarly, parents of young children find working at home to be an attractive way to be around while their children are growing up. Previously, parents would have sighed wistfully at the notion of being home for the kids. Today, parents have seized upon the home office as the key to the quality time of their lives.

Lots of officially designated free-lance people—writers, photographers, artists—work at home. Most doctors are self-employed, although their lances are anything but free. Many of them have offices in their homes. Many therapists—for our mind, body, or pets—work at home. Architects, contractors, consultants in all sort of industries, mail-order moguls, and lawyers are among those who work at home.

It can get complicated. About ten years ago, Felice and Boyd Willat, a Los Angeles couple, created a loose-leaf organizer that would help busy people keep track of every aspect of their lives. Thinking it was a good idea, the Willats started designing and marketing the Day Runner from their home. Fortunately, they have a very large home. Other people—as in customers—also thought the Day Runner organizer was a good idea. The business grew.

"We had three bedrooms upstairs," recalls Felice Willat, "and that was the only living space we could call our own. But we had every other room devoted to departments. We had accounts receivable and accounts payable, and a reception area. Our garage was the art department. My office had been the den. The downstairs extra room was used as a computer room. We'd have our conferences in the backyard. It would get dark and cold but there was no other place to go."

Actually two houses were on the property, and both were stuffed with departments and working people. At one point, the Willats had sixty-five people working in their home office. Inevitably Day Runners moved to a downtown office. It wasn't staff size that inspired this rendezvous with the moving van. It was another reality. In addition to their sizable home office, they also had manufacturing and warehousing facilities, each of which was in a separate location.

"We realized," says Felice Willat, "that it would be interesting if we had everything under one roof." The Willats do not plan to move the business back to their house. They like the separation between home and work. Perhaps the specter of sixty-five people busy-beeing away in one's castle is a bit daunting. Still, Felice Willat places great value on the years in which Day Runner was run from home. "This company would not be what it is today," she says, "if we had not started out in our home."

Can you base the business of your desires at home? Probably. Coralee Smith Kern of the National Association of the Cottage Industry has compiled a list of more than 125 professions pursued by people working from their homes. It ranges from accessories manufacturer to writer. The list's last four words are "and so many more."

The home-based business fits into the category of small business. The motivation of those who want to do it at home differs markedly from the rest of small business, according to Leone Johnson, a Venture Development market analyst. "For the people who want to work at home," says Johnson, "there is a desire to be involved in one's family. There is a noncomformist life-style. There is a desire to stay away from office politics and dress codes. There is a real rationale besides starting your own business and being successful. There is a philosophy about running your own life."

Not everybody who works at home is self-employed. Many folks discovered that to ply their trade as staffers, they needed to bring work home. Their next step was to create an environment at home in which they could vice-president away to their heart's delight.

Of course, most people do not start working at home because they have read the tea leaves and want to be part of the next trend. More likely, people shrewdly appreciate the very obvious attractions of a home office. The rent is cheap, the commute is a breeze, the hours are flexible, and there's a minimum of sexual harassment in the office.

Hugh, an editor at a major publishing firm, works at home one day a week. "I have an office at home," he says, "with a phone on my desk; but, you know, people are reluctant to call me there. I get a lot of work done."

Mark, a traveling salesman for a small educational textbook firm, had a squash racquet under his arm as he stepped out of our apartment building. No, he wasn't on vacation. "I convinced my company," says Mark, "that when I returned from my territory it wasn't necessary for me to go to the company's offices in Connecticut every day. All I needed was a phone and a computer and I could take care of everything that had to be done. I save four hours of commuting time every day, and I have time for my family and this." He swung his racquet. It wasn't long before Mark started his own company.

Fred, a public relations counselor, says, "It took me a while to get used to working in my home. First, there was guilt—the feeling I had to work every day. After a year, I decided I could take weekends off. Six months later, I realized I could take an occasional afternoon off with the knowledge that I could make up any work that I happened to miss. It got to be more fun and I got to see my daughters grow up."

Working in your own home office is a way to reclaim, or at the very least enjoy, your personal identity. Not everyone is at home in a home office. The good thing about a home office is that there's no one there telling you what to do. The bad thing, of course, is that there's no one there telling you what to do.

The words *discipline* and *structure* get bandied about a lot among those who are considering a home office. These concerns are both real and phony. Sure, you should work in some kind of a structure. The discipline and structure come from how you work and what your business needs—not from how your old boss did things. When you work at home, you are not a cog; you are the machine. Machines do not need the same structures that cogs do.

For some, working at home is an enduring life-style. Others find it a wonderfully helpful booster rocket that sends them on their paths.

Angelo Valenti is a consultant who advises small and medium-size businesses on the intricacies of excelling, expanding, and even making money. He began his business in his Brooklyn home in 1980.

"My appointments were in Manhattan," explains Angelo. "I was getting two or three appointments scattered through the day. For six months the way I handled it was by knowing where all the great telephone booths in the city were. For example, the Algonquin Hotel has phone booths where you can sit down."

Valenti would often find himself, between appointments, spending an hour or so in a phone booth making calls and catching up on paperwork. "It got to be a little crazy," said Valenti. He decided to rent office space in Manhattan so that he could call on his clients and prospects more easily, and they would find his office convenient to visit.

*   *   *

I'm assuming that the people curious enough to own this book fall into one of two categories. There are those who already have a home office and are looking for ideas that might give them an edge. Then, there are those who contemplate setting up a home office. I feel there's plenty of useful information for both. Not only will I provide some good ideas about setting up a home office, but I will provide lots of ideas about how to make the office work for you so that you can enjoy your work and your life.

A simple notion will take us through the book: If you have a home office, then you are a home officer. You are the king of the castle, the captain of the ship, the chief executive officer of your office.

The entire real estate of your concern may not take up more space than half a desktop. No matter. You are the home officer. All departments report to you. You have a switchboard and a mailroom and accounting, computer, marketing, and other departments. In the following pages you will encounter good strategies to make all these departments work for you rather than against you.

Congratulations again, because you're on your way.

CHAPTER 2

The Telecommuting Option

Telecommuting is the system by which an individual, although a fully salaried employee of a company, works at home full or part-time. *Tele* pays respect to today's telecommunications marvels, which often make it feel as if the main office is just down the hall from the home office.

Telecommuting seems, for some, to be the best of all possible worlds. You get a salary and benefits and yet you work at home. I personally don't like the part where you accomplish this by being an employee. Still, it has its advantages. If you want this brand of employment, how can you achieve it?

Two people who have excellent perspectives on telecommuting are Beverly Campbell and Gil Gordon. On May 10, 1989, you could hear the sound of necks snapping as home office hotshots turned to look at California. It just had been announced that the Los Angeles County government was going to start a telecommuting program. Beverly Campbell, chief of the Policy and Support Division in the Chief Administrative Office, was in charge.

Gil Gordon, through his firm Gil Gordon Associates, consults to corporations that wish to set up some sort of telecommuting program. His business is structured so that he does not advise individuals who seek to telecommute. Still Gordon has provided us with some useful information, starting with the arguments that could persuade an employer to use you to telecommute.

"Put yourself in your employer's shoes," says Gil Gordon. "Sell it to them from the perspective of what's good for the company."

Los Angeles County was sold on the idea by an article that appeared in *Personnel* magazine in October 1988. The legislation was proposed in January 1989. Then came that press conference in May. Campbell and company were cooking. In June, the first telecommuter clocked in. She works for the tax department. (Why am I not surprised?) By the end of the year several hundred Los Angeles County government workers were telecommuting.

"I've asked people," says Campbell, "to not just look at what the job is now but at what the mission of the department is, and how the job can be structured so that telecommuting can assist in getting the job done. That's what the Probation Department is doing.

"It has a crying need for space. We don't have enough room to house all the probation officers that we need. We have a backlog in producing adult court reports. Right now the deputy probation officer produces the report and it's transcribed by a transcription service or by employees that can do that sort of work.

"They're looking at having these reports restructured so that a tele- commuting deputy probation officer can enter the information directly, produce the report, and also eliminate the need for transcription ser- vice. They can hire additional probation officers, plus the reports will be more timely."

Los Angeles County has discovered that space-sharing and produc- tivity are two powerful arguments for telecommuting. However, em- ployers may yawn when your arguments use terms such as *personal growth* and *children's emotional development.* How does not seeing your face make the company work better?

Gil Gordon says there are a number of questions for you to think about. For example, can telecommuting make you more productive? Will it let you continue as an employee instead of resigning if you can't get this option? Perhaps the company is short of office space. If you telecommute would that give Charlie or Mary the chance to use your office three days a week instead of using the conference room?

If you want to be considered as a likely telecommuting candidate, make sure your performance at the salt mine is above reproach. Eval- uate yourself before you even talk to the boss. Identify those areas where you need improvement. Raise your level before you raise the subject. Also measure your supervisor. You'll fail if the boss is less than enthralled with the idea.

"Frankly, we do get a lot of resistance from supervisors and man- agers," says Beverly Campbell. "Some feel that they can't supervise someone that they don't see. They have to be people who evaluate work based on the timeliness, quantity, and quality of the work and the cost it takes to produce the work. That's opposed to things that are easy to supervise. Did the employees get there on time? Did they leave on time? Were they absent today?"

Campbell says supervisors who follow the latter approach tend to be wrong for a telecommuting project. When you get the go-ahead, be sure to first stand pat. Planning is necessary before making another move.

"Analyze the way the job is done in the office," says Gordon, "and where all the pieces fit in. Then, make an appropriate schedule. Look at the timing, the sequencing of days. You may be a person whose schedule allows you to be home three days a week. Because of the need to attend meetings, pick up mail, drop off finished work, whatever, those days may have to be Monday, Wednesday, and Friday, as opposed to Tuesday, Wednesday, and Thursday."

If your job demands that you be very accessible to the public, as well as to other departments of your company, it may be wise to telecommute only one day a week. If you're really what Gordon calls a "heads-down worker," you may enjoy a four-days-at-home schedule every week. An insider at one computer software company says to "beware of the out-of-sight, out-of-mind syndrome." Telecommuters in her company were always the first to be laid off. It turned out they never came into the office because they lived a few states away from it.

Getting your phone calls requires some planning. A call-forwarding arrangement at the office is one solution. The company directory can include your home office number and the days when it should be used.

Set up a file at home of basic reference material that you use most during the day. Create what Gordon calls a "telecommuter agreement." It's a document that defines and clarifies all the specifics of the working arrangement.

"We have an agreement," says Campbell, "that's worked out with the department and the employees. It spells out core hours they're expected to work and be available, what equipment is to be used and who purchases it, what we do about the telephone lines, and an overview of what the project is. It sets forth the tasks, duties, or responsibilities and that the arrangement can be terminated at the request of the employee or at the discretion of the department. It spells out that their work hours, overtime, and vacation and other benefits will be as it is already in our county code. We don't change compensation for telecommuting people.

"The agreement specifies that the department can look at the employee's work site. That's basically to make sure that it's safe and appropriate. We do consider the home environment to be an extension of the work site. Therefore, in their county work space at home they're covered by workers' compensation. It states that the employee has to be willing to participate in surveys and evaluations of the program. We are going to do a rather formal evaluation of how it is working.''

''Be willing to start slow,'' says Gordon, ''and remain patient. Try to strike a deal where you work at home for one day a week for the first month or two. Just work at that low level so that everybody can become comfortable and see that the whole place isn't going to pot just because you work at home.''

Once you telecommute, you have a number of responsibilities to yourself and to your company. First, you have to be honest with yourself. After immersing yourself in telecommuting, you may discover that you and it are not meant for each other. According to Gordon, this period is where telecommuters might discover if ''they are self-motivated; they can work away from the office several days a week without the social hub-bub of the office; they are compulsive snackers; they are soap opera junkies'' among other such truths.

''We want to emphasize,'' says Campbell, ''that this is a management tool. There are lots of benefits for employees, but that's not why we're doing it.''

CHAPTER 3

The Reality of Working at Home

Now that we've contemplated the joy, the philosophical superiority and the utter inevitability of working at home, let's get real. This life has its own set of problems, otherwise I guess fewer people would do it. You can solve some problems, wait for others to go away, ignore a few, and adjust to a few.

The business problems are the easiest to consider. You either beat them or you die. All of these can be conquered. Second, if you live with other people, harmony and the ties that bind may need the intensive care unit. Also, there's the outside world: friends, neighbors, and acquaintances who don't understand what you do and can conspire against you by making demands on your time.

Then, there are the little hotfoots we give ourselves—habits, such as procrastination, that thwart productivity. These are the worst. We know our secrets. We know our rationalizations. We know our scripts. No wonder we have so much disdain for our games. Self-contempt notwithstanding, we can put out these fires. We also know our strengths and we get to experience our achievements every month, every week, every day. In a sense, we're fighting fire with fire. Our allies are the flames of passion, commitment, ability, and maybe even some dumb luck.

BUSINESS BUMMERS

Zoning regulations have done more for indigestion than this year's crop of chili peppers. Quite frankly, when I started working on this book, I thought of zoning as some silly abstraction. I didn't understand why people I respected spent so much time talking about it. I thought they were paying lip service to boring regulations that don't really matter.

I was wrong.

It is the very bureaucratic vanilla of zoning rules that makes them so terrible when they strike. The ordinances declare what kind of activities and buildings are allowed in which neighborhoods and districts that come under the local government's jurisdiction. They also can stipulate under what circumstances and restrictions commercial activity can take place.

Zoning regulations sometimes bar the very presence of a business. Otherwise, they might limit the physical space, or the number of employees, or the type of vehicles that can go to and fro. For example, I heard of a New Jersey dentist who can have only one assistant because local zoning regulations forbid more than one employee in commercial enterprises in the community. This restriction limits the growth of his practice.

Zoning laws are real. They are designed to protect community flavor, not to mention sight and smell. Some residential neighborhoods get irritated by such little details as sudden truck convoys, the presence of noxious chemicals, the clatter of machinery, and the appearance of garish signs.

A letter published in the *New York Times* real estate advice department, "Q & A," complained about an entrepreneurial neighbor in a section made up of one-family houses. "Two and sometimes three vans are parked along the curb," says the letter writer. "The apron to the garage is frequently stacked with pipes and lumber, and both side gardens are filled with construction material." Apparently, the source of this consternation ignored pleas to reform.

The *Times* replied by saying that the less-than-cooperative contractor probably was in violation of zoning rules and published the city's Buildings Department's phone number for complaints.

It would be wise to be mindful of the zoning regulations, even if you're in the type of business that does not call attention to itself. Before asking local government what the rules are, check with your lawyer and accountant. They're in a good position to know the facts. Someone at the local chamber of commerce also might give you the facts.

Once you possess the facts, you can decide if zoning regulations will interfere with your business. Ask yourself these questions:

1. Do the current zoning regulations apply to your business?
2. If so, can you still do business the way you want to?
3. Do zoning restrictions affect your ability to make your business grow?

4. Can you modify your business to conform to the zoning rules?
5. If you can make the necessary alterations, would the resulting business structure be worthwhile and fun?

What do you do if the regulations are against you? I certainly wouldn't advise you to do anything illegal. As best as I can see, there are two reasons why the zoning cops will come knock-knock-knocking at your door. First, an irate neighbor might complain to the authorities after tiring of some quality-of-life blemish (the three old vans in your driveway and construction material on your lawn story).

Second, the act of applying for local licenses or permits can call attention to your code violation. It can be a rude shock if you're told that you can't do business in your home. You might be told that you can, but that there will be additional fees and taxes each year. You can hope that the ordinances are old and will be overlooked. Indeed, your lawyer or accountant is in the best position to know the local enforcement culture. I would suggest that compliance not only is your civic responsibility but also is a good strategy.

As we stagger through the 1990s, we are privileged to witness financial crunchitis at every level of government. Local governments, in search of revenue, are doing everything but clawing through garbage cans in search of deposit bottles. What better way to raise money than with laws already on the books. Some people feel they are in compliance with the spirit of the regulations if they rent a post office box and list it as their business address.

Depending on your business, it might be possible to get a variance, which is something like a dispensation. The difficulty and cost vary from community to community. You certainly can make a case if you are not the scourge from which the community must be protected.

In their book, *Working from Home* (Jeremy Tarcher, 1985), Paul and Sarah Edwards describe possible reasons that a variance might be permitted. Your request might be accepted if you can show that what you are doing is comparable to an occupation that is acceptable. (Different communities have different notions about which professions may be practiced at home.) Also, you might be able to gain approval by demonstrating a definite hardship if you are forced to forego your business. It could help to show that closing you down would be a blow to the community. This argument requires community support.

It should be noted that these reasons are offered as possibly acceptable ones. In no way are the Edwardses trying to predict what a zoning board finds acceptable or unacceptable. They suggest that you attend zoning hearings to see how they work and how your planning boards think.

The Edwardses also say that "regardless of how well prepared you are, it's wise to consult an attorney." And they are right! Again, your lawyer might know if your wonderfully reasoned arguments would make any difference in the case.

Some people believe in lobbying for new legislation that repeals anachronistic zoning regulations. If you're just starting your business, you may not have time to carry placards, round up petition signatures, write to your local elected and appointed officials, and scream slogans through a bullhorn. If your business is established, you still may not have the time, but you may have no choice. The alternative may be the dismantling of your business, at least at the present location.

Home officers also face the specter of not being taken seriously because they do not work in a "real" office. How do you purge customers and potential customers of this bias? Two different solutions have provided fairly reliable results. One school holds that deceit works wonders.

Adherents reason that if your clients never tiptoe across your doorstep, then they don't know your dirty secret of independence and they don't have to know. They freely can imagine the decor in your suite of offices. They can imagine what magazines sit in your reception area. They can speculate on the placement of pastel panels that separate one cubbied worker from another. People use several tactics to reinforce this illusion.

Most important, they don't spill the beans. They always say "my office" instead of "my room." They conjure mythical beings and assign them important tasks so that customers are likely to receive letters from the "office manager" and the "accounts receivable bookkeeper."

Their letterheads and other business forms are impressive and expensive. Their business cards announce a "direct line" instead of simply a phone number. Instead of using a phone answering machine or service, they use a voice mail service, which requires the touching of tones by the caller and suggests a corporation with an up-to-date phone system. Everything they do hints at a rich resource system.

I find it all a bit silly. On the other hand, I respect the fact that people know their own industries. Often sharp insights into the marketplace mind-set inspire such camouflage.

The other approach to being taken seriously is to let it all hang out, but *be professional.*

PROFESSIONALISM

Textile broker Gary DePersia finds that his use of his Sharp computer and Sharp fax machine conveys a sophisticated professionalism. He makes sure that his clients and contacts know he's been at his desk since 8:30 A.M. This tends to dispel the "did I wake you" queries he used to receive at 10:30 A.M.

Symbols enable others to perceive our professionalism. Gary De-Persia uses electronic equipment associated with a *gen-u-ine* office, and therefore he's real to other textile brokers.

A letterhead suggests you are serious and have been around for a while. The manner in which you market yourself is important. When a prospect wants more information, do you have something (a brochure, a catalog sheet, an order form, a background report) ready to go? Is it attractive? How well do you follow up? Do you do enough of those things that suggest the kind of consistent quality performance that characterizes professionalism?

Let your customers see your life-style as an advantage for them. Their money does not go into supporting your overhead. It allows you to give them the quality and care they deserve. They should delight in knowing that the 5:00 bell tolls not for thee.

William Bradford Ross, Jr., of Chevy Chase, Maryland, finds an extra marketing edge in working at home. Ross is in real estate and helps people find capital. "We live in a lovely house," says Ross, "and I use it as strategy. I stress the idea that working at home denotes success."

Judith Lederman, a Dobbs Ferry, New York, public relations and advertising counselor, discovered that her clients appreciate her commitment to both family and business. "A lot of people I deal with are family people themselves," says Lederman. "While they're not working at home, they understand what it's like to have a family. If anything I get support. They're very supportive if they hear Jason in the background."

While accentuating the positive, keep the negativism at bay. Never use your family or home circumstances as an explanation for goofing up, even if it's the truth. My wife owns and operates a wonderful store, The Scouting Party, in the Park Slope section of Brooklyn. One day she called a supplier to ascertain the whereabouts of a long-overdue shipment of holiday-related items. Jane was treated to a medical report about the terrible flu that afflicted her vendor's baby.

Jane is the last person in the world to put the opportunity to sell a few things over the health of a child. She just wishes that somebody had made a two-minute phone call to let her know about the delay. She then could have exercised some options in preparing for holiday sales. Failure to fulfill is unprofessional. Ample warning that "fulfillment is not possible at this time" is customer service. Family mishaps and woes should never be cited as reasons for business obstacles, especially when family and business share the same address.

A phone with a "hold" button does a lot to mute the aura of nonprofessionalism. Sometimes unavoidable or unexpected distractions crash into your office while you're on the phone. A discreet "excuse me a moment" and a genteel depression of the hold button leaves the party at the other end in the blissful dark. It's crisp, businesslike, and you can yell at your kids all you want.

Another business problem that hits home but really is endemic to all small businesses is good old cash flow—more specifically, the collection of moneys that you are owed. For example, a major client might be a major corporation that prefers to roll around heaven all day to paying lowly but deserving vendors. I mention this here because it's a real problem; but we deal with it later on in Chapter 13, "Debt and Taxes."

FAMILY ADJUSTMENTS

When you put an office in your home, you alter the fragile ecostructure, which can disrupt the local inhabitants, namely the people with whom you share your home. A home office can be compared to a sudden, lengthy visit by Great Aunt Matilda. Everything can go topsy turvy.

After baseball executive George Weiss retired, his wife was quoted as saying, "I married him for better or worse, but not for lunch."

"I think you need to sit down with the people you live with," says small business consultant Angelo Valenti, "and talk about what it really means to have a business in one's home. You may be taking people's physical space away. When you once were available, you no longer may be available. It helps to work together to manage this thing called change."

Then there's the question of children. Dr. Joan Kinlan of Washington, D.C., is a child psychiatrist who has a small practice in her home and a set of (at the time of this writing) two-and-a-half-year-old twins. When Dr. Kinlan works in her downstairs office, a babysitter is upstairs with the children.

"When I'm with a patient," says Dr. Kinlan, "and I hear my children crying, I want to run upstairs to their room. If they're crying hard, I do.'' Dr. Kinlan has learned that when she leaves a session to attend to her children, her patients do not resent the interruption. They are distressed by the crying also, and glad that the problem is being handled. Moreover, she finds, they are comforted by seeing that Dr. Kinlan is a caring person.

Apparently being a child psychiatrist with children provides an edge. While waiting for their sessions, her patients may see her children playing on the patio and go outside and join the fun. Dr. Kinlan finds that it's a good experience for her patients and her children.

There are downsides that might be peculiar to the psychiatric profession. Dr. Kinlan tells of a colleague's four-year-old daughter who had had it with these people coming to her house and stealing her mother's attention. When one patient showed up, the little girl looked her in the eye and said, ''My mommy can't see you today. She's sick.'' ''Oh,'' said the patient, and left.

Dr. Kinlan finds that sometimes her children play with toys in the office playroom, which is fine except that sometimes they take the toys up to their room. ''This can be a problem when the patient comes back ready to continue fantasy play, and the toy isn't there,'' says Dr. Kinlan. Dr. Kinlan frequently makes a sweep of her children's room to ferret out office toys and restore them to their rightful place.

Dr. Kinlan's approach is creative and knowledgeable, and based on personal circumstances, not least of which is the age of her children.

What do you do when the children you stayed home to be near actually want your attention?

''The child must understand,'' says Dr. Louise Bates Ames, associate director of the Gessell Institute of New Haven, Connecticut, ''that just because you're there, he or she can't run in and ask for things and expect your attention.''

According to Dr. Ames, children need to know that you can't stop working and attend to a crisis, unless what's going on really is a crisis. She emphasizes that the child's ability to judge the situation depends on his or her age and level of development.

Agreeing with this point, Dr. Alex Weintrob, a New York City child psychiatrist, noted that one should look at the child's tolerance of separation, style, temperament, sophistication, tolerance of frustration, ability to delay gratification, level of intensity, and ability to be distracted. For example, if the child is not easy to distract with activities that do not require your constant involvement, it is not fair to this child to receive only limited attention.

''The more language a child has,'' says Dr. Weintrob, ''the more the child is able to understand. You can explain the similarities and differences between working at home and working outside home. You can say, 'I can spend some time with you now, and I will go back to work.' There still can be some frustration because you are 'leaving'; but the upset child knows you are there and may not feel abandoned.''

Dr. Ames says that children who are six and under generally cannot be expected to decide whether or not they should interrupt you. Some sort of supervision by you or another adult is required. Again the level of supervision varies, according to the child's development.

"A four- or five-year-old child might be watching television, or coloring, or working with a puzzle quite comfortably," says Dr. Ames, "and the person looking in on them can be doing housework or some other thing.''

The hardest lot befalls a parent of a child who is three or younger. Children in this age group need active attention from one or both parents. Parents (usually mothers) who feel that they can handle the needs of an infant and a home business experience a rude shock, not to mention serious exhaustion. This problem can be eased to the extent that one can rely on a babysitter or caregiver. When resources are such that you are on your own, possibilities are severely limited.

"You've got to plan your work to take place during their naptimes and after they've gone to bed," says Dr. Ames. "You can't do it before they get up, because they get up so very early.''

Dr. Ames points out that balancing child care and a home-based business involves more than the infant and the parent. It relies on everybody in the household. "There's got to be a schedule," she says, "and everybody's got to respect it, and you've got to respect your own schedule.''

Let's not pin the rap of Grand Theft: Time on children alone.

"People who live in your building," notes one Manhattan author, "who go out to other places to do their work never quite accept the fact that you are running a business. They seem to feel that you are a convenient package-acceptance service among other things.''

A Los Angeles consultant knows the feeling. "My friends and associates often don't take my schedule seriously," she says. "For example, they expect me to drive forty-five minutes to meet them for lunch, or they want to talk long on the phone.''

The essential problem is that friends and relatives see you in a situation they associate with rampant sloth and therefore devise trespasses upon your time. Either their behavior or yours gets modified. At stake is not a game of dueling calendars but the survival of your business.

When intruding friends start bending your ear, get off the phone quickly. Explain that you have another call, you have an appointment, you have a deadline, or you have to go to prison in two hours and some matters need clearing up. As a courtesy, ask if there's anything you need to know before you hang up. Tell them you will call them later, in two days, over the weekend, whatever (and do it).

If you have a business line and a home line, put an answering machine on the home line especially when other household members are out. Let the machine answer that phone. It has the time and the concentration. You don't.

The basic rules to convey are that you are not there. You only seem to be there. The fact that you are at home means that you do not have spare time. You only have spare time when you are not at home.

When all else fails, you might try being unreliable. If somebody badgers you into doing something, agree to do it and then forget about it. You won't be asked again. We deplore passive-aggressive behavior, but it can get results. Those who remain your friends will understand.

INSURANCE

Another avenue for angst is the cost and availability of health insurance. Welcome to the world of hardball. If you grow faint at the thought of medical bills, imagine how insurance carriers feel. Blue Cross would rather spring for a second opinion than deal out dollars for the surgery called for in the first opinion.

In my opinion, the very best strategy would be a national health insurance plan that guarantees medical care to all citizens. Four out of five doctors say don't hold your breath. In the meantime, the next best tactic is to be married to a salaried someone whose employer has a good health plan. If you work for a company with a health insurance plan, discreetly inquire about what happens if you leave.

You may be able to continue with the plan because of a Congressional act, the Consolidated Omnibus Budget Reconciliation Act (COBRA). Basically, COBRA lets departing employees and/or dependents continue coverage in the same plan for eighteen to thirty-six months. The business must have at least twenty employees. Federal or church employees are not eligible. The company doesn't have to pay for the coverage, and in fact may add a 2 percent service charge.

"COBRA," writes Katherine Hogue, in *The Complete Guide to Health Insurance* (Walker & Co., 1988), "primarily protects the following groups: divorcees and widows and dependents of deceased, unemployed or Medicare-eligible employees." Further legislation extended its umbrella to people (and their dependents) who are retiring from companies in Chapter Eleven reorganization.

You may or may not be able to assume the policy. Even if you do, the terms are likely to be different. What should you know? There are commercial insurers and group insurers. With commercial insurers, even those offered through organizations, the numbers reflect the likelihood of your staying fit and perhaps even alive. With group insurance, rates reflect the mortality or (if you prefer) vitality characteristics displayed by a pool of people. Some group rates may be higher than some individual rates depending on the group and the individual.

Whatever you do, consider getting a major medical plan. The higher the deductible (the amount you shell out in one year for medical expenses without being reimbursed by the insurer), the lower the premium you pay. Also be leery of the "dread disease" policies and the "you cannot be refused" policies you see advertised on television. Each "dread disease" policy covers only one affliction. In the words of one health insurance industry spokesman, "If you try covering disease by disease, you'll be paying a small fortune."

The aforementioned TV-hawked policies are supplementary. They're designed to work in conjunction with another policy. They do not stand very well on their own. A number of organizations offer insurance plans. If you're thinking of joining, try to learn the health plan terms. Many groups view this information as proprietary.

Kathleen Hogue, author of *How to Beat the High Cost of Health Insurance* (Walker & Co., $24.95), feels a group plan is definitely worth exploring. "Explore group access at a chamber of commerce, a small business association in your area," says Hogue. "Sometimes these are groups of very small companies that have banded together for more clout with an insurance carrier.

"People shouldn't ignore professional, civic, or religious associations to which they belong or to which they have a right to belong. If you are a member of any profession, remember there might be a policy lurking in the background. Bnai Brith has excellent policies for their members.

"You might investigate," Kathleen Hogue continues, "depending on where you live, a county farm bureau or a state farm bureau. These organizations, at least in our area, do not really require that a person be engaged in the business of agriculture to be a member. They will accept a person for membership just on the payment of a fee."

In all groups, the nature and availability of health insurance plans may vary from region to region. Also, you may be qualified to join an organization, and you may be a member long enough to apply for health insurance. But the insurance carrier may advise you to take a walk not only because such exercise is healthy but also because your individual situation contains too great a risk.

"If you've got a child who's a diabetic," says Hogue, "or you see a counselor for depression or anxiety, they may not take you into the plan. They may exclude from benefits all payments for that existing condition anywhere from six months to forever, which is slightly different from excluding you but it has the same effect.''

In desperately seeking insurance, you'll be running down a number of leads and talking to a number of sales agents. Compare each policy. In looking at the benefits offered, think awful thoughts. At your age, and in your condition, are you more likely to face trauma by getting hit by a bus or having a heart attack? View the terms of each policy in light of this self-examination.

"If you are below the age of forty," says Kathleen Hogue, "and you are indeed in perfect health you may in fact get a better deal on the open individual market. You may be able to find a high deductible plan that has good back-end benefits but in the short run doesn't pay for very much. It would be relatively cheap, and could serve a young person in his or her twenties or thirties. Also, say you're looking for a health insurance plan for your nineteen-year-old secretary. You might pay as little around here [Cleveland] as forty dollars a month with no maternity benefits.''

Kathleen Hogue shares another useful option. Health Maintenance Organizations (HMOs) that accept federal funds are required to advertise an open enrollment period one month a year. This is probably a simplification; but during this month they have to take anyone under fifty-five, except for nursing home residents and mental hospital patients. There is a catch. Apparently, they do not use the most attention-getting advertisements. They're likely to whisper their messages in the "Legal Notices" section of the newspaper.

What if you'd like to pursue this? Hogue advises a phone call to the HMO of your choice. The conversation may go as follows:

YOU: Hello, are you having open enrollment this month?
THEM: Nah!
YOU: I see. When will you have the open enrollment period?
THEM: We haven't decided that yet.
YOU: Okeydoke. I'll call you again.

And you do. And you keep calling them until it is time.

PERSONAL PLAGUES

The most maddening plagues to rain upon home officers are those we construct ourselves. "We have met the enemy," says Pogo, "and they is us." All our fears, controls, doubts, emotional baggage, and other such marching buddies come up front and take a bow.

The need for discipline jabs at the self-image of many home officers—but in a most surprising way. For many, there's always some more work that can be done, even if it's midnight, even if it's the weekend, even if you just wanted to go out and play.

"The problem with working for yourself," says Tony Stewart of Home Office Software, "is that there's nobody there to tell you to stop. Stopping is very important to doing a good job. Take at least one day of the week completely off."

When you get back to your desk, according to Stewart, you'll notice that the world has not collapsed. You may even find that you're bringing a fresh perspective to the work.

Also, as one public relations consultant put it, "There's no psychological separation between work at home." Says Bob Beaudoin, "Last week, I went to Westchester to do a bit of cycling. It was the first time I had any appreciable distance from the office." He is the senior partner of Bull & Bear Marketing Group, New York, New York.

Beaudoin acknowledges that his feelings are complex. "I did the commute in, the next morning, with all the people in from Westchester and I thought, geez what a horrendous commute; I'm glad I don't have to do it. But by the same token I was a bit jealous because when they get on the train for the night they're probably not thinking about work so much anymore."

The solutions vary. People use time management systems, such as the Alan Lakein method. A major principle of these systems is that people should learn to distinguish between priorities and nonpriorities. If it's not a priority, it can wait.

Some people get so frazzled that they dare to take a nap at midday or sneak off to the movies. They learn that flexibility can work for them. Some people put doors on their offices, and make sure they close the doors behind them when they've stopped working. With experience, many people get to understand their genuine time needs. They still may work long hours but the schedule is out of choice rather than compulsion. The dirty secret is that most people who work at home love their work.

PROCRASTINATION

That other time extreme, procrastination, is complex. Many who do not work at home fear the prospect of having no Mommy in a three-piece suit telling them what to do. A boss sets goals, priorities, deadlines. Fear of disapproval or worse spurs us to complete tasks we otherwise don't care about. It is, the reasoning goes, this dread of getting fired that separates humans from the other animals. If there were nobody telling us what to do, how could we get anything done?

Many who feel this way do not have the experience of working for themselves. They do not know what it is like, in an occupational context, to do something because you want to and because it helps you grow.

"Sometimes," says photo researcher Laura Ten Eyck, "it's hard to just wake up and go to work when there's no one checking up on you. But when it gets to the point where it becomes a part of your life-style, you feel great about yourself, because it really is hard and not everyone can do it."

I believe that most people who fear they will succumb to sloth are not really looking at their own resources. The same people who will work into the wee hours on a hobby or drive themselves beyond fatigue for volunteer work wonder if they have enough discipline for their professional lives. They need to know that they carry the fire with them.

My father frequently reminded me that "Procrastination is the thief of time," a sentiment first expressed by eighteenth-century poet Edward Young. Theft is a good image, especially since it conjures George Washington Plunkett's distinction between "honest graft" and "dishonest graft." (The latter happens when you benefit but the citizens don't.) There's creative procrastination and paralyzing procrastination.

Author Dodi Schultz explains creative procrastination well. She even rebels at calling procrastination a problem. "It's a challenge," says Schultz, "and an opportunity—greatly expanded, in fact, by working in a home office—and limited only by the practitioner's imagination. Plus, of course, one's own tastes and predilections.

"As we all know, procrastination cannot consist of mere time-wasting activity such as lolling about and munching bon-bons while perusing trashy novels (unless one makes a living by writing trashy novels—in which case, this is not procrastination either, but work). It has to be useful, constructive, or offer some redeeming social value (such as cleaning out the closet, or the garage, or the freezer—possible only if you work in a home office).

"I happen to have at my elbow a shelf of bird-identification books that I use to further my education whenever I observe avian visitors to the yard just outside my office window. I also write frequent letters to my local legislators. I am always seeking new ideas. If you subsequently publish a book on creative procrastination, please be sure to let me know."

Of course, even when she dawdles, Dodi Schultz is incredibly productive. Her attitude should suggest two home office realities:

1. Working at home allows you to integrate your work and your life.
2. Even when we do procrastinate, our flexible schedules allow us to get the job done on time.

Now let's hear it for those others who genuinely are paralyzed by delay. Some animals when startled by their predators flee. Some turn and fight. Some go into shock and appear dead. Humans, when stalked by fear, anger, and anxiety, procrastinate. Are you worried about the shame of failure, unpleasant encounters with certain individuals, or emotionally wrenching or physically exhausting activities? Are you dismayed by the enormity of the task? Are you irate that this task prevents you from doing what you really want to do, or that you're doing somebody else's work?

The childish inhabitants of our minds persuade us to shirk with wonderfully simplistic arguments: Just say no. If you don't start, you can't fail. If you avoid the work, then the work can't turn your life into hell. If you don't do it, then you get even with those who are trying to make you do it.

Fortunately, adult notions also dwell within our minds. People have reported success when they have applied any or all of the following mature insights:

1. The sooner you start something, the sooner you finish it and get it out of your life.
2. Listen to your feelings and identify them.
   a. If you sense fear or anxiety, try to put your concerns into perspective. Remember that what we imagine and anticipate tends to be more devastating than what actually happens.
   b. Remind yourself of other times when apprehension delayed

you; yet when you finally went ahead, albeit timidly, you were able to achieve your objectives.

3. If you sense anger, try to locate the causes of your rage. Is it related to this project or something else? Identifying the source of your anger can give you enough power to proceed.

4. If the job just seems too large, break it into smaller more manageable pieces. (And do them!)

More probably can be said about procrastination, and I'll try to say it later.

ANXIETY

Anxiety can mug us in a variety of ways. We all have worn scripts that we know by heart, and yet we manage to trip ourselves. When we catch ourselves behaving in a personally stereotypical fashion (making lists instead of working, going on errands instead of working, getting unnecessarily involved with paperwork when a project needs attention) we should say, "There you go again."

"I worked at home," my cousin tells me, "but I had a problem because I knew where the refrigerator was." Eating when you're not hungry is one of life's more famous problems. Some people (present company included) hurl sacrifices of food down the old volcano to appease the anxiety gods. Some ingest copious quantities of protein and carbohydrate fuel to reward themselves. We resist these impulses (often successfully) when we're in somebody else's offices, because we know it doesn't look right; but when we're working at home—ohhh mama, yum!

As with procrastination, noshing is a way to ward off one or another perceived threat. When you suddenly rise from your chair, and walk trancelike toward the fridge, make yourself conscious. Ask if you're truly hungry. Ask what you're really feeling uncomfortable about. See if you can calm yourself with a different pacifier or reward, such as strolling around the block, exercising, or filing (papers or nails). If you still must stuff your face, get real crazy and eat something healthy like fresh vegetables.

Molly Groger presents an interesting view of eating. She's developed a technique called Eating Awareness Training. Her thesis is that if we train ourselves to get in touch with our appetites we will eat better and more wisely.

LONELINESS

Another rude shock sets people who work at home all atremble. The solitude is haunting. "I used to be very lonely when I first started working at home," says Laura Ten Eyck of Ten Eyck Photo Research. "Now, I'm used to being alone and enjoy it. I think it's healthy to be alone for a good part of each day. You know yourself better."

It seems that people miss being part of the gang, part of the team, part of the tribe. In offices that you have to travel to, you'll find banter, colleagueship, and sharers of the load. You have a shared language and shared goals. You have intense relationships, some of which even might be social. You have—here is a phrase from the past—a safety net.

Of course the further away and the longer ago this work experience was, the better it seems. All of those details that define the standard workplace are gone when you work at home.

Tony Stewart of Home Office Software accurately describes one big side effect of the isolation that can come from working at home. "I feel that working at home essentially alone all day is a tremendous focuser and enhancer of the emotions. When I'm happy, I'm ecstatic. When I'm depressed I am miserable. When something doesn't work out too well, I feel as if I've screwed up my life. Something good will happen next week, and I'll think, God, I'm going to be rich. On a regular job, you share everything."

Most home officers who successfully cope with the solitude have adopted two strategies:

1. They accept the fact that they are by themselves. Often they realize the benefits outweigh the disadvantages. They are able to focus themselves on the work and profession of their choice without being encumbered by the meaningless distractions of a company's culture.
2. They forge a new tribe. This one is made up of the people with whom they do business, as well as colleagues and peers. In addition, they make an extra effort to stay in touch with their friends.

Some people discover that they miss the structure that comes with working for somebody else in another location: all the details of grooming, dressing, commuting, arriving at the corporation by a certain time, and relating to certain businesspeople.

When he first started working at home, consultant Angelo Valenti found himself impressed by the importance of doing dishes and other personal chores. "By the time I actually did get to work," he says, "it would be eleven or twelve o'clock."

He reasoned that for him the best way to get to work on time would be to get ready for work. Upon rising, he showered, shaved, dressed, and was at his desk before 9:00 A.M.

"It's like the musicians getting dressed up for a gig," says Angelo. "I'm here to play." He discovered an additional benefit. Sometimes when he called a lead, the prospective client would say, "I'm excited. Can you be here in two hours and we can get started?" Angelo was ready.

RESOURCES

The Complete Guide to Health Insurance, by Kathleen Hogue, Cheryl Jensen, and Kathleen McClurg Urban (Walker & Co., $24.95). This is an essential how-to-cope book. It details all the intricacies of health insurance. It gives a basic course in "How to Analyze and Compare Contracts." The book contains much good advice on claims and benefits. There is much material on nursing home insurance and Medicare. Hogue and Urban founded the Cleveland-based Mediform Inc., a medical insurance management business. Among other things, Mediform helps people get their claims processed. Contact: Walker & Co., 720 Fifth Ave., New York NY 10019; (212) 265-3632.

Eating Awareness Training (EAT, $75). A six-week course is packed into six hours of material found on this set of five EAT audiotapes. The technique, developed by Molly Groger, teaches you to be alert to what your body wants. You listen to one hour per week and practice the awareness skills and techniques. There also is a Q&A component containing answers to the most commonly asked questions keyed to the lessons. The taped course is based on the workshop Groger directs in California and her 1983 book, *Eating Awareness Training* (Simon & Schuster, $5.95). Groger says that people make eating "an intellectual, emotional, and psychological issue when it's really a normal life-sustaining function of the body, a basic instinct. When you interfere with your basic instincts you're in trouble." Contact: EAT, P.O. Box 4045, Malibu CA 90265.

CHAPTER 4

The Executive Suite

One day, in one section of one department of one division of a major corporation, the manager laid down the law. "The vice-president is coming by tomorrow. I don't want him to think we do sloppy work, so get those desks cleared off." The vice-president did indeed notice the pristine desks. "Doesn't anybody do any work around here?" he fumed.

The worst part of the story is that it happens to be true. The vice-president and the manager had their own well-honed notions as to what constitutes an environment in which work gets done. The only thing omitted from their cherished formulas was reality. How do the individuals in that department work best?

In your home office you don't have to pay attention to anybody's stupid rules but your own. Neat desk. Sloppy desk. No desk. It all depends on what you think and how you work. And that's the way it should be. After all, it is your executive suite. In fact, the downtown company office is designed specifically to accommodate the needs of a whole bunch of different people, and the corporation for which they work, which translates into everybody in general and nobody in particular. Your home office is built around how you work, feel, and live.

FIRST THINGS FIRST

What is the first thing to consider when setting up your home office? Somewhere along the way you're likely to change it.

Manhattan astrologer/author Debbi Kempton-Smith says she "added furniture, including carpets and computer, slowly." Attorney Thomas Atkins decided to replace his vertical filing cabinets with lateral filing cabinets because they "worked better for storage and space."

29

You may want to scrap your answering machine and hire an answering service or vice versa. You may want to move your desk toward the window or away from the window. You may want to deep-six the typewriter and adopt a computer. Perhaps an evolution in the nature of your business (a different pool of prospective clients, different products or services, time spent differently in or away from the office) will demand a reconfiguration.

Bob Nadler of f/22 Press, a New Jersey publisher of books and computer software, installed his home office years ago because he wanted to moonlight as a writer. (At the time he daylighted as an engineer.) He began by writing about photography for magazines. Then he wrote books. Then he published books. Then he developed and published software. "I first put in a couple of typewriters," he says, "then built a darkroom, then a studio, then additional desks, then added computer program duplication facilities."

Presumption of change helps. Even if you have all the furnishings and equipment you'll ever need, you are wiser to make the office imperfect and temporary on the first pass. You will adjust and improve as you go along.

If you're starting on a skimpy shoestring, that's fine. The trade-off is simple. The less money you spend on your home office, the more time and effort you have to expend to accomplish various tasks. People used index cards before computers were available, and as recently as last month index cards were still being sold. What luck!

THE RENTAL OPTION

Leasing is one middle ground between buying just the right stuff (that happens to come with the wrong price tag) and doing the space in early Salvation Army. Obviously leasing tends to raise the long-run cost of furnishing space, but it does have advantages.

It reduces your start-up expenses. Instead of paying many thousands of dollars at one time for quality, useful furniture, you pay several hundred dollars up-front (including such start-up fees as deposit). Afterward, you might pay under $150 a month.

Furniture renters say that leasing for a business enables you to take a 100 percent deduction as a business expense, rather than having the furniture as a depreciable asset. It would be wise to discuss the possible tax advantages with your accountant.

Renting also might be smart when you literally do not know where you will be in three or six months. Your business may change in such a way that what you've bought today may not help you enough in the near future. Your business may grow so quickly that you will have to move it to another space in or even outside your home.

Renting can make sense for short-term or seasonal projects that require more staff and/or work space. Howard Rothkerch, of International Furniture Renters (IFR) in New York City, Hartford, and Westchester, says when preparing to lease make sure you've measured your space carefully. Remember to include the doorways. It can be embarrassing to discover that the elegant desk you've picked just won't make it over the threshold.

"Make a realistic assessment of how long you'll need to rent," adds Rothkerch. Yes, he notes, your business will be going great guns in three months, but you may not have the time to go shopping for furniture. Renewing the lease another three months will cost you more than it would have cost if you had signed a six-month lease at the start. The longer the term of the lease contract, the lower the monthly cost.

I asked Rothkerch to describe the IFR terms and conditions:

• The minimum charge is $400 over the period of the lease. Whether you rent for one day or three years, you're going to pay IFR at least $400.

• The up-front payment is based on several factors. There is the monthly rent, of course. Let's say it's $100. Then, there's an insurance waiver fee, which is in case your insurance doesn't cover the stuff you've rented. (In order to get that coverage in your policy, the items would have to be written into the policy.) Essentially, IFR self-insures. This fee is 5 percent of one month's rent. There's sales use tax. Pick-up and delivery charges depend on the quantity of furniture and start at $40. The security deposit, which is refundable, is 1.5 times the monthly fee. The first payment on a $100-a-month rental would be about $300.

• Normal wear and tear of furniture (for example, a scratched glass table or a coffee-stained desk) is expected, and not penalized. Charges are assessed for unusual events, such as a dog mistaking a desk for a fire hydrant, a broken chair leg, or a burn hole in the upholstery. IFR makes the repairs in its shop and then charges for them.

Earthbound considerations also are tied to change. Beware of putting overwhelming obstructions (such as heavy furniture) in front of electrical outlets and/or telephone jacks. The results could lead to backache when the need to change haunts your office.

LOCATION, LOCATION, LOCATION

Where exactly will you put your office? The three big secrets for a successful retail business are location, location, and location. And so it is with your home office.

"The very first thing that needs to be done," according to Dan Droz, furniture designer and professor at Carnegie-Mellon University, "is to assess the level of distraction you can or must accept. The second issue is truly how much time you need to spend sitting. Most of the time in a corporate situation you don't have very much space. You can't really roam around with a phone on your arm, for example. You have to be centered in one place. When you're working at home, that needn't be the case. For example, I have an office at home but I do a lot of my reading in another room. Sometimes when it's nice weather I do drawing and other work on the porch or on the deck."

Your distraction quotient and the degree to which you need your activities to anchor you heavily influence the space you claim for your own. There's still another big rule: Your office should accommodate the stuff you're going to cram into it and the way you like to work. Do you want isolation or should your office be centralized? Do you need wall space on which to hang posters, charts, assorted memos, and so forth? Does gazing through a window make you more or less productive? What kind of furniture and business machines will you need? Will clients come through your hallowed doors? When clients appear, neatness counts. There's an additional interesting consideration: If you have or plan to have customers who happen to be disabled, it would be wise to create an office and entrance that are accessible.

Most people seem to prefer at least one separate room. As attorney Thomas Atkins puts it, "My office is in a totally separate room, selected because of the fact that it was capable of being isolated from the rest of the house whenever necessary by its location and its door."

My office used to be the apartment's dining room. Even though the table has been replaced by a desk, we still manage to find a place to eat. Although I am with family I usually keep the door open because I like to be available if somebody needs me.

Don't feel glum if you don't have the luxury of an extra room. A writer I spoke with is a home officer who lives in a typical Manhattan space: a one-room studio apartment with kitchenette. Her office uses a large portion of the apartment's available space. Her sofa bed enables her to keep domestic furniture at a minimum. Her desk is where a couch otherwise might be. She expertly scavenges space. Bookcases stand in the apartment's small foyer area. Boxes of supplies as well as her answering machine crouch in her closet. Brightly colored two-drawer file cabinets—tomato red and chrome yellow—sit below the bamboo desk.

She selects all office accoutrements with an eye toward a style that resonates with flamboyance. Sleek richly hued Eurostyle telephones ring with abandon. Her floppy disks are safely kept in a teak diskette cabinet. For each buying decision, she not only asks what brand but what style and what color.

When surveying your home for your office's location-to-be, don't just look for an unused area. Be prepared to steal space. Don't ignore space because it's unworkable. You might be able to make it workable.

That's what happened to Manhattan textile broker Gary DePersia. In the past ten years, he tried several times to run his business, Aegis Associates, at home. He lives in a compact duplex apartment. His upper floor is on the building's ground-floor level. The lower floor is the building's basement. For each of the first three working-at-home forays, he would set up shop on the kitchen table located on the upper level. At the beginning of each workday, he would locate the papers he needed, and at the end of the day he would put everything away. Essentially he created and disassembled his office daily. He did not even consider the basement because he feared it would be like working in a dungeon.

He just didn't feel organized enough at home. After each of the first three episodes he found himself abandoning the home and renting office space downtown. One day, while on the lower level, where he sleeps, he suddenly noticed a space where he could put an office. It was a dark area occupied by a piece of prosaic furniture. DePersia visualized a design that would ward off claustrophobia. Three months later, after an orgy of weekend and evening do-it-yourselfism, his office was ready. The unfinished white wood paneling and the brilliance of overhead track lighting made him feel quite at home.

Computer consultants John and Kathy McMullen (of McMullen & McMullen) live in an upstate New York barn. They selected the site because of their business. It seems that a couple of hundred years ago folks built barns atop hills. Facing one way, the barn had three stories, and facing the other it had two. Each side had its own entrance. The extra floor was on the lowest level, and that's where the animals lived. Thus, the farmers could bring hay into the two-storied side and just drop the cow chow down. The McMullens liked the idea of using separate entrances to reinforce the line between living and working quarters. Now, they do intricate consultant things where once the live-stock used to feed. The first order of business was to pour concrete over the dirt floor.

Angelo Valenti moved his office from his living room to a large living room closet. The closet's accordion doors made the difference. Up to that point, whenever Valenti saw his desk, he felt there was some work he could or should do. "At ten o'clock in the evening after dinner I would be coming to the desk," says Valenti. "Even when I wasn't working, my eye would wander over to the incomplete work, and I could not be around work. The accordion doors made it possible for me to open and shut my business for the day."

The location you select may not satisfy all your criteria. However, you should not forget the whole idea. As Mick has observed, "You can't always get what you want." Do the best you can with what you have.

SETTING UP ISN'T HARD TO DO

Now that you know where your office will be, it's time to take care of one more technicality. Just what will be in your office?

What you put into your office is entirely dependent on how you best work and the demands of your business. You don't have to duplicate famous cubicles in which you've worked. Those are set up in accord with the company's goals and policies. You are building an office that takes advantage of how you like to work.

Work Surface

We've already touched on the controversies raging about neat desk versus sloppy desk. The other orthodoxies worth looking at are what shape desk, and should there be any desk at all.

I use a big scarred behemoth wooden desk that I bought used for thirty-five dollars about ten years ago. It has wonderful drawers just ideal for holding typing paper. Unfortunately, I don't use very much typing paper. I mostly use continuous-form computer paper that sits in a box on the floor and snakes through my printer. The desktop neatly holds my computer, printer, telephone, answering machine, and other stuff.

To paraphrase, or more accurately, slaughter Shakespeare, a home office is the dream that stuff is made of. It's not so much that you have to have room for the stuff you have, as it is that you have to have access to the stuff you need. For example, even those out of school find themselves consulting books—professional directories, almanacs, yellow pages, and other assorted reference works. In addition, computers require manuals and software housed in looseleaf binders. Thus, for many people, the home office setup would include easy access to books. Some home office furniture has a shelving configuration.

Recently, I moved the desk next to one of my bookcases. I have nine-foot-tall lawyer's-office walnut bookcases. By planting the desk next to the bookcases, some of the walnut shelf space becomes work space. Reference books also are within reach.

When selecting a desk, Gary DePersia, the textile broker, was much smarter than I was. He knows that he likes things spread out when he works. Thus, he decided on a U-shaped desk. When he couldn't find what he wanted, he built one.

John Stossel, the television reporter, craved a desk that would let him see everything. Otherwise, he felt, he would never find what he needed. He discovered a nineteenth-century desk that has lots of cubbyholes.

Tony Stewart transformed the alcove just off his living room into his office. He has what he calls a "conventional desk." Behind the desk is a wall crammed with bookcases. Four filing baskets hang beneath the bottom bookcase shelf. They are set aside for the day's incoming mail, pending for his assistant to handle, things that have to be filed, and magazines that either have references to his program or might be good places in which to get his program mentioned.

Not everyone reaches heaven by riding a desk. In her previous apartment New York author Dodi Schultz used "a couple of large 3- by 6-foot worktables." When she moved to her current apartment, she actually had the same kind of work area built in. "It's simply a formica-covered wood slab," she explains, "resting on a lot of two-drawer file cabinets. I also had desk-to-ceiling bookcases with adjustable shelves built in."

Dan Droz may not have achieved a paperless office, but he has a deskless home office. "Most of what I do," explains Droz, "is read and think and use a pencil. The system I have is a movable table—something like a hospital tray—with a light attached to it and a lounge chair. That's my work space. I have one of these tables virtually in every room in the house in which I will work. They're very small. They adjust in height. They have a little flat part on which you can put a cup or glass. They convert any sofa, any chair, that I happen to be sitting in into a workplace."

Bush Industries (Jamestown, New York) has developed some insights into what works in a home office. Bush, a leading manufacturer of office furniture, wanted to be a player in the home office market and set about to study its (or rather our) needs. "We put together a task force," says Bruce Anderson, the company's director of design. "It was comprised of people who use typewriters, engineers, marketing people, design people. We went out and bought all the equipment that we knew people would have in a home office. The computer of course is most obvious; printers both in the narrow and extra-wide width and all the fax and copier machines and then we started trying to figure out how these could be used."

The width for most home office desks, Bush found, is no more than 50 inches. Bruce Anderson says the two prime dimensions in a desk are its depth and height.

"For writing," says Anderson, "you want around a 30-inch height. For a keyboard you want 26- or 27-inch."

What other features did the Bush task force deem tops in taps for the home office? Compactness was seen as a virtue. Added to this ideal is the notion of lots of storage capability. This criterion covers not only places to shove reams of paper but extends to the keyboard that gets placed on a tray. It hides under a desktop and is rolled out when needed. Bush's fax stand was adapted from its file cabinet. You can hold the various fax supplies including paper (rolls or cut) in its drawers. Without the facsimile machine on top, the fax stand can roll under most Bush units. Bush home office hutches have adjustable shelves to allow for the fact that different computers and monitors have different sizes.

Please Be Seated

"What is a chair, after all, but a horizontal platform designed to keep one's rear end off the floor," asks Doug Stewart in *Smithsonian* magazine.

What are the best available chairs these days? Is there really a perfect chair? If so, is it affordable and accessible? If not, will it be designed before the common cold is cured?

Start with the notion that the chair should be comfortable and allow you to work. Typical work consists of typing at a keyboard, talking on the phone, writing notes, reading, mulling, and scheming. These activities and others influence how you hold your back and whether you're leaning forward or backward.

Apparently sitting up straight is not a good idea, no matter what your momma said. It makes the spine do too much unnatural work.

Slightly reclining allows your weight to be distributed over the back of the chair. A chair that reinforces some reclining rather than sitting ramrod straight is desired. Let us not neglect the chair that preserves the integrity of the *lordosis*—the S-shaped curve of the spine. A chair that allows you to maintain that curve helps you to lumbar along.

Free-lance medical writer Mark Fuerst helped his lordosis by putting an ordinary throw pillow on the back of his chair. When pressed for further details, he explains that it was not too soft, and furthermore he had it around and it matches the color of the chair. Fuerst added that the pillow makes an appreciable difference.

Typing and other forward-leaning chores demand extra support for your lower back. Leaning back and musing can put an extra strain on your upper back. If the point at which your chair pivots is in the chair's center, then when you tilt back, the seat's front rises and the circulation in your thighs goes bye-bye. The chair works better when the pivot point is in the front. Chairs that swivel and have casters to roll make it easier (and more fun) to access different parts of your work space.

It helps to know what to search for when looking for a chair. Thanks to my research on this book, I was able to spend much more for a chair than I ever would have before. But it's really good. My chair tilts forward and backward, has a dynamite pivot point, gives good support, and is comfortable. For the record, I bought it at Dallek's in Manhattan, and the chair (Programma 5010-22) was manufactured in Italy. Mr. Dallek doesn't know if any other American store stocks the Programma.

Office chairs seem to be divided into two main categories: secretarial and executive. Secretarial chairs are designed for people who bounce up and down and do lots of keyboard work. The chairs happen to have less padding, and the major ergonomic feature is lower back support. Executive chairs tend to be plush and high-backed (the latter, no doubt, because the occupants are so high-minded). With these, there's a greater emphasis on upper back support.

Then, there is the question of nomenclature. Although these two basic categories dominate, furniture manufacturers may look at their market research and come up with different designations. Secretarial chairs also can be called task or function chairs. Executive chairs also may be called management chairs. Then again, some manufacturers may prefer to call secretarial chairs management chairs. A more executive-like management chair not only has lumbar support but has an adjustable back. I guess that makes it an upper management chair.

Because he does very little computer work at home, furniture designer Dan Droz does not have an office chair in his home office. Instead he uses a big comfortable lounge chair with an ottoman.

Keyboards

You are going to need some sort of mechanical device for, at the very least, your correspondence and invoices. In the long run, a computer makes most sense. Its innate ability to keep a file of form letters and reports, help with financial planning and analysis, and destroy aliens from space makes it a perfect home office tool. It may be that your typing needs are minimal and do not demand computerized assistance. It may be that your typing needs are advanced but you cannot afford a computer. So be it!

Electronic typewriters have become popular in the last few years. They are not to be confused with electric typewriters. Although both use electricity, the electronic typewriters take advantage of microchip strengths. Varying degrees of memory enable them to retain a line or pages at a time. The memory enables the user to make corrections before the typewriter keys commit to paper.

Electronic typewriters are to computers what elevators are to automobiles. When you enter the elevator you just press a button and you're on your way, but the journey is kind of limited. The procedure of starting a car is more complicated, but once you're off, you've got so many more places to go. The computer is an anything machine. You can continually find new ways in which a computer can help with your business. An electronic typewriter is for typing. Its memory helps slay one of the most grisly aspects of typing: doing it over.

The electronic extras also include the simplification of such basic tasks as setting margins, underlining, and carriage return. Computer owners use typewriters for dashing off quick notes and typing envelopes. If you buy a new typewriter, make sure you know where to get ribbons for it and how much they'll cost. They may be in a store near you or you may want to get them by mail order or both. Check the impression the typewriter's keys or rotating ball makes. Is that the impression you want?

You probably can get a good bargain on a used typewriter. More of them show up these days in yard sales, classified ads, and second-hand stores. When buying a used typewriter, try to get the instruction booklet that came with it. Usually, the booklet tells you what kind of ribbon to get and how to change it. It also describes useful features that may not be apparent. If the seller does not have it, contact the manufacturer. (Your library probably can tell you how to locate the manufacturer.) It's a good idea to invoke the aforementioned instruction manual "rule" when buying any piece of used equipment. In deciding the outside price you will pay for the typewriter, don't forget to factor in some repair costs up front.

I caution against computeroid devices called word processors. They're billed as the less-expensive, easy-to-learn, all-you'll-ever-need alternative to orthodox computers. As you and your business needs expand, a computer expands with you. Word processors are much more limiting. They're not that much easier to learn, and they're not cheap enough to warrant their purchase over a computer.

Copiers

The affordable personal copier has brought big-time help to the home office. We now can get copies as we need them. No longer is it necessary to run to the bank, library, or copy shop for photocopying. The personal copier should not be confused with the heavy megaton machine that sits in corporate lairs. There are limitations on the personal copier's talents. Most only do one sheet at a time, and, in fact, the blank sheets only go in one at a time. Other one-sheeters do have paper trays. Personal copiers continue to make sense until you're traveling in the thousand-copies-per-month zone.

Just the Fax, Ma'am

At the time of this writing, the fax (short for facsimile) machine is the most hotly hyped item for small businesses. As of December 31, 1988, Venture Development's research shows that fax penetration into the home office is fairly small (1.2 percent). Those who have them love them. For the price of a phone call you can instantly transmit a facsimile of a piece of paper from one spot to another. That second spot is wherever there's another telephone line and fax machine. It can be in a different office, a different city, or even a different continent.

Ring-a-Dingy

Most home offices use telephones. (I qualify this because I've read of at least one home-based businessperson who because of religious beliefs has no telephone.)

Your phone system offers a wonderful array of flexibility. The telephone itself can have all sorts of built-in features such as storing phone numbers in memory, redialing, and alarm clock. You can have one, two, or more phone lines. You can buy extra services from your telephone company such as conferencing, call waiting, and call forwarding. Then, there are the answering machines with which you can do all sorts of weird things.

Talk That Talk

Gripping a microcassette recorder and dictating your memos, letters, and "to do" notes is one way to get a grip on your effectiveness. According to a Westinghouse Productivity Quality Center study, dictating tends to be 70 percent faster than writing by longhand. If you follow this path, remember that you're the person most likely to transcribe these thoughts later.

Speak slowly, so that when you're transcribing you can keep up with yourself. Spell out any names and addresses that you'd otherwise have to look up. "Spell out" numbers (e.g., "one-five" for 15 and "five-oh" for 50). Speak in an even, calm tone. If you're going to give an instruction or label (e.g., "This is a letter for the New York Stock Exchange Ethics Committee"), pause and modify your speaking pattern.

Look for these helpful features when shopping for a microcassette recorder:

- *Cuing or electronic indexing.* During dictation, you push a button and stick a beep onto the tape, which makes it easier to find the spot during transcribing.
- *Automatic backspace.* Normally when a transcriber stops and then starts a tape, a couple of words get lost. This feature restarts by automatically backing up a few words.
- *Pause.* Sometimes the words do not jump trippingly off the tongue. You may need a few seconds to collect your thoughts. When in doubt, press the pause button.

Lighting

When Paul Cozad thinks about lighting, he has more on his mind than just the brightness of lamps. Cozad is the president of Human Factors Consultants, Inc., an ergonomics company in Rochester. His specialty is perception. The quality of lighting in your office, according to Cozad, depends on the placement of the lamps as well as the color of your walls and work surface.

"You have to understand what light does to the eyes," says Cozad. "It takes a certain amount of energy in order for your eyes to operate, albeit only a small amount. You want all the energy you expend for seeing to go toward something that's expeditious, toward whatever you're trying to do. You don't want any erroneous type of light that you have to take into account."

When the eyes adjust to disturbing conditions energy gets sapped. A light source shining in your eyes is one no-no. Deciphering material that is in shadows also takes work. So does catching glare peripherally from other light sources or shiny surfaces. When the eyes use up energy just to compensate for visual turbulence, you tire more easily.

"Light that you use for working directly on your desk," says Cozad, "should be an indirect type of lighting. It's mandatory that the working space be lit with the type of lighting that does not get directed into a person's eyes."

When we're talking lighting, the term *lamp* applies to what I in my less enlightened days would call a *bulb*. A *fixture* is the thing on the wall or ceiling that holds the lamp. The object on your desk that holds the lamp is a desk light. Hence, a desk light should be shaped so that the lamp is shielded and no glare gets into your baby blues.

You create a shadow when you get between the light and your work surface. It's a dandy way to explain how eclipses work; but it's hell on the eyes. A good position for the lamp is slightly to the right or left, so that the light flows over your shoulder. The rule of thumb, according to Wesley E. Woodson in his book *Human Factors* (McGraw-Hill, 1981), is light over the left shoulder for righties and light over the right shoulder for lefties.

"If possible," says Paul Cozad, "a person's work space should have lighting from more than one direction to minimize the shadows. At my desk, I actually have two 24-inch fluorescent bulbs which are mounted 16 inches above the surface. My desk is 5 feet wide. In essence the light runs almost across the front edge of my desk."

You can ward off the curse of peripheral glare. Shield other lamps in the room. Keep overhead lights dim. If light streaming through a window captures your eye in a most uncomfortable way, curtains, shades, or blinds may remedy the situation.

According to ergonomics specialist Rani Lueder, president of Humanics, bad lighting literally can be a pain in the back. It seems that people, especially those working at computer monitors, adjust their postures to avoid glare and reflection and other such games that lighting plays with the eyes. It's like sleeping in the wrong position.

"A lot of studies," says Lueder, "have found a majority of office workers have a problem with glare and reflection and get into a frozen posture. Their physical problems are greatly accentuated as well as their productivity problems."

The type of surface you work on has a lot to do with how well you see. "The surface should be a darker color," says Paul Cozad, "so that whatever you are working on becomes the main object in your sight."

Cozad notes that pads of yellow paper are preferable to white paper pads. Even though black ink on white paper yields a greater measurable contrast, psychologically people "distinguish a greater contrast with dark marks on yellow paper."

Color in the room is not only important because of contrasts but because it helps define the light. "The walls," says Cozad, "should be a softer color—never bright or harsh. For office work, you really want to keep away from some of your major colors—the blues, the reds, the greens. Even an off-white would turn into a bluish-white. Beige is a very good color.

"You're better off with the softer wood tones for your furniture. The broken lines caused by natural grain or its simulation is pleasing to the eyes. You see, eyes need a novelty. If you have anything that's just too plain without being broken up by various lines, the eyes tire a lot more. That's why, believe it or not, people can work really better when they have a cluttered desk." The business about cluttered desks has nothing to do with lighting, but I think of it as a piece of life-affirming information I am obligated to pass on.

"The most perfect type of lighting," says Cozad, "is to take a little piece of the sunshine that comes through the atmosphere and have that on your desk." Barring that, most people would be served by artificial light that mimics outdoor light such as a fluorescent light that gives a bluish tint.

Low Tech

The glamorous high-tech weapons, such as computer and fax machine, overshadow but do not diminish the importance of that army of paper, metal, and plastic office helpers. What are some of the basic office supplies?

Author/astrologer Debbi Kempton-Smith likes Duo Tang colored pocket folders. They are letter-size folders with pockets that "you can cram a lot into." Attorney Thomas Atkins finds that "the Pendaflex-type filing system is a must both for efficiency and capacity."

Manhattan author Dodi Schultz says, "I have come to value my 'solar' calculator which is powered by the light of my desk lamp. It's far superior to having to replace those tiny disc batteries [using tiny jeweler's screwdrivers to take the cases apart]."

You need all kinds of paper. Stationery with your letterhead is at the top of the list. Most everyone feels that the letterhead should be distinctive and impressive. Many have criticized the practice (which I have followed) of printing out a letterhead on a dot matrix printer. They're probably right. (Since writing these words, I've gone back to an officially printed letterhead, and I must admit it's more presentable. When my stationery came back from the printer, I made a few hundred offset copies for lower-priced letterheads.) You need paper to scribble and write notes on. You need paper for your typewriter, computer, fax machine, and copier.

You might need dedicated forms (i.e., invoices, from-the-desk-of's, etc.). Now that you've squirreled away some paper, you might want to think about pens.

Consider owning and even using a fountain pen. It's often considered a status symbol and rightly so. After all, so many fountain pens can boast of elegant design, gold-plated nibs, and luxury price tags. The well-made fountain pen conveys the personality of its wielder. It's ideal when you're signing a document and you want your signature to look official. It also lends your spirit to handwritten notes, because as you write with your new pen the point (nib) gets modified by your style of writing and the angle at which you hold the pen to the paper. Essentially, the fountain pen nib becomes custom-crafted for your touch. In fact, a fountain pen improves penmanship to the degree that it slows you down. When you become old slow hand, then you earn a bit of extra legibility. (Conversely ball and roller pens are better when you need to be a quick scrawl artist.) Pen purists must despair. Today's fountain pen makers are very much enamored of cartridges as opposed to bottled ink.

Things that attach things to other things also are useful. These include paper clips, staplers, and tapes. You'll want some sort of calendar that lets you know and even plan where you're supposed to be. I'm actually ridiculously proud of the calendar decision I made. For years, I've tried to deal with the simple task of tracking and scheduling my days. I've had every type of chronological configuration from week at a glance to days of our lives to hard-cover daybook to pocket calendar, and so on. The problem, or should I say challenge, is that when on the phone making an appointment, I'd just reach for any slip of paper (usually a torn envelope) to jot down my note. Then I'd misplace the slips of paper.

I decided to get a 15-by-20-inch calendar. Each page is a different month of the year. It rests on my desk and no doubt thinks it's a desk blotter. Instead of reaching for a scrap of paper, I just bring my pen to the calendar. I know that daybooks and pocket calendars are much more efficient. Unfortunately, they don't work for me, and fortunately the desk calendar does.

I happily bragged to one friend about my decision, and he was horrified.

"That's the wrong way to do it," he told me.

"You're absolutely right," I said.

"So?"

"What so?"

"So why don't you get a small or compact calendar that you can carry with you at all times?"

"This works for me."

"But what will you do if you're in somebody's office and they want to make an appointment with you?"

"I'll tell them," I said, "that the date sounds okay to me but my calendar isn't handy, so I'll doublecheck when I get back to my office and call to confirm."

"My way makes more sense," he grumbled.

It helps to know the most efficient way to do something, but if it doesn't work for the individual, then the approach is worthless.

CATALOG

Artisan Work Center (Bush Industries). This modular furniture is made of oak solids and is oak laminated. This collection consists of a 50″ by 30″ desk, hutch, return (the piece that's perpendicular to the desk), pedestal, pedestal with drawers or doors, bookcase, two-drawer file cabinet, and fax stand. Contact: Bush Industries, One Mason Dr., Jamestown NY 14702.

Work Station (Soundesign, $159.95). This four-piece ensemble (the WS4002) is definitely a low-price spread. Made with a walnut finish, the work station consists of a desk (27½″ h by 43¼″ w by 23¼″ d) with one large drawer, a hutch (9¾″ h by 42″ w by 10¾″ d), a printer stand (27½″ h by 22″ w by 14¾″ d) with two shelves, one for paper and one for supplies, and an adaptor, the piece that bridges the printer stand and desk. The desk basically is a work surface on which you can place some pieces of equipment. The hutch has a six-cube organizer for things like memo pads, pens, paper clips, postage, and so forth. It

(Above): Artisan Work Center

(Right): Soundesign Work Station

SteelWorks Organizer
with Desktop

also is appropriate for computer monitor and books. The adaptor is both cosmetic and an additional flat surface on which to put something. You assemble the pieces with a screwdriver. Contact: Soundesign, Harborside Financial Center, 400 Plaza Two, Jersey City NJ 07311; (201) 434-1050.

The Organizer (SteelWorks). A combination file drawer and stash-the-stuff cabinet, this compact piece measures 13″ h by 12″ w by 27″ d. It has a storage cabinet with lock in which you could put books or supplies, two letter-size drawers, and a file with built-in rails to accommodate hanging folders. The organizer is all steel with an enamel finish and comes in gray or black and white. Contact: SteelWorks, Inc., First and New York Aves., Des Moines IA 50313; (800) 383-7414.

Vertical Filing Cabinets (SteelWorks, $30 to $50). The three-drawer cabinets in this economical line have one filing drawer and two ''storage'' drawers. Both drawers in the two-drawer version can be used for filing. Both sizes are made of steel with an enamel finish. The drawers glide easily on nylon rollers. Whether two- or three-drawer the cabinet's dimensions are 15″ h by 18″ w by 28″ d. The three-drawer model includes a bonus six-compartment drawer organizer tray. The three-drawer cabinets are available in mauve, white, black, and slate blue. The three-drawer versions can be obtained in those colors, as well as gray, red, and almond. Contact: SteelWorks, Inc., First and New York Aves., Des Moines IA 50313; (800) 383-7414.

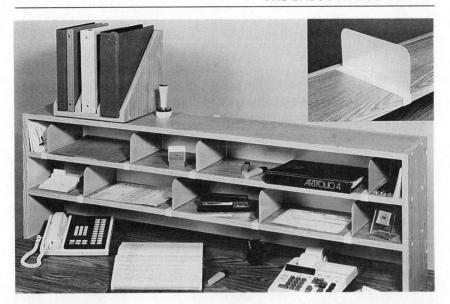

Timberline Space Saver

Desk Tops (SteelWorks). These functional flat surfaces plus one or two file cabinets equal instant desk. The 40"-wide models 181 and 189 come with a set of square tubular legs at one end. The other end sits atop the file cabinet. The legs, which simply get attached to the top with screwdriver and pliers, are designed to work with 28", 29", or 30" file cabinets. The 54"-wide model 185 does not come with legs. The color choices are oak and white. Contact: SteelWorks, Inc., First and New York Aves., Des Moines IA 50313; (800) 383-7414.

Timberline Space Saver (Buddy Products, $91.75 to $198.95). These are really one-, two-, and three-shelf hutches to add to your work surface. All come with steel dividers for convenient organization. You can move a divider to any spot on the shelf. The space savers are 18⅛" high and 10¹⁵⁄₁₆" deep. Their widths range from 30" to 58". They come in oak or walnut laminate. Contact: Buddy Products, 1350 S. Leavitt St., Chicago IL 60608; (312) 733-6400.

Space-Saving Revolving Bookcase (Hammacher-Schlemmer, $165). A little more than 2 feet high (26¼") and 17¾" wide, this bookcase is said to have the equivalent of 6 feet of shelf space. There are eight shelf compartments, each of which is 11" high and 9½" wide. The bookcase is solid oak with a lacquered oak finish. Contact: Hammacher-Schlemmer, 147 E. 57th St., New York NY 10022; (800) 543-3366.

FileAround (Kartell USA, $120). This little cart is a hanging file folder holder on wheels. You can wheel it next to you when you need

Hammacher-Schlemmer
Revolving Bookcase

FileAround

Day Runner Classic
Organizer

access to your files or let it sleep discreetly out of harm's way, depending on your needs. Measuring 26¾" h by 17" w by 24" d, the black or white cart holds about 2 feet worth of material. It can accommodate both letter- and legal-size folders. Contact: Kartell USA, P.O. Box 1177, Greenville SC 29602; (800) 845-2517.

Rotary Book Organizer (OfficeTech). This desktop bookcase turns, making it compact and making your most consulted books accessible. Constructed of sturdy plastic, it provides extra inches of shelf space on a 12" square base for books, manuals and/or binders. Contact: OfficeTech, P.O. Box 97105, Redmond WA 98073-3715; (206) 885-6460.

Square Element (Kartell USA, $66). Now we can say a square element is moving into the home office universe, and it's perfectly okay. The element in question is a neatly designed two-part stacking piece that is convenient for storage. One section has a little door. A tray sits on top for organizing, or more likely, piling. Optional casters cost $12. Contact: Kartell USA, P.O. Box 1177, Greenville SC 29602; (800) 845-2517.

The Classic Organizer (Day Runner, $55 to $275). What some people desire is not just a calendar, mind you, but an organizer. This modern

Design House Desk Organizer Base with Daily Calendar

classic is set up as a three-ring looseleaf binder. It enables you to enter and consult your schedule, memos, addresses and phone numbers, expenses, receipts, and other such paper files that you create. For example, you can keep a file of restaurants, or taxicab numbers, or gift shops, and/or fax numbers. All the separate sections fit into the same binder. The Day Runner also holds credit cards, checkbook, business cards, pen, and pad. Finding is fun with such two-color pages as month-in-view weekly planning calendar; today pages for nitty-gritty scheduling; contact pages for keeping up with the fleeting whos, whats, and whens; and expense report pages. It is a way to keep all your wits about you or at least conveniently accessible in the same package. It's available in a variety of sizes, from pocket to executive, and a variety of covers, from snazzy to exquisite. Contact: Day Runner, 3562 Eastham Dr., Culver City CA 90232; (213) 837-6900.

Desk Organizer Base (Design House, $10). The clean-lined plastic base holds the standard no. 17 desk calendar. In addition, it has scooped-out hollows in which you can (in an orderly fashion, of course) place pens and pencils, erasers, paper clips, rubber bands, and Post-it notes. It's available in gray or black. Contact: Design House, 185 W. Englewood Ave., Teaneck NJ 07666.

Walltrak

Daily Desk Calendar (Design House, $4.50). This is a standard no. 17 calendar. The pages measure 3½″ wide by 6½″ long. Each day including Saturday and Sunday gets two pages. The left side is for the schedule, and it's arranged in half-hour notations from 7:00 A.M. until 5:30 P.M. The right side is for notes. Contact: Design House, 185 W. Englewood Ave., Teaneck NJ 07666.

Walltrak (Bretford Manufacturing). The manufacturer applies the good old shelf-and-bracket wall unit notion to a computer center. Pre-drilled aluminum tracks get mounted to the wall, and the shelves hang from the track. The Walltrak Computer Center consists of two 56″-wide shelves, two 32″-wide shelves, a computer keyboard drawer that can slide out when needed, three vertical tracks, and one horizontal track. Contact: Bretford Manufacturing, 9715 Soreng Ave., Schiller Park IL 60176.

Gem Clip Dispensers

Gem Clip Dispenser (Plus U.S.A. Corp., $1.95). This rounded paper clip abode feels quite good in the hand. When ready for a clip, give a little shake. The dispenser is magnetized so the clips come out gently and slowly. You load just by pulling the two halves apart. Available in satin-finish charcoal gray, white, or blue. Contact: Plus U.S.A.; (800) 289-PLUS.

Stoppers (The Slencil Co., $5 and up). Keep objects in their place on your desk by using these coiled tethers. A reusable double-faced tape attaches the Stopper base to your desk. The coil (similar to a telephone wire coil) runs from the base to the desk item (stapler, scissors, tape dispenser, etc.). Slencil also makes Coil Pens. It's the same principle only the coil is attached to a pen. Contact: The Slencil Co., Consumer Products Dept., 36 S. Main St., Orange MA 01364; (508) 544-2171.

Executives' Choice Desk Light (Electrix). Shielded by the 20″-wide shade are two light-giving 15-watt fluorescent lamps. A short gooseneck gives a bit of maneuverability. The desk light is black with walnut trim. Contact: Electrix, 45 Spring St., New Haven CT 06535; (203) 776-5577.

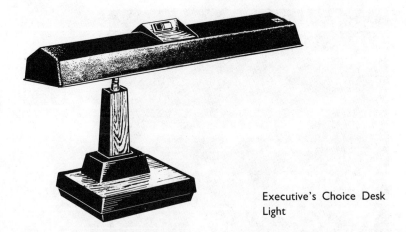

Executive's Choice Desk
Light

Desk Lamp (Waldmann Lighting Co., $296). The 209 is a respon-
sive task light. Its built-in parabolic louver lets you control and direct
the rays while reducing glare that otherwise would bounce from the
computer monitor. The fixture's arms can move both horizontally and
vertically. You can position the lamp even more precisely by swiveling
the head. The fixture uses two 9-watt compact fluorescent lamps. The
colors are matte black, white, chocolate brown, beige, slate gray, and
burgundy. The 209 can be mounted with a clamp, bracket ($8), or
table base ($42). Contact: Waldmann Lighting Co., 9 W. Century
Dr., Wheeling IL 60090; (312) 520-1060.

Folding Tables (Barricks Manufacturing, $82 and up). When you
have an occasional need for an additional work surface, a folding table
may be an appropriate solution. Barricks offers a range of suitable
tables, including the square Safari (starting at 30″ by 30″), $82; the
circular Fold-N-Roll (it's on casters and the narrowest has a 48″ diameter), $231; and the Port-A-Fold, which has a built-in handle (the
smallest is 24″ by 60″), $137. The company also manufactures folding
conference tables, as well as unfolding (I guess that's nonfolding) oc-
tagonal oak and laminate conference tables. Contact: Barricks Manufacturing, P.O. Box 1612, Gadsden AL 35902; (205) 442-2600.

Architect's Light (Electrix). The Ultima's bell shape and swiveling
arm (stop your swiveling) help you direct light to the task at hand.
There's a metal shade and weighted base. The Ultima works with a
100-watt incandescent bulb. Contact Electrix, 45 Spring St., P.O. Box
9575, New Haven CT 06535; (203) 776-5577.

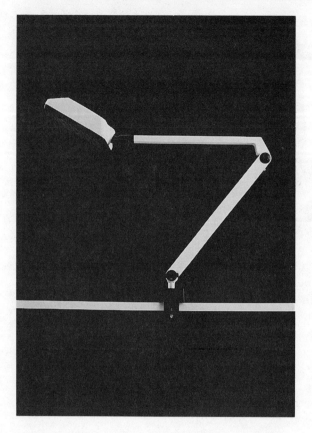

The Waldmann 209 Desk
Lamp

Fax Markers (Schwan-Stabilo, $1.79). Use these writing instruments to highlight phrases on fax paper. They manage to make marks on thermal paper without eradicating, smudging, or discoloring the message. The fax markers are not really designed to write notes onto the paper; however, the chisel tip, really intended for underlining, will let you sneak in a brief jot. They're available in six colors: blue, red, yellow, pink, orange, and green. Contact: Schwan-Stabilo, 101 Dividend Dr., Peachtree City GA 30269; (404) 487-5512.

Flat Stapling (Max Business Machines, $11.95). Using standard mini-staples, the Max flat-clinch stapler does its work by leaving, in its path, staples that lie flat rather than curved when they close. The results are piles of paper that stack flat, and no scratching or snagging by bulging staple ends. Contact: Max Business Machines, 585 Commercial Ave., Garden City NY 11530; (516) 222-2184.

Barricks Folding Tables

Hideaway Home Office (Hammacher-Schlemmer, $995). It's a cabi-
net that opens to reveal shelves, hutches, surfaces, and filing cabinets.
One might think of the Hideaway Home Office as part telephone
booth, part Murphy bed, and part Swiss army knife. It's 44″ tall. The
width, when open, is 64″, and when closed it's 32⅛″. It's 29″ deep
when open, and 20″ deep when closed. The compact piece is made of
solid oak and oak veneer. Contact: Hammacher-Schlemmer, 147
E. 57th St., New York NY 10022; (800) 543-3366.

Palm-Sized Microcassette Tape Recorder (Sony, $189.95). Luxuriously
small, the Sony M-88V tape recorder has plenty of features. It's a two-
speed recorder with pause control and cue/review. It can be voice-
operated (i.e., start when it hears something and stop at a silence, such
as when you're framing your next thought). There is a built-in speaker.

Ultima

It comes with a tie-clip microphone and an earphone that doubles as a mike for telephone use. The M-88V weighs just 5.6 ounces and is 3.6″ h by 2.1″ w by 0.94″ d. Contact: Sony Corporation of America, 9 W. 57th St., New York NY 10019.

Sidearm Task Light (Luxo, $199). Luxo's FL-18 is an asymmetric light. The 18-watt fluorescent bulb's bright glow is cast from the side. The task light's four reflectors spread the illumination evenly. The light can be effective, even though it's positioned outside the work area. The manufacturer says that placing the FL-18 about 17″ above the work surface helps to avoid glare. Contact: Luxo, 36 Midland Ave., P.O. Box 951, Port Chester NY 10573; (914) 937-4433.

Paper Cutter Plus (Ingento). It's as if a fashion magazine did a makeover of the staid paper cutter that haunts every mail room and

art class. The result is Ingento's Paper Station. Not only does the
Paper Station have a sleek design but it's useful. Built into the pack-

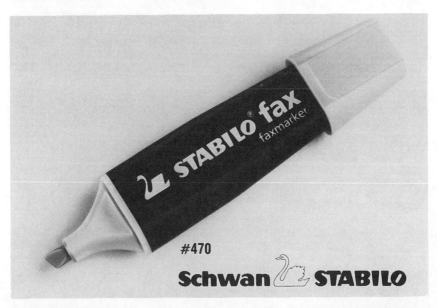

Fax Marker

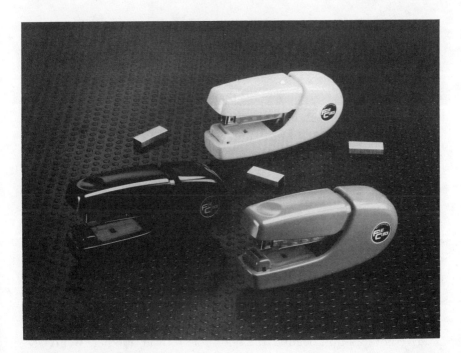

Max Flat-Clinch Staplers

Sidearm Task Light

age are clear-tape dispenser, stapler, storage tray, and staple remover. Its best use is for paper trimming, particularly around the copier and fax machines. For example, the good, clean edges satisfy those FAX machines that won't take paper with perforated edges. The manufacturer recommends that you cut up to ten sheets at a time. The Paper Station can slice through heavier cardboard and corrugated material, but more force is required. The tape et al. are thoughtful accessories for the kinds of chores that accompany copying and faxing. The Paper Station is available in office supply stores and a number of catalogs. Contact: Ingento, 2245 Delany Rd., Waukegan IL 60085; (800) 327-1336.

GBC One Step (General Binding Corporation, $99). Not half a Texas dance, but an ingenious (and inexpensive) binding system that allows you to bind up to thirty sheets. It's especially helpful for those people who insist on having attractive-looking reports and other sorts of presentation material. You assemble your pages, place them in the GBC folder, stick the whole mess in the One-Step, wait 60 scconds, and you've got a bound beauty. It's advisable to wait another twenty seconds for the glue to dry. The secret is in the folder, which has a line of silver nitrate ink, the adhesive, and two terminals. The One-Step itself does not heat up. It just goes zap! And the glue melts. There's a temptation when using the One-Step to close the cover, just as we might with a microwave, a waffle iron, or some other appliance. Resist. It doesn't work when the lid is shut. The cover is just for storage. The folders with a 1/16″ spine accommodate between two and fifteen sheets. The 1/8″ spine is best for between fifteen and thirty pages. Contact: General Binding Corporation, One GBC Plaza, Northbrook IL 60062; (800) DIAL-GBC.

Not Fade Away (Pentel, $1.29). When you want to make an unfading impression, the MR205 is appropriate for legal or banking documents. Pentel says that it's the first waterproof pen that resists fading. Contact: Pentel of America, 2805 Columbia St., Torrance CA 90503.

Twist-Erase Pencil (Pentel). People who use automatic pencils appreciate erasers. All too often, the lead outlasts the erasers, and darn, the pencil no longer feels useful. The Twist-Erase gives its owner eight and a half times more eraser than conventional automatic pencils. Contact: Pentel of America, 2805 Columbia St., Torrance CA 90503.

Copier Paper That Glows (Miami Valley Paper, $17/200 sheets). Razzle-dazzle copier paper with fluorescent colors (red, orange, green, pink, and canary) certainly captures attention. The fluorescent-coated paper can be used in plain paper copiers. It's perfect for such tasks as announcements, brochures, and instructions on handling hazardous wastes. Some high-level managers in federal agencies use Copy-Glo to indicate their place in the pecking order. (If you get a memo on screaming orange paper, then you jump to it.) Copy-Glo's manufacturer, Miami Valley Paper, mostly makes fluorescent labels and tags. This paper also can be used in plain-paper laser printers. Contact: Miami Valley Paper Co., 413 Oxford Rd., Franklin OH 45005; (800) 543-7905.

Sortkwik (Lee Products, $1.90/85). This fingertip moistener helps when counting, collating, sorting, and generally pushing around pieces of paper. For example, it helps when diving into a pile of photocopies. Glycerine is a major ingredient. Many bank tellers use Sortkwik for the heavy-duty counting of currency. Just smear a bit on your fingertips. (The heavier your touch, the more you use.) Sortkwik comes in three sizes: 3/8 ounce up to 1 3/4 ounces. Contact: Lee Products, 800 E. 80th St., Minneapolis MN 55420; (800) 356-8969.

Canon PC-7 Copier

Dallek Furniture (Dallek). This retailer deals with 33,000 manufacturers around the world. Its major activity seems to be the filling of New York City skyscrapers with desks, credenzas, and the like. The staff is knowledgeable and helpful. Even though I was dressed casually to the point of sloppiness, my salesman gave me his full attention and treated me quite respectfully. Mr. Dallek says that he receives orders from all over the world. ("People see my ads in the *New York Times,*" he explains.) Contact: Dallek, 269 Madison Ave., New York NY 10016; (212) 684-4848.

Business Forms (NEBS, free catalog). It seems there's a form for every possible piece of information that you want to store and/or pass on to a customer. Somebody somewhere arrived at exactly the right location on a piece of paper for every necessary fill-in-the-blank space. That same somebody knows exactly what information is a must. NEBS (New England Business Service), a mail-order house, seems to have every specialized form in stock. Some are even more specific, as they are for particular businesses or industries. You also can get forms custom-printed. Contact: NEBS, 500 Main St., Groton MA 01471; (800) 225-6380.

Copier (Canon, $2095). The PC-7 is a versatile copy machine. It has fixed settings for enlargements (122 percent) and reductions (70 percent, 78 percent, 86 percent). When in the Zoom zone, it goes from 70 percent to 122 percent by 1-percent increments. The maximum original size it takes is 10″ by 14″. You can feed paper manually or use the 100-sheet cassette. You can change the ink color to blue, light blue, brown, red, or green just by changing the toner cartridge. It has a stationary top and it will run off eight copies per minute. Contact: Canon USA, Home Office Products Sales Division, One Canon Plaza, Lake Success NY 11042; (516) 488-6700. For information about dealers call (800) 892-0020.

Spelling Electronic Typewriter (Smith-Corona, $429). A 75,000-word dictionary rests on the shelf of the Smith-Corona XD-7600's internal electronics. When you enter a typo (nobody misspells, of course) the XD-7600 gently beeps. Don't worry if you type a little bit more and it takes a while for the tone to reach your brain. You press the "find" button; the machine goes back to the point of error, erases the boo-boo, and automatically types in the correct spelling. If the new spelling is longer than the old one, the typewriter automatically respaces for up to ten lines. The typewriter has a 20,000 K (approximately ten double-spaced pages) memory. Thus, you effortlessly can do over any page, or you can store frequently typed letters. It has a two-line by forty-character display, and automatically does bold, underlining, paper feeding, and centering. Contact: Smith-Corona Corporation, 65 Locust Ave., New Canaan CT 06840; (203) 972-1471.

Discounted Office Supplies (Performing Artists Diversified, various prices). This commercial stationer (known as PAD) is not really in the mail-order business, but will sell office supplies at a 10 percent discount to readers of this book. It is included in this section because of the discount offer, plus PAD has an interesting story, plus I do some writing for the company. Singer/songwriter Steve Sawyer created PAD as a way for performers to keep body, soul, and rent together. Many performers find it a particularly attractive alternative to waiting on tables or driving a cab. Customers benefit from the positive service attitude that results. Contact: PAD, (800) DOO-WOPP, or fax order to (212) 643-0527.

Furniture Rental (IFR or FRAA). Those living in the New York metropolitan area may want to turn to International Furniture Rental, which has showrooms around the area. The photo on page 62 was supplied by IFR. To find out if there's an IFR near you, call (212) 421-0340. Also, the Furniture Rental Association of America (FRAA) provides toll-free referral services. To find a member near you (and to get a free copy of the brochure, "A Consumer Guide to Renting Furniture"), call (800) FOR-RENT. In Ohio, Alaska, and Hawaii, call collect (614) 895-1273.

RESOURCES

What to Buy for Business ($95/year). The publisher issues six detailed handholding guides on a bimonthly basis. Each guide takes you through the maze of a specific business machine category (computers and printers, copiers, fax machines, phone systems, typewriters,

Furniture Leased from IFR

computer software). Concise books, they are somewhere between 80 and 120 pages in length (depending on the subject). The treatment is readable and informative. A typical guide offers user polls on reliability and service, a "best buys short list," background material on the subject, a bunch of "what you need to knows" about specific categories of the machine being covered, and buying tactics. The bulk of the guide is devoted to product profiles: detailed evaluations of most if not all machines in the field. In alternate months *What to Buy for Business* sends its subscribers an update bulletin that reports on new, updated, and discontinued models and price changes. The publication does not accept advertising. Individual issues cost $20 (including shipping). A subscription is appropriate for those who not only want to buy but want to stay sensitive to what's available. Just buying individual issues makes more sense to those home officers who only want information about one or two types of machines in the course of a year. Contact: What to Buy, Inc., 350 Theodore Fremd Ave., Rye NY 10580; (914) 921-0085.

Sunset Home Office & Workspaces (Lane Publishing Co., $6.95). This book corrals a number of home office setup ideas under one roof, or at least within one binding. Its sixty-three color photographs and fifty-three drawings and diagrams, plus its straightforward approach, combine to provide guidance about how to use space, what space to use, and what to think about when selecting furniture, lamps, and office machines. It also has instructions for seven do-it-yourself office furniture projects. Virgos will appreciate the pristine work surfaces seen throughout the book. Brand names are not provided for the various pieces of furniture shown, but you can bring the book to a furniture or office supply store and say "give me one of those." Contact: Lane Publishing Co., Menlo Park CA 94025.

Viking Office Products Catalog (Viking, free). Although not targeted at home officers, the 200-page catalog is crammed with items that you no doubt will recognize, and perhaps even want. The products are discounted, sometimes up to 50 percent. Service is fast and good. Contact: Viking (800) 421-1222.

Reliable Home Office Catalog (Reliable, free). This is the first office products catalog directed straight at us. The products were selected to appeal to our sense of style and taste. You'll see lots of bright colors and attractive design. You'll also see an emphasis on space-saving through items that are compact or offer storage possibilities. Contact: Reliable Home Office, P.O. Box 804117, Chicago, IL 60680-9968; for credit card orders call (800) 621-4344.

IKEA (IKEA Inc.). This chain of furniture/housewares stores started in Sweden and seems to be expanding all over the world (including the United States). I learned that several design and ergonomics consultants do not hesitate to send their clients to IKEA. Check out the store's desks, chairs, closets, and storage items. The furniture is attractively designed, sturdy, and inexpensive. It's also ready to assemble (RTA), which means you put it together in the privacy of your own home. A significant snag for some might be the fact that (at least at the time of this writing) IKEA does not do mail order. However, the chain does seem to be popping out new branches all over the country, and there is a catalog. Contact: IKEA (215) 834-0180 for the store nearest you.

Furniture by Mail (Home Works). This small catalog features furniture that is mostly for computer setups. The materials used include solid oak, melamine, or veneer (teak or oak). It's RTA all the way. Contact: Home Works, P.O. Box 31544, Raleigh NC 27622; (800) 544-4902.

CHAPTER 5

Professional Help

A wonderful Italian restaurant grows in Brooklyn. It's called The Two Toms, although I believe nobody named Tom is remotely connected with it. My wife and I first sampled it because of a hearty recommendation from a car service dispatcher. The next time we were in the car service, we reported our pleasure and gratitude to the dispatcher.

"It was a delight," I said. "Thank you."

"You're welcome," he said. "I'm going to have to try it myself one of these days."

"You've never been to Two Toms?"

"No," he said, "but all the drivers tell me it's very good."

When seeking counsel on business matters, you'll find many repositories of knowledge and experience are out there waiting for your questions. Probably lawyers and accountants rank among your chief advisors. The trick is to get lawyers and accountants who aren't too rank.

Yes, accountants tell us what's deductible and do our tax returns, but there's life after April 15. "Avoid getting Uncle Louie as an accountant," says Angelo Valenti, a consultant to small and medium-size businesses. "You know Uncle Louie. He works for a Big Eight company, but he doesn't really have the time and he's doing you a favor." He also doesn't understand the accounting requirements of your business.

Hiring an accountant whose strengths are taxes and bookkeeping is really hiring half an accountant. As Valenti puts it, getting an accountant who's trained mostly to do taxes is having someone "handle my history, rather than create a future. An accountant can help you with spreadsheets and projections and things like that."

And yes, lawyers assist us with our wills, but there's life after death.

It would be most pleasant if the lawyer knew about the legal needs of small business in general, and your business in particular. If we're lucky, the accountants and lawyers we pick function informally as outside directors. They give us information about the business climate.

REFERENCE WORK

Referrals are the best way to go when it comes to picking a professional. Of course, if you'd like, you certainly can haunt archives and go through lists provided by professional associations and read professional journals for signs of flash and scholarship. You can develop a list of professionals and subject them to rigorous interview and scrutiny. You also can empty the Sahara with a teaspoon.

By talking with peers, you have a chance to take a shortcut along the learning curve. You're more likely to get an accurate sense of performance by talking to users rather than vendors of professional services. You must, however, take a human nature quirk into account. People don't like to say bad things about other people, even if those bad things are true.

First, you must decide whose judgment you really trust. Who among friends, acquaintances, colleagues, competitors, vendors, brothers-in-law would you even ask for a referral? Otherwise you might get the kind of accountant depicted in a "Saturday Night Live" skit:

"Got a horrible acne," he asked. "Use a lotta Clearasil . . . that's an oil depletion allowance. You say your wife won't sleep with you? You got withholding tax coming back. If she walks out on you—you lose a dependent. But . . . it's a home improvement—write it off!"

In addition to esteem, there's another practical matter. Think about the people you get referrals from. Does the way they work with their professional advisors have any relevance to the services, attention, and experience you want? Do they give their lawyers and accountants the same role you intend to give your lawyer and accountant? Are they in the same business or industry that you are? Is or was their business about the same size as yours? Do they have the same special business needs you have?

OTHER QUESTIONS

In addition to asking about these matters, you'll want to know a few other things. How do the professionals do business? Are they casual? Are they formal? Do they make house calls? Do the people who are giving referrals care if their lawyers and accountants understand the peculiarities of their particular businesses? How interested are the professionals in the start-up aspects of business?

Make it clear to each person from whom you seek a referral that you'll be talking with several people. Otherwise, they will feel a bit miffed if the match is not made. Feelings range from annoyance that their time has been wasted to insecurity because of a sense that you felt their lawyer or accountant isn't up to scratch.

When seeking referrals there are additional questions to ask. The best is, "What can I do to get the best use out of this accountant or lawyer?" This question is nonthreatening. It allows the recommender to supply you with negative traits framed in a positive context. Possible answers might be, "You've got to stay on top of him because sometimes he's so busy that he doesn't follow up like he should." Or "She's got a bit of a temper, but she really knows her stuff so don't bother her with stupid questions."

Other questions may be more mundane, but are eminently useful. What have the accountant and lawyer done for you? How did they go about doing it? Have there been new questions concerning the matter? How have they handled or advised you to handle these questions? Was there something you neglected to tell them about the matter that has come back to haunt you? Do you think their fees are fair? What are their staffs like: pleasant, surly, smart, dumb? Was there anything they were supposed to do for you that they didn't? If so, why? Do you give them all your accounting or legal work? If not, what do you have them do and why? With some artful listening on your part and maybe a bit of luck the answers to these questions will tell you how your friends and acquaintances really feel about the professionals they recommend.

If no one you know can suggest a lawyer, or you wouldn't take a lawyer recommendation from anyone you know, there is another source: referrals from the local bar association. But be warned.

"Generally," notes William A. Hancock in *The Small Business Legal Advisor* (McGraw-Hill, 1986), "this route will not be very productive for business problems. It works fairly well for personal injury problems, probate matters, or other *personal* legal problems, but corporate lawyers may or may not be in the local bar association referral system, and the people at the local bar association may be little, if any help."

However you end up with the names of lawyers and accountants, you will want to set up appointments with the professionals. First find out if any consultation fee is required. If there is a charge it should be moderate.

When interviewing prospective lawyers and accountants, you needn't put on your district attorney costume. The idea simply is to find out

if the two of you are right for each other. Frankness on both sides is a
virtue. The purpose of asking questions is not to elicit answers. The
goal is to get useful information. The distinction is crucial. An answer
is merely a response to a question. It may or may not be satisfying.
Useful information is the data you need to make a good decision. The
data may be contained in the answer. They even may be found in the
manner in which the question is answered.

Generally, an answer provides partial information. Don't feel that
the professional fulfilled the social contract just by answering. Ask a
follow-up question. ("Could you please clarify something you just
said?" "Are you saying that's something I have to do or something I
don't have to do?" "You said this is an area of the law you know a
little bit about. What have you done for clients in this area?" "Do
you handle it or does somebody else in your firm handle it?")

The first set of questions concentrates on how the lawyer or accountant views your business. "What do you think I need in the way of
professional advice and service?" "Who are some of your clients?"
"Are any of them similar to me in any way (e.g., size, nature of the
business, special problems or concerns)?" "What do you typically do
for them?" "Have you done anything of a special nature that I also
would require?"

Then you'll want to know how you and the professional will work
together. They have to know what style client you are, and you have
to know how they like to run their offices.

"How far in advance do you give notice of filings, paperwork, or
information required of me?" "I like to use the phone a lot. Is there
a time of day when you prefer I do or don't call you?" "Can I call
you at home?" "If you're not available, can someone else in the office
help me?" "Do you have an answering machine, answering service,
voice mail, or beeper?" "How do you like to work with your clients—
housecalls? frequent or infrequent contact? formal relationship? social
relationship?"

Mercy me! We almost forget money. I wouldn't raise the "how
much" question at the start of the interview, but I wouldn't forget to
ask it. How much do they charge for their services? What's included
within this charge? How are the charges broken down? What services
cost extra? If a partner, associate, or staff member does the job, what
is the fee structure? When do they bill?

HOW TO MAKE FRIENDS WITH FEDS

If you want to learn something from the U.S. government (stop your snickering), you have two choices. You can contact the agency or department that you think administers the program or bureau that you think deals with the situation you are addressing. Then you call the agency *they* refer you to; then you call the agency *they* refer you to; then you call . . .

Or you can call a Federal Information Center (FIC). The FIC staffers know their way through the maze. They can tell you about publications, programs, and even government courses that answer your questions; and they can tell you just which government doors to knock on. Federal Information Centers are not exclusively for businesspeople. They field all sorts of queries from people in every walk or jog of life. Nevertheless, an FIC can be an excellent resource for business. They're particularly adept at helping people in their travels through SBA and IRS. The FIC people also might be able to tell you about government rules (ranging from federal procurement procedures to regulations) that might have a direct bearing on your particular business. The Federal Information Center staffers prefer phone calls to letters.

"When a letter comes in," explains one staffer, "the question is frozen. We may not know what is meant. If we're on the phone, we can ask you about it. We'll say, 'let's step back a moment and discuss what you meant, what you really wanted here.' We can help focus your question."

Ask your question as simply and directly as possible. Don't get into the trap of weaving acronyms, jargon, and program titles into your question. Your use of the wrong terms in an assured fashion may accidentally send the FIC staffer in the wrong direction. Also, please respect their time. The Federal Information Center personnel has endured cutbacks during the 1980s. (Oh, wasn't that a time?) The staff is generally attentive, courteous, and pressured to get to the next call.

Even if a query stumps the FIC folks, they know enough to help narrow the search. You'll find seventy FIC offices scattered throughout the country. Here is the list:

ALABAMA
Birmingham:
 (205) 322-8591
Mobile:
(205) 438-1421

ALASKA
Anchorage:
 (907) 271-2898

ARIZONA
Phoenix:
 (602) 261-3313

ARKANSAS
Little Rock:
(501) 378-6177

CALIFORNIA
Los Angeles:
(213) 894-3800
Sacramento:
(916) 978-4010
San Diego:
(619) 557-6030
San Francisco:
(415) 556-6600
Santa Ana:
(714) 836-2386

COLORADO
Colorado Springs:
(719) 471-9491
Denver:
(303) 844-6575
Pueblo:
(719) 544-9523

CONNECTICUT
Hartford:
(203) 527-2617
New Haven:
(203) 624-4720

FLORIDA
Fort Lauderdale:
(305) 522-8531
Jacksonville:
(904) 354-4756
Miami:
(305) 536-4155
Orlando:
(407) 422-1800
St. Petersburg:
(813) 893-3495

Tampa:
(813) 229-7911
West Palm Beach:
(407) 833-7566

GEORGIA
Atlanta:
(404) 331-6891

HAWAII
Honolulu:
(808) 541-1365

ILLINOIS
Chicago:
(312) 353-4242

INDIANA
Gary: (219) 883-4110
Indianapolis:
(317) 269-7373

IOWA
From all points in
Iowa: (800) 532-1556

KANSAS
From all points in
Kansas:
(800) 432-2934

KENTUCKY
Louisville:
(502) 582-6261

LOUISIANA
New Orleans:
(504) 589-6696

MARYLAND
Baltimore:
(301) 962-4980

MASSACHUSETTS
Boston:
(617) 565-8121

MICHIGAN
Detroit:
(313) 226-7016
Grand Rapids:
(616) 451-2628

MINNESOTA
Minneapolis:
(612) 370-3333

MISSOURI
St. Louis:
(314) 425-4106
From elsewhere in
Missouri:
(800) 392-7711

NEBRASKA
Omaha:
(402) 221-3353
From elsewhere in
Nebraska:
(800) 642-8383

NEW JERSEY
Newark:
(201) 645-3600
Trenton:
(609) 396-4400

NEW MEXICO
Albuquerque:
(505) 766-3091

NEW YORK
Albany:
(518) 463-4421

Buffalo:
(716) 846-4010
New York:
(212) 264-4464
Rochester:
(716) 546-5075
Syracuse:
(315) 476-8545

NORTH CAROLINA
Charlotte:
(704) 376-3600

OHIO
Akron:
(216) 375-5638
Cincinnati:
(513) 684-2801
Cleveland:
(216) 522-4040
Columbus:
(614) 221-1014
Dayton:
(513) 223-7377
Toledo:
(419) 241-3223

OKLAHOMA
Oklahoma City:
(405) 231-4868

Tulsa:
(918) 584-4193

OREGON
Portland:
(503) 221-2222

PENNSYLVANIA
Philadelphia:
(215) 597-7042
Pittsburgh:
(412) 644-3456

RHODE ISLAND
Providence:
(401) 331-5565

TENNESSEE
Chattanooga:
(615) 265-8231
Memphis:
(901) 521-3285
Nashville:
(615) 242-5056

TEXAS
Austin:
(512) 472-5494
Dallas:
(214) 767-8585

Fort Worth:
(817) 334-3624
Houston:
(713) 653-3025
San Antonio:
(512) 224-4471

UTAH
Salt Lake City:
(801) 524-5353

VIRGINIA
Norfolk:
(804) 441-3101
Richmond:
(804) 643-4928
Roanoke:
(703) 982-8591

WASHINGTON
Seattle:
(206) 442-0570
Tacoma:
(206) 383-7970

WISCONSIN
Milwaukee:
(414) 271-2273

Small Business Administration (SBA)

You've heard it said all over the place. Now read it here. The Small Business Administration (SBA) is a sterling resource for the new and established home officer—not so much because of the SBA loans that do exist (but don't hold your breath) but because the Small Business Administration has three solid programs under its umbrella.

SCORE (Senior Core of Retired Executives) is an organization of volunteers drawn from the ranks of retired businesspeople who are willing to share their expertise. The SCORE policy is to try to get you counseled by a volunteer who's familiar with your field. SCORE is most appropriate for those in the start-up phase of their businesses.

The SBA's Small Business Development Centers (SBDC) are particularly helpful for those who are off and running with their businesses. Various colleges and universities have been designated as SBDC sites. The professors and their willing students will look at a particular challenge (we're not supposed to say problem) and suggest remedies. Chances are you won't live happily ever after, but you can get an informed solution that will help you, even though the service is free.

As with the SBDC, the Small Business Institute (SBI) is more equipped to help businesses that already are established. Again, there's an academic affiliation. Here, the SBI assigns a graduate student to analyze a business need and to make recommendations. For example, you might like to advertise your business, but you don't know the most effective space and time buys for your budget.

In addition to the counseling, the Small Business Administration runs seminars and issues publications. One seminar I attended recently was about how to start and run a business. It went from 8:00 A.M. to 4:00 P.M., with coffee and lunch breaks. The attendees were an excellent advertisement for the American Dream—all ages, races, sexes, and all with a vision. The speakers managed to be encouraging, realistic, patient, and informative. There was very little if any hype. The seminar cost $10, which included a handout pack complete with government pamphlets that sell for $5.

The SBA has prepared more than fifty folders and booklets under the general heading of ''Business Development Publications.'' They deal with financial management and analysis, general management and planning, crime prevention, marketing, personnel management, and new products/ideas/inventions. The average price seems to be $1. The five-page publication called ''Thinking About Going Into Business?'' asks and answers thirty-five questions. The questions can lead you to some good basic resources.

Now about those SBA loans. First, the SBA doesn't make loans. It makes guarantees to banks. If the bank lends you money, and somewhere along the way you stop making payments, the government has to pay the bank a large portion of the loan.

Various SBA funds are available to guarantee loans in certain communities. The applicant (that's you) is expected to have collateral, a strong business plan, and documented means with which to pay back the loan. If I have all of that, one might wonder, what do I need the SBA for? What indeed? An SBA guarantee might not be called for, and that's good news. It cuts down on the paperwork. On the other hand, there may be individuals who have just about everything but the confidence of a bank's loan committee. For one reason or another, there still may be a perceived risk. In such a situation, the SBA loan program takes the worry out of being close.

Before contacting a bank, check with the Small Business Administration for a list of banks that currently deal with SBA loans. At the bank, request a loan officer who has had specific experience in dealing with SBA loans. If you have trouble finding out where in the SBA you should go for anything, don't forget to call the Federal Information Center. They'll tell you which line to stand on.

PERSONAL TRAINERS

New York metropolitan area home officers have a real resource in Angelo Valenti, a consultant to whom we already have referred. Valenti, founder of The Organizational Resource Co., Inc. (New York, New York), works with small and medium-size businesses. What does he do?

"I train them to make money," says Valenti. "I advise them about business planning, project management, raising capital, putting in marketing, and how to delegate and hire staff."

Valenti's clients pay The Organizational Resource Co. between $3,000 and $6,000 over several months. The more work Angelo does, the higher the fee. For example, it would cost the client more if Valenti actually wrote a business plan than it would if he advised the client on how to do the business plan.

I met Angelo Valenti at a Small Business Administration seminar where he was a featured speaker. As best I can figure out there's no clearly defined national association made up of people who do what Valenti does. Still, you'll find his peers around the country. They are the people speaking at other SBA courses. They also may be teaching classes at continuing education programs in universities, libraries, and so on. Look for the courses on how to start a business or how to write a business plan.

Business associations represent another source for the goose that hopes to have a golden egg. "After I opened the business," says Judith Lederman of JSL Public Relations, "I affiliated myself with a few different organizations: the Advertising Club of Westchester, the Westchester Association of Woman Business Owners, and Women in Communications. I had been at an all-time lonely point after the first six weeks of business. I didn't have anybody to bounce ideas off; there was no one to share or celebrate with when I got a good placement or a good client. The affiliations gave me a forum in which to meet people and network and share ideas.''

She found a number of tangible rewards. The contacts she made helped her quickly locate reliable professionals and services. Otherwise she would be spending a great deal of time tracking down people she needed. She also learned of a well-managed college intern program that, in fact, helped her hire a motivated assistant.

Several national membership organizations devote themselves specifically to the concerns of people who work at home. Typically, they offer a health insurance plan, discounts on various products and services, and publications. The newsletters are likely to contain information about tax matters, more effective marketing, useful products, and relevant government programs. The mix on these and other such topics varies according to the organization.

There is another interesting, albeit indirect, advantage to membership in these groups. Major corporations see the handwriting on the rec room wall. They know there is indeed such a beast as a home office market. It seems they are torn between greed and fear. How can they get a juicy piece of this market? How can they avoid being shunned by this market? The answer to these and associated questions leads them to wonder, What does the home office market really want?

For some of their research they turn to home-based business organizations. The directors of these groups consult to businesses. And now we get to that famous indirect advantage. In a sense, the directors act as lobbyists for their members. They accurately tell the corporate clients what product features are genuinely significant to home officers. They detail what home officers care about. They report trends and concerns, wants and needs. The results are products and services well-suited to the members, and, for that matter, the at-large population of people who work at home. You will find a few worthwhile organizations described in the Resources section below.

RESOURCES

Is Exporting for You (SBA). This eight-page booklet essentially answers its question with a hearty, ''Sure if you know what you're doing.'' It does have a useful chart that shows you which organization (federal or otherwise) you can go to for particular export information. Contact: U.S. Small Business Administration, P.O. Box 15434, Fort Worth TX 76119.

The Business Plan for Home-based Business (SBA, $1.50). This workbook (designated as Management Aids No. 2.028) is specifically designed to help people who work or intend to work at home come up with a business plan. The booklet contains a series of questions. They spur you to describe such things as the form of the business, principal activity, customer profile, market potential, competition, pricing, terms, sales plan, duties and responsibilities of all involved, banking plan, financial planning, and cash flow projection. The answers, when put together, form your business plan. The thirty-page book also has a worksheet to help you decide what kind of business you might want to enter. It is okay. It does not mention any kind of professional agenting or consulting business. Contact U.S. Small Business Administration, P.O. Box 15434, Fort Worth TX 76119.

Feasibility Checklist for Starting a Small Business (SBA, $1). This five-page questionnaire (designated as Management Aids No. 2.026) forces you to shine a flashlight in your own face in the dead of night and tell the truth. By answering its 117 questions honestly, you'll be able to see how ready you really are to launch a business. (Even if you've already started your company, the news might be a bit of a shock.) Some of the questions are as follows: List your product/services suppliers. Are there any causes (i.e., restrictions, monopolies, shortages) that make any of the required factors of production unavailable (i.e., unreasonable cost, scarce skills, energy, material, equipment, processes, technology, or personnel)? What minimum income do you require? What do you know about consumer shopping and spending patterns relative to your type of business? Are you aware of the major risks associated with your product? Service? Business? Contact: U.S. Small Business Administration, P.O. Box 15434, Fort Worth TX 76119.

The Small Business Legal Advisor by William A. Hancock (McGraw-Hill). This book explores the legal side of a variety of small business activities and situations. I believe the author really would be horrified if you used the book as a substitute for a lawyer. Use it instead as a travel guide to legal land. It explains issues and gives the kind of background that helps you establish your legal policies. In many cases you would require the services of a lawyer to make these policies effective and real. Topics covered include obtaining a good lawyer; partnerships, corporations, and hiring; buying an existing business; franchising; pensions, profit-sharing, and deferred compensation plans; occupational safety; business forms; patents, trademarks, and copyrights; insurance; and white-collar crime. Contact: McGraw-Hill, 1221 Ave. of the Americas, New York NY 10020.

Business Assistance (U.S. Department of Commerce, free). Specific questions of the where-do-I-go and how-can-I-get nature can be directed to this office. For example, a Minnesota company that was beginning to target its product to power plant operators wanted to find a quick way to locate such facilities. The Business Assistance Service told the company about the Energy Department's directory, "Inventory of Power Plants in the United States." Someone else wanted to know about the rates of duty on imported ice-hockey skates. The Business Assistance specialist sent along the relevant page from "Tariff Schedule of the United States Annotated." The most frequent queries this service receives concern government procurement, exporting, marketing, statistical sources, and regulatory matters. Contact Business Assistance Service, Office of Business Liaison, Room 5898 C, U.S. Department of Commerce, Washington DC 20230; (202) 377-3176.

Mancuso's Small Business Resource Guide by Joseph Mancuso (Prentice Hall Press). Written by the president of the Center for Entrepreneurial Management, the guide is an excellent compendium of associations, publications, and services. There's information about more than sixty categories ranging from accounting to women entrepreneurs. Strategically placed anecdotes and illustrations also pop up in this 557-page volume. Contact: Prentice Hall Press, 15 Columbus Circle, New York NY 10023.

The Coopers & Lybrand Guide to Growing Your Own Business by Seymour Jones, M. Bruce Cohen, and Victor V. Coppola (John Wiley & Sons, $19.95). The authors hold key positions with Coopers & Lybrand's Emerging Business Services Department. As one might expect of a book written by a Big Eight accounting firm's executives, this guide is particularly strong in its coverage of money issues. Chapter topics include finance sources, business plans, management of assets, accounting controls, employee benefit plans, tax strategies, estate tax planning, and going public. You'll find only passing references to marketing. Contact: John Wiley & Sons, 605 Third Ave., New York NY 10158.

The American Home Business Association. The AHBA counts among its membership lots of consultants in various industries, medical and therapeutic professionals, writers, and publishers.

"We have," says AHBA President Dee Denton, "the whole group of new people who worked for large companies and now take on clients to whom they consult."

The organization, which has 28,000 members, issues a monthly newsletter that seems to focus primarily but not exclusively on various money matters. Regular topics include getting more clients, structuring fees, tax information, business expansion, and saving time. AHBA membership includes authoritative answers to a member's individual questions. The AHBA forwards questions to one of its forty-eight experts. The answer goes back to the member by mail within a couple of days. Sometimes an AHBA staff member can answer the question immediately.

AHBA's buying service provides members with products at a 25 to 55 percent discount, as well as discounts on car rental, hotels, car purchases, and long-distance calls. Contact: American Home Business Association, 60 Arch St., Greenwich CT 06830; (203) 655-4380.

National Association for the Cottage Industry. Started in 1982, the NACI has as members an extremely broad spectrum of people who work out of their homes. The organization's strength, according to Coralee Smith Kern, founder and executive director, "is that the people who have surrounded themselves with the NACI are the experts on the public policy issues of home work." Kern says that NACI stays current with "what's happening in terms of zoning and labor law across the United States. . . . We know the position on home business taken by every state's governor, department of commerce, and department of community affairs."

Benefits include health insurance and a credit union, as well as car rental discount and long-distance phone service. Its bimonthly newsletter, *The Cottage Connection,* covers public policy issues, particularly those pertaining to zoning and legislation. You'll also find articles about how to run your business. Among the pieces in a representative issue were "Coping with Isolation," "Measuring Advertising Results," and "Trademark Registration." Contact: National Association for the Cottage Industry, P.O. Box 14850, Chicago IL 60614.

The National Association of Entrepreneurial Couples (NAEC, $100/year). NAEC is made up of couples who live and work together. Founders Frank and Sharon Barnett not only coined the term "copreneurs" but wrote the book *Working Together: Entrepreneurial Couples* (Tenspeed Press, 1989). The book is one part celebration of copreneuring, and one part how-to handbook. The Barnetts report that entrepreneurial couples share a high degree of communication, continual feedback, mutual trust, and a vision for where the enterprise is going. Copreneurs also are subject to many of the same problems. NAEC grew from response to the book. The young organization has membership in thirty states that ranges from couples running large corporations to couples running small businesses. Members are not necessarily home officers. Benefits for members include a quarterly newsletter, discount long distance phone service with U.S. Sprint (10 percent or higher), a buying service that provides discounts of up to 40 percent, and discounts to both NAEC events (seminars and the like) and events that the organization endorses. Each new member also receives a copy of *Working Together*. A newsletter subscription without membership costs $30 a year. You also can purchase a copy of *Working Together* from NAEC ($12.95 including postage and handling). Contact: National Association of Entrepreneurial Couples, P.O. Box 3238, Eugene OR 97403; (503) 344-1566.

Center for Entrepreneurial Management (CEM) ($96). Joseph Mancuso, founder and president, likes to say, "It's okay to be independent, but you don't have to be alone." Established in 1978, CEM has about 3,000 members. It is not specifically for people who work at home. Rather it is for people with "an entrepreneurial attitude." Many members are in the start-up phase; and, on the average, members tend to be running one-million- to two-million-dollar companies. According to Mancuso, membership benefits are mostly educational. They include subscriptions to *Inc.*, *Success*, *Venture*, and CEM's own monthly newsletter, *Entrepreneurial Manager's Newsletter*, which smoothly blends solid information with insights into the entrepreneurial mind (there's a whiff of appropriate rah-rah here) and CEM news. New members also receive *The CEM Membership Book* that includes sections on "How to Write a Winning Business Plan," "How to Buy a Business with Very Little Cash," and "How to Get a Business Loan Without Signing Your Life Away." Mancuso arranges nationwide meetings and events for the membership. (These do have admission prices.) Other benefits include discounts on books and tapes, travel, and credit cards. Advice-seeking members are helped at no charge. Their questions typically concern buying or selling a company, banking, raising of capital, and assembling and working with a board of directors. Mancuso thinks members make the best use of CEM when they come to meetings.

"Information in the mail is passing," he says. "You sort of let it accumulate, but if you actually come to something we do, you tend to take action."

Contact: Center for Entrepreneurial Management, 180 Varick St., New York NY 10014-4606; (212) 633-0060.

How to Really Start Your Own Business (Inc. Publishing, $29.95). With this videotape, a select group of nine entrepreneurs from a variety of businesses give you the inside track on such topics as "Testing the Idea," "Finding Good People," and "What It's Really Like to

Run Your Own Business.'' Also within the tape's ten "chapters" are clear tutorials on cash flow and raising money. This tape is an excellent primer on both inspirations and perspiration. Contact: Inc., (800) 372-0018.

Peak Learning (Audio-Renaissance Tapes, $11.70, including P&H). This is a perfect how-to audio tape for people who work at home. It's all about how to do something that we generally enjoy doing—that is, using our brains. Author/educator Ronald Gross has assembled some absolutely fascinating approaches to boosting the power of the old gray matter. The techniques include ''mind mapping'' new information, discovering and using your own personal learning style, tapping your creativity, and driving toward your goals with auto-suggestion. Contact: Audio-Renaissance Tapes, 9110 Sunset Blvd., Los Angeles CA 90069; (800) 333-3969.

Audio Tape Catalog (Nightingale-Conant, free). This catalog is definitely American. Its pages are filled with descriptions of audio cassettes that preach the gospel of self-improvement. The emphasis is on business. Some of the available programs are Edwin C. Bliss's ''Doing It Now'' (about procrastination), Hermine Hilton's ''Executive Memory Guide,'' ''Word Bank'' (a power vocabulary) from Simon & Schuster, ''Getting to Yes: How to Negotiate Agreement Without Giving In'' by Roger Fisher and William Ury. The sixty-three-page catalog offers tapes on such subjects as selling, negotiating, building success, and the law. Many tapes featuring Zig Ziglar, Leo Buscaglia, Robert Schuller, Wayne Dyer, and Napoleon Hill can be found. Contact: Nightingale-Conant Corporation, 7300 North Lehigh Ave., Chicago IL 60648-9951; (800) 323-5552.

Dial-A-Writer (American Society of Journalists and Authors, negotiable). If you ever need something written for your business (a letter, a press release, a pamphlet, a study, a book, etc.), you might want to hire a professional. For those who can't find a satisfactory pro, or who wish to spend as little time as possible looking, the Dial-A-Writer referral service might help. The ASJA is an organization of professional nonfiction free-lance writers. I happen to be a member, so this is a shameless plug. But it's a useful shameless plug. The organization has more than 700 different members scattered around the nation and in various well-known countries. You explain the details of your project to Dorothy Beach, director of the service. She puts you in touch with one or more appropriate members. She selects the names on the basis of their expertise in your area, background, and/or location. Contact: Dial-A-Writer, ASJA, 1501 Broadway, Suite 1907, New York NY; (212) 398-1934.

The Elements of Style by William Strunk, Jr., and E. B. White (Macmillan). Many good books tell businesspeople how to write. This is the reference work to which writers return. Among its many virtues is its brevity. Its eighty-five pages contain everything you need to know to write with clarity and color. Contact: Macmillan Publishing Co., 866 Third Avenue, New York NY 10022.

Inc. (Inc. Publishing Corp., $3/issue, $25/yr). Describing itself as "the magazine for growing companies," *Inc.* is a finite but powerful resource for home officers. Its focus clearly is on small and mid-size companies. *Inc.*'s notion of small may be mega to most of us. Still, much of the information is solid, either immediately applicable or— if nothing else—practical information that deserves being filed in a corner of the mind. It really is an anthology of instructive case histories (bombs as well as skyrockets), ideas and trends, news, and resources. Contact: Inc. Publishing, Subscription Service Dept., P.O. Box 51534, Boulder CO 80321-1534; (800) 234-0999.

National Home Business Report (Barbara Brabec Productions, $18/yr). This quarterly publication splendidly serves its readership of home-based businesspeople. Subscribers are people who tend to be running smaller businesses. Brabec defines the breakdown as "product-oriented where they do crafts, sell the products of others, or produce books and newsletters; and service business—everything from gift-shopping to handwriting analysis." The NHBR owes its lively, information-laden approach to Brabec's extensive knowledge and her close contact with readers. Many readers will submit items or articles on how they've dealt with specific challenges. The result is a networky feel and a good range of concerns and solutions that subscribers can relate to. It should be noted that Brabec is the author of *Homemade Money* (Betterway Publications, $18.95, including postage and handling). Its accurate subtitle is "A Definitive Guide to Success in a Home Business." In addition to everything else, the book presents lots of good marketing information. It and her other offerings are described in her free catalog. Contact: Barbara Brabec Productions, P.O. Box 2137, Naperville IL 60566.

The Organizational Resource Company (fees vary). This is Angelo Valenti's company. Angelo, whose insights are laced throughout *Your Home Office,* considers himself a coach to small businesses. He consults on such vital areas as business plans, marketing, raising capital, project management, productivity, strategic planning, and personnel recruitment. Contact: The Organizational Resource Company, 40 W. 38th St., New York NY 10018; (212) 382-0771.

Working from Home, 2nd edition, by Paul and Sarah Edwards (Jeremy P.

Tarcher, Inc., $12.95). Their background as successful work-at-homers and their separate training (he's a lawyer; she's a therapeutic counselor) give this book a solid grounding. The book covers areas we look at here. Their perspective is a bit different, and they give more attention to legal and interpersonal issues. The Edwardses also host a very good weekly national radio show, and operate the "Work at Home" forum on CompuServe. Contact: Jeremy P. Tarcher, Inc., 9110 Sunset Blvd., Suite 250, Los Angeles CA 90069.

Business Books (Self Counsel Press, various prices). The emphasis here is on self-help with a strong emphasis on business. The publisher is a subsidiary of a Canadian company. There is a strong Northwest regional list, as well as an effort, wherever possible, to have material that is useful to the Canadian market. Self Counsel's business list overflows with solid texts, including its books about how to start and run particular businesses; works dealing with finance and accounting; and some savvy introductions to marketing. Contact: Self Counsel Press, 1704 North State St., Bellingham WA 98225; (206) 676-4530.

Your Library. Unfortunately, the library as a business tool is one of our better-kept secrets. Yes there are all those books, magazines, and reports that will give you information for and about your business. But today's library is exceptionally exciting (in an understated way, of course). You still can get information even when it's not on file in your local library. Libraries can borrow from other libraries in their cities and maybe even states. Some libraries are set up to get information via fax from other institutions. Many libraries can go online with computer data bases for you and charge you the cost, which is fairly inexpensive. (I heard something like $6/hr.) Most reassuring is that when you must find out something, a librarian usually will be able to tell you exactly where to look. The system works.

Skills for Success by Dr. Adele Scheele (Ballantine Books, $3.95). Although not specifically directed at people who operate home-based businesses, this book is a solid primer on how to cultivate those skills that make others (and yourself) aware of your achievements. Contact: Ballantine Books, 201 E. 50th St., New York NY 10022.

You Are the Message by Roger Ailes (Dow-Jones, Irwin, $24.95). Ailes is best known as the political consultant who helps presidents and various leaders of the free world communicate, particularly on television. You may not be running for or from office, but this book can represent a good investment for you. Whether you deal with media, do public speaking, or even communicate one on one, you will benefit from Ailes's practical advice on how to focus your personality and your message for maximum effectiveness. Contact: Dow-Jones, Irwin, (800) 634-3966.

Secrets from a Stargazer's Notebook by Debbi Kempton-Smith (Bantam, $4.95). We all know that timing is important. Many of the wheel-and-deal, do-or-die set use astrology as an aid to finding the right timing. Some use it to get a fix on people they might have to work with or against. This book is good for those interested in adding astrology to their selection of tools. It contains much information and just as much zest. Contact: Bantam Books, 666 Fifth Ave., New York NY 10103.

Video Catalog (Video-SIG, $4.95). Independent video productions, costing $14.95 each, are described in this book. Home officers might benefit from the handful of business-oriented tapes that range from telephone technique to interviewing prospective employees. Not to be ignored are personal development tapes. Also, you may find that the roster of instructional and documentary programs harbors a videotape that might be useful to your particular business, whether you use it to drive home a specific point to your clients, or to better understand a topic. Contact: Video-SIG, 1030 East Duane Ave., Suite C, Sunnyvale CA 94086; (800) 245-6717.

CHAPTER 6

Management Information Services

Every business that has at least one computer has a computer department. This is true whether the business is a many-computered huge corporation occupying a building that has the same name as the corporation, or whether the business sits on a desk in the corner of someone's living room. Of course, in the big-time Ozymandias Corporation, it is not called a computer department but rather MIS for Management Information Services, or maybe DP for Data Processing. The computer is as important a business tool as the telephone. You too should be thinking about your own MIS department.

There is a clinical term for what happens when someone contemplates the purchase of a computer. It is called "going bananas." Suddenly you feel that this decision is the most important one you ever made in your life. Forget about choosing someone to share your life with. Forget about standing in a voting booth and deciding who you want as the leader of the free world. There is a feeling that the computer you buy determines whether you are the shrewd, savvy, forward-looking cookie you always knew you were or a hopeless schlemiel.

A good part of this concern comes from the belief that a computer is an investment—something that grows or decreases in value. In my opinion, it is not so much an investment as it is a tool. It's something you use, like a box of paper clips. The differences between various brands of computers are of some consideration, but one shining truth should prevail: All computers do the same things. They just do them with different degrees of sophistication.

82

COMPUTER BASICS

For those who are currently computerless, and for those who are curious, here is a short course on everything you have to know about computer science. Three key elements are data, program, and memory. Data are the given information (words and/or numbers) with which the computer works. The program is the list of instructions that tells the computer what to do with the data.

Memory is probably the hardest aspect to explain, and the easiest to use. Memory is the vessel that holds the work. First, there is the computer's internal memory, officially referred to as random access memory or RAM. It functions only while the computer is switched on. The amount of RAM (for example, 512K) describes the amount of program and data that can be crammed into the computer while the machine is on. When you enter information, the computer relates the entry to the program and the data in its memory. The computer sorts, compares, discards, and builds—all at lightning speed.

What do you do when you're ready to turn the computer off and you want to preserve all your precious work? You use external memory, usually in the form of a floppy disk or hard disk. The data you've saved are in a "file." When you're ready to roll again, you load the file you saved into the computer's RAM.

This is where the computer really begins to shimmer.

If the file you've saved is a letter or a report, just an appropriate updating here and there, and *poof!* you can print out the new version without retyping the whole document. If you've entered orders that you've received during the month, you can quickly see what's been taken out of your inventory, or what invoices have been sent out, or just how you're doing. It's easier to look up a single phone number on your Rolodex than to consult the computer. Nevertheless, the computer excels in helping you look, instantly finding a batch of numbers according to area code or zip code, finding clients who haven't ordered in at least sixty days, or finding clients who buy at least $700 worth of merchandise per order.

Many programs are designed to be used by people who are not hampered by any trace of computing knowledge—people like me. We don't see any of the inner workings of the program. We're not bothered by knowing any of the steps the machine goes through. All we need to know is that we press a designated key and get an expected effect. Everything else goes on inside the machine where it can't scare the horses or the humans. Usually, the more a program can do, the more you have to learn, but you don't have to learn it all at once. You learn it as you need it. When you discover that you need to learn a new trick, you just turn to the documentation ("computerese" for instruction manual) and look up the needed command in the index.

Yes, documentations are a form of punishment. The publishing industry, however, offers a variety of books about every specific computing topic imaginable. Usually, these are clearer than the documentation. As you repeatedly use the item you've looked up, it becomes part of your repertoire.

I used to use a word processing program called Perfect Writer. To get various typographic effects (italics, boldface, underlining) you put the particular word or phrase within parentheses, preceded by a command. One day I was on the subway scribbling some notes. When I came to a phrase that I wanted underlined, I didn't do what normal people would do and scrawl a line underneath. Without thinking, I enclosed the words in parentheses and preceded them with the appropriate Perfect Writer command "@U." What happened, of course, is that the computer maneuvers for underlining had become absorbed into my system.

A vigorous computer education industry has burst forth. Private training centers, adult education programs, instructional videotapes and, of course, tutorial computer software are all available. Corporations are hefty consumers of these electronic schoolrooms. In many cases, the prices reflect this demand.

My basic rule for all computer programs is, What at first is complex soon is reflex, so don't get a complex. Other appliances are goal-oriented. For example, a dishwasher washes dishes. Computers are process-oriented. They lend order, speed, and precision to any task to which they've been assigned. Other devices go to work as soon as you press the *on* button. In this respect, a computer is more like an automobile. Turning a key in the ignition is not enough. You still have to change gears and step on the pedals and turn the steering wheel. With a computer, after you turn it on, you still have to press buttons and perhaps insert disks to get it going. Once you're in the program, all you have to do is cruise.

The thought of being dogmatic makes me cringe, but the sooner you get a computer into your home office, the better off you will be.

SO WHAT KIND OF COMPUTER
SHOULD YOU GET?

Let's take a look at the likely candidates. But before we do, let's nibble at two more technical concerns. The fact that there are different disk operating systems is something you have to appreciate. Once you understand it, you can toss it out and manage to live your life without ever raising the issue again.

Unfortunately, the easiest way to define a disk operating system (DOS) is that it helps the computer operate the disks. That really doesn't take us too far, does it? So let's journey through history. In earlier computer days, the machine was able to perform its functions because a human stationed at the machine sent commands by turning various switches on and off at the right times. The switcher performed very much like a Swiss bell ringer. This was a human operating system. There was a universal desire to automate. Information was sent by tape and so we had tape operating systems. The emergence of disks brought us DOS.

If the disk is formatted for the computer's DOS then the computer can "read" files on the disk, and also "write" files to the disk. Otherwise, the computer is a wonderful brain that cannot express itself. A program that is written for one kind of disk operating system just won't work in a computer that depends on another type of DOS.

The second consideration is the chip. Computers have many chips, but only one is "the chip." It is the main brain of the operation. Again, different kinds of computers are based on different chips. Within the same family of compatible computers, you find simpatico but different chips. Their differences denote their technical capacities.

When we talk about what kind of computer, we're really talking about what kind of disk operating system and what kind of chip.

The IBM Choice

During the first years of the personal computer, a number of machines—each with a different operating system—took hold. These included the Apple, the Atari 800, the Tandy, and the Commodore PET. (By the way, while avoiding work recently, I came across the July/August 1977 issue of *People's Computers* magazine which contained a news item about the then-impending PET. It gives a good sense of how far we've come, and I quote: "The PET Computer by Commodore will be rolling off the assembly in early September at a bargain price of $595. . . . The PET is a self-contained factory assembled unit that contains a 6502 microcomputer, keyboard, CRT display (40 columns, 25 lines), 1000-baud tape cassette and memory. For $595, you get 4K of user memory [or 8K for $795] . . .")

Along came the Osborne and the Kaypro 2. These had three big selling points. All the necessary hardware—computer, keyboard, monitor, disk drives—was assembled in a carry-away package. A basic library of software was bundled with the machine at no extra charge. They used a powerful operating system—CP/M—that offered many advantages. When I acquired my Kaypro 2, many knowledgeable people predicted that CP/M was definitely going to be the standard operating system everyone awaited. Other CP/M computers came out.

Still, a significant portion of the potential business market held out. It didn't want to know from CP/M. These people weren't going to buy a computer until they heard the word of God. As it turned out, a press release from IBM sufficed. IBM's entry was the reassurance that corporations and hesitant individuals needed. Computers may be the last refuge for brand loyalty.

When IBM first introduced its personal computer (PC), it also introduced a proprietary disk operating system—PC-DOS. The sudden relative popularity of the PC fueled the introduction of software (particularly for business) for the PC. The availability of software made the PC more popular, and voilà more software. Other manufacturers eyed the market, but there was the problem of PC-DOS. The introduction of MS/DOS (a viable PC-DOS alternative) made it possible for manufacturers to make IBM-compatible machines and software without being licensed by IBM.

At the time of this writing, the IBMs and IBM compatibles are howling happily in the marketplace. (According to a survey sponsored by Fuji Photo Film USA [a manufacturer of diskettes], 38 percent of home office users have IBM or IBM-compatible PCs, 31 percent own Commodore computers, and 12 percent own Apple computers.) More people have been buying into the IBM approach. In turn, more software creators are producing programs for the IBM family. More peripheral manufacturers are churning out devices that easily hook up to PC-DOS and MS-DOS machines.

As best I can tell, during the last five years most of the new business software has been for MS-DOS and PC-DOS. It's going to continue this way for at least the next three years. Each piece of new software represents an opportunity to do something faster, smarter, better, more efficiently, more effectively. An IBM or IBM clone would be a very practical choice. The price need not make you blue because the IBM compatibles are cheaper than IBM computers.

When I began to work on this book, I didn't have an IBM or IBM-compatible computer. I had (and have) a CP/M computer. I borrowed an MS-DOS computer from its manufacturer, HeadStart. I felt that since I was going to talk about MS-DOS programs, it might be nice if I also used them.

HeadStart also interested me because the company has leaped into the home market (office and otherwise). Many other manufacturers direct their marketing at corporate buyers for very understandable reasons. In the first place, a corporation doesn't have to be sold on the need for having computers. A corporation buys more than one machine at a time. The corporation is less fussy about little details such as price. The corporation's needs are perfectly suited to features provided by more expensive technology. Chief among these needs is that more than one person and, very often, more than one department, will deal with the same data.

Harry Fox, president of HeadStart, feels that in this environment the microcomputer industry is preoccupied with "offering the latest and greatest hardware" and doesn't consider sufficiently "developing useful applications to go with that hardware."

"The truth of the matter," says Fox, "is that what we'll call for the moment an XT computer—which can be categorized as a single-user, single-tasking desktop or laptop product—probably will fulfill the need of 90 percent or more of potential home office users.

"Unfortunately, a lot of people get sucked into expensive hardware, high-speed products, high-capacity drives and waste their money. With what they could save by buying a less powerful machine, they'd be able to buy important things like modems, decent software application packages, and other useful accessories that are out there."

It's not exactly a coincidence that HeadStart manufactures exactly the kind of computer that Fox extolls. He has set sights on a marketplace of 96 million American households, and he has a strong feeling about what technology is appropriate and will be greeted as such. He discusses the computer as a tool, and gives a useful analogy.

"You can buy a really fine hand drill for $29.95," says Fox, "if you're not a professional carpenter but somebody who occasionally has to drill holes. To spend more than the $30 on a reputable product is throwing out money. Suppose you go out and buy a $1,000 drill set which has variable speed, autoreversing, and a bunch of special features, and it takes special ultra-hard bits for cutting through metal. If all you're going to do with that tool is once or twice a year cut a hole into a door or hang a picture or something like that, you're overkilling. The other side of the coin is if you're going to need to do lots of special things and spend $30 on a product and it's going to break because you're using it for the wrong application, that's also wasting money."

Macintosh, Amiga, and Atari ST

Apple's Macintosh, Atari's ST, and Commodore's Amiga are in the same family of computers, although each has a different operating system. They offer ease of use, which really means that it's easy to learn how to use them. They also have won much praise for their graphics and sound capabilities. These qualities attract people working in the visual arts or in music. The Macintosh is the most entrenched of the three and has the most software available. Also, the Macintosh successfully penetrated the business market, which means it's trusted by people who wear suits. An equally important meaning is that lots of good business software is available for it. Both the Amiga and the Atari have significantly lower prices than the Macintosh.

L. R. Shannon, writing in the January 31, 1989, *New York Times,* quotes an Atari executive who said that the Atari and Amiga computers are in the PC ghetto. "Users of IBM-compatible and Macintosh computers," explains Shannon, "prefer to pretend that Atari and Amiga computers do not exist, even though the machines are better in some ways and more cost-effective for many users."

After favorably reviewing a new Atari model, Shannon writes, "Most computers used in businesses are IBM compatibles (or Macintoshes) with vast libraries of interchangeable software and security of dealing with well-established standards. A [Atari] Mega ST sets its own standard, a wonderful one but one with limited or nonexistent compatibility with other operating systems."

Shannon concludes by saying that the lone hobbyist or the user with specialized interests could benefit from an Atari, but the business user wandering through the IBM or Macintosh landscape had better be skeptical of the Atari. This wisdom may be conventional, but conventional wisdom is what determines standards.

Others (A Sneaky Alternative)

The computer setup you have your eye on may cost more than you're able or willing to spend when you start your home office. Many would counsel you to wait until you get exactly what you want. I firmly believe that any computer—even the outmoded one for which there is no real new software—is better than no computer.

About three years ago, a discount camera chain had a sale on Atari 800 computers that offered the computer and a printer for $400. A writer friend of mine snatched one up, and was able to increase his productivity as a writer. A few years ago, when my Kaypro 2 started wheezing and grinding to a halt, the repair bills added up to one statement: It was time to get a new computer. Fortunately, I was put in touch with a seventy-year-old woman who lived in New Jersey who wanted to get rid of her Epson QX-10 (like the Kaypro 2, a CP/M computer). She had hardly used the Epson, but she wanted to get a Macintosh so she could communicate with her grandson in Arizona. She sold me the computer and printer for $300.

If your finances encourage you to get a so-called outmoded computer, do it. The computer doesn't know it's outmoded. It will give you word processing, spreadsheeting, and quick information access capabilities. Having these perks—even through a slow, limited, outmoded computer—will help you more than not having them.

If you compare an available cheap computer (ACC) to the newest, the fastest, the best, you'll be sick and sullen. If you compare your life with an ACC to what your business would be like with no computer at all you will be wise and practical.

Of course, there's a downside to an ACC. When new applications come along, they're simply not written for the outmoded computers. There's no real desktop publishing program for my Epson QX-10. On the other hand, despite the thousands and thousands of programs that you can dip into, there are only a few types of programs that you're likely to need.

The other downside doesn't occur until you get a new computer. The question is what do you do with your old programs and disks? Programs for one operating system will not work with a computer using another DOS. They will be history. Your files, however, can be used. There are programs that make conversion possible. There are companies that do conversions for you. Also it's possible to send files from one computer to another directly or indirectly with a modem. Modems are discussed later in this chapter.

What Kind, Already?

First check your budget. If you can afford an IBM clone, do it. The MS-DOS systems tend to be less expensive than the official PC-DOSers manufactured by IBM. A compatible will put you in the mainstream of computing life. I know that having your own home office means that you're likely to swim in any old stream that you choose. I assure you that an MS-DOS computer won't make you a pod person. It'll just make it possible for you to have the widest assortment of software, be able to add peripherals to your computer with a minimum of fuss (because they're often configured for IBM or IBM compatibles), and exchange disks with clients and colleagues who probably have the same type of operating system.

If your work demands extra attention to graphics and/or sound, then the Amiga, Macintosh, and Atari ST are likely to be the best choices. These also might be appropriate if you want an "easier" computer to learn. (Of course, even laboratory critters can learn to press buttons in sequence, and they're not smart enough to start their own businesses.)

If the work you do encourages the use of a particular program available for only one kind of computer, then that's the computer to get. If you have a primary client who uses a particular type of computer, that's the one you should get.

If you can't afford the computer you were intended to have, then get an ACC. Use it, and as soon as you can afford something more suitable, scrap the old one. Don't worry. You'll have gotten your money's worth from it.

HeadStart President Harry Fox has some good advice for those who venture into a computer store. "We're a society of smell, touch, feel, and see," says Fox. "If you can't see it, touch it, feel it, and smell it, don't buy it. That's my advice, plain and simple. When you go into a store and you look at a computer, have that person behind the counter demonstrate to you what you are paying for. Physically show you what it is. If they're telling you that the machine has X amount of mips or works at a certain megahertz speed and that's the reason you should buy it and spend more money for it, don't buy it for that reason.

"If the salesperson can show you that it comes with a really solid keyboard that's easy on the fingers; it comes with a certain number of drives or hard drives that let you access information; it's IBM compatible and they prove it to you by pulling IBM-compatible software; it has things like a mouse or the ability to plug a printer right in without buying accessories; when they can show you the applications either included with the system or offering extra; when they show you how to use the machine—that's how you decide to buy it. The wrong reasons are that somebody told you to buy it but you don't know why they told you or this happens to be the newest and latest model."

It's not a shock that computer store salespeople are there to sell. What may be shocking is that consumers (you and me) too often uncritically heed what salespeople say. The experiences and knowledge of computer consultants John and Barbara McMullen confirm this.

"The majority of people who do something with numbers on computers," says John McMullen, "are best served by Lotus 1-2-3 on an IBM computer. For some people who work with numbers, spreadsheets really aren't appropriate—perhaps equation solvers are. Those people might walk out the door with 1-2-3 and an IBM computer because that's what comes to mind with the computer salesman. That's what they sell. A computer store can't stock everything.''

A magazine once hired the McMullens for a covert mission—shopping. ''We did an undercover thing for *INFOworld*,'' says John McMullen. ''We found the worst computer salesman and the best in the same store. We found men were treated better than women, and men in suits were being treated better than men in jeans. People asked Barbara if she was gathering information for her boss. At that time she was an officer of a 2,400-member computer club and in *Who's Who in Women*.''

Regardless of which computer you get, a few other blipping, blinking additions will help out in your home office.

PRINTERS

The first time I saw a manuscript advance steadily from my Atari printer, tears came to my eyes. It was so easy. Words were jumping onto the page, and all I had to do at that point was watch. In those days (the beginning of the previous decade) the hotly argued choices were daisy wheel versus dot matrix (the D-styles). The daisy wheel output looks like a typewritten copy. And no wonder. As with a Selectric ball, the wheel holds complete characters. Each time the wheel strikes the ribbon, a fully formed letter or number goes onto the pages. Though faster than typing, the daisy wheel is molasses compared to dot matrix printers. With the dot matrix approach, pins strike the ribbon, leaving dots in their wake. The proximity of the dots to each other and, in varying degrees, the gullibility of our eyes connect the dots.

While daisy wheel printers have offered type clarity, the dot matrix variety offered speed (measured in characters per second or CPS) and the ability to do designs (otherwise known as graphics). These days, both D styles are classified as impact printers. (They hit the ribbon; the ribbon hits the paper.) The dot matrix quality has soared so much that the daisy wheel, though still around, might be a bit déclassé.

There are two categories of dot matrix: 9-pin and 24-pin. The 9-pinners are perfectly fine for draft work and yeoman work. Most offer a near-letter-quality (NLQ) type style that is fairly presentable. The 24-pin dot matrix printers offer more speed and more dots per dollar, which makes for some fine-looking pages.

For every yin there's a yang and so we also have nonimpact printers:

laser printers and ink-jet printers. They send fully formed, well-defined characters to the paper. The laser printer technology makes it a kissing cousin of the photocopier. It creates a page at a time, rather than a character at a time. Ink jets spray the characters onto the page. Both do it with speed, measured in pages per minute (six and up) rather than characters per second. They do it quietly. There is no ghostly machinery making steady unnerving noises. And they do it expensively. Laser printers start at $2,500. Ink jets cost $1,500 or a bit less. The prices used to be much higher. If speed, quality, and comfort are important, then nonimpact printers are very much to be considered.

When you buy a printer, you are limited by your ability to mediate between your piggy bank and your desires. Whatever you do, make sure you see what the printer's output really looks like. Are these the characters that you're willing to hang out with?

GET YOUR MODEM WORKING

The modem is the device that hooks up your computer to your phone line, so that information can gallop back and forth between your computer and somebody else's. That other computer may be a client to whom you send or from whom you receive a file. It might be a great big computer in the sky (CompuServe, Dow Jones, Knowledge Index, etc.) that houses scads of data bases from which you ingeniously extract valuable information.

There are a few facts to note about modems. Hayes basically set the standards for modems. Other manufacturers offer Hayes-compatible modems, and the Hayes versions tend to cost more. As usual, they all work well enough.

The measurement we look at in a modem is bauds per second (bps). It describes the rate at which characters shoot through the phone lines. The higher the rate, the faster the information goes from one end to the other. And—you guessed it—the higher the rate, the greater the cost. The modem is a one-time expenditure, but each use incurs an expense. The faster the bps, the shorter the connect time. At first, 300 bps was the standard rate, 1,200 bps moved in and, at the time of this writing, 2,400 bps is establishing a beachhead. In order to use a modem, you need software. It is not terribly complicated, and will be discussed later.

Modems themselves are blank little boxes that deserve little meditation once they've been installed. What they allow you to do, however, is absolutely glorious. Your computer plus a modem plus another computer and modem equals telecommunications—the ability to send and obtain useful information (a.k.a. data) from anywhere. After all, businesspeople have learned that what we don't know will absolutely slaughter us.

"Accessing information," says HeadStart's Harry Fox, "quickly and conveniently from a PC versus spending half your life in research or never even finding information in the first place is probably the greatest computer tool." The modem is one broad bridge for information traffic.

Information Utilities

Sometimes referred to as online services, information utilities are those great faraway sources of information. The info is packaged several different, exciting ways. With your modem you log on to a service and spend a few minutes to research a subject in a data base (perhaps the Business Magazine Index), send messages to other users of the utility, check to see if you've received messages, check on a special-interest group (SIG) bulletin board geared toward your profession, or type of computer, or area of expertise and/or obsession, and see what notices have been posted. You might want to find the best air travel bargain and order the tickets. You pay according to the amount of time you spend online. It's like paying the electricity for the amount of time you keep your lights on.

SURGE PROTECTORS

It is wise to get a surge protector as quickly as you can. These devices protect computers, printers, phones, fax machines, and the like from a tidal wave of electrical current that suddenly rushes through the lines. These surges (a.k.a. spikes) can be caused by heavy electricity in the atmosphere. They also have exceedingly domestic causes, most notably big-motored household appliances such as refrigerators or air conditioners that switch on and off.

The surge of power can overload computer chips and damage or erase the memory. The surge protector "clamps" the spike when it happens, and regulates the amount of voltage that courses through the system. You plug the surge protector into the electrical outlet and in turn plug the various devices you wish to safeguard into the surge protector. It comes either as a free-standing strip or in a wall-mounted form. The Underwriters Laboratories has studied surge protectors and has come up with a rating (UL 1449). Labels on surge protectors for which the rating has been applied and received indicate the maximum amount of voltage that can pass through the wires. Lower is better.

Think of the internal wiring as being connected to the two or three prongs of the appliance's plug. The prongs (and the wires) are designated as hot, neutral, and ground. The surge floods through one wire and leaps from one point to another. The most basic surge protector gives hot to neutral protection. More sophisticated devices offer hot to ground and neutral to ground protection. Some surge protectors also deal with the electrical spike's stepbrother, electromagnetic interference (EMI) and radio frequency interference (RFI). Some also provide phone line protection.

CD-ROM

The same type of compact disk that holds music is being ogled by the computer industry because it can hold great amounts of information. Already law libraries are being put on CD to interface with computers. CD-ROMs are inserted into CD-ROM drives. Steve Jobs' Next Computer uses a compact disk variation both as a library and as a medium on which to store new files. At the time of this writing, the technology is just filtering into public use, but it's on its way and worth thinking about.

"We're spending a lot of time and effort," says Harry Fox of HeadStart, "to bring the $100 encyclopedia into the home on a CD-ROM. It not only saves space but allows people to update themselves on a 5″ disk affordably. That's not long-term future. That's short-term future." (At the end of 1989 HeadStart unveiled a computer that uses CD-ROM technology.)

OTHERS

There's a host of other accessories to make your computing life easier, surer, smarter, neater. They include boxes in which to store your diskettes, stands on which to place your printer, and so on. We will look at a number of these in the catalog.

SOFTWARE

As impressive as your computer might be, it is nothing without software to give meaning to its life. Below are the prime programs.

Word Processing

Probably the most popular and most readily valued type of program, word processing gives you a staff of corresponding secretaries. Bare-bones word processing allows you to write, store, and edit your prose. Your time is spent in writing and honing rather than typing and re-typing. More sophisticated packages allow for typographical and layout nuances, specialized features such as footnotes, and a variety of time-saving tricks.

Spreadsheets

The advent of the electronic spreadsheet is said to have given a rich vitamin B shot to computer sales. Based on the multicolumned tabular sheets of yore, a spreadsheet allows you to process columns of numbers (as well as columns of words stating what those numbers represent). You can do all sorts of mathematical stunts with those numbers. Change a number or formula and see what happens to the whole col-umn. Compare one column to another. From this number processing, you can derive all sorts of financial information from the "what if" to the "what happened."

Data Bases

Computernauts love to prate about how any body of information is a data base. They'll say things like, "The phone directory is a data base," "*Encyclopedia Britannica* is a data base," and "Your address book is a data base." I think they stop short of saying, "Your mother is a data base," as they know that such an observation can lead to a fight. The data base, then, is a collection of facts. A data-base program allows you to sift through the facts, at lightning speed, and find just those you wish arranged in whatever order makes sense to you. Data processing is another example of the computer's special ability to access information.

Integrated Programs

Integrated programs combine word processing and spreadsheet and data-base applications. You can pluck information from one module and plant it in another (e.g., you can patch data-base info into a report you're preparing on the word processor). You get three for the price (sometimes hefty) of one. You use a lot of the same commands throughout for moving the cursor and manipulating, which makes learning all three modules easier. Some people who have heavy needs in a particular area may prefer to have both an integrated program and a powerful program dedicated to word processing, spreadsheet, or data base.

Graphics

These programs are dedicated to making pictures and designs, including charts.

Telecommunications

This program tells your computer how to talk to the modem. The results, depending on the sophistication, are ease of use and some good tricks for communicating with other computers. Sometimes a manufacturer will include a free telecom program with the modem. Communication modules also can be found in some integrated packages, as well in some word processing programs. Then there are stand-alone telecommunications programs that you can buy.

Desktop Publishing (DTP)

A DTP program allows you to lay out a page by combining art and words on the computer screen, without one touching a pair of scissors or getting a whiff of rubber cement. The advent of laser printers, computers with more memory, and more accomplished word processing and graphics makes these programs sensible and desirable. In the home office, desktop publishing programs are great for composing newsletters, advertisements, brochures, manuals, and so on. We will talk a little more about DTP programs in Chapter Eleven.

Memory Resident Programs

These programs get loaded into the computer's memory along with the main program you're using. You pop a resident program into view when you need it. They do little gofer chores. A resident program might include a calculator, a memo pad, and a calendar. You might stop in the middle of word processing to do a little math problem. Someone might phone you to make an appointment, and you might call up your calendar.

Utilities

The above categories deal with ways that the computer helps you be more productive with your various tasks. Utilities help the performance of the computer itself. They deal with finding files more easily, having the disk (hard or floppy) work better, compressing data so you can get more information in a file, rescuing damaged files, and so forth. One particularly useful utility program is the "shell." It acts as a mediator between you and MS/DOS so that you can cruise through your programs without learning some of those tedious computer commands.

When you're ready to buy a type of program, you'll probably go through the usual choreography. You'll check reviews of this program in computer magazines. The reviewers for *PC Computing, PC Resource,* and *Home Office Computing* magazines usually do a responsible job. They carefully explain what they test the programs for, and what features they deem important. You might check reviews in trade or professional journals. These can be genuinely unreliable. The evaluations might be gems or the products of uninformed minds. There's a certain giddy propriety in falling in love with advanced features. Try to remember what you want this software to do for you.

There's another good tactic, particularly valuable in the case of expensive software. Ask the store or software publisher for a "demo" disk. As the name suggests, you get a chance to try out the package in the privacy of your home. A demo has the features of the program, and allows you to discover what working with the program is like: what it does, how it feels, whether it solves your problems. Companies usually charge between $10 and $75 per demo, depending on the program. Usually, if you buy it, this charge is deducted from the program's price. Demos also might be available directly from the software publisher.

Whichever software you buy, there's a particular section of small print worth checking. It is called "System Requirements," and usually can be found both in an ad and on the program's packaging. The system requirements tell you what kind of computer operating system the software is intended to work with, as well as the minimum amount of internal memory needed.

As you approach C-Day (the day you absolutely must get a system) you might want to consider hiring a computer consultant. It's likely to cost between $50 and $100 an hour. A consultant can be particularly valuable if you are particularly busy or steadfastly ignorant. Good consultants can do anything or everything for you. They can advise you on the computer system and packaged software to buy. They also can create special software just for you. Essentially they take an existing program and modify it for your business's special needs.

As with everything else, the best way to get a consultant is through personal contacts: friends, colleagues, associations. Of course, if a consultant is referred to you, be sure to ask your contact those salient questions. What did the consultant do for you? How much did it cost? How did it work out? Was the consultant's advice any different from what you were going to do? Could you understand what the consultant was saying? Was the consultant available to troubleshoot or do fine-tuning after the equipment was purchased and installed?

The important questions to ask consultants, according to John McMullen, are "Who have you done work for; do you have a client list; can I call them; have you done anything in my industry; have you ever done anything with the setup I have?"

Unfortunately, computer consultants do not have to be licensed. Many who call themselves consultants are, at best, programmers. "They know how to write a BASIC, C, or FORTRAN program," says John McMullen, "but they don't have the foggiest idea of how to please a client or how to be more aware of business practices. Sometimes people can get burned like that."

If you can't locate a computer consultant with whom you are comfortable, you might turn to the Independent Computer Consultants Association. Now nearly fifteen years old, the ICCA has about 2,000 members around the country. The organization has a code of ethics. Its membership requirements, though less than restrictive, do call for some degree of professionalism (see Resources section).

CATALOG

SOFTWARE

Wordbench (Addison-Wesley, $149–$189). *Home Computing* magazine's reviewer gave this word processing program four stars. The package, easy to learn and use, helps writers as well as other people who find themselves creating something lengthier than correspondence. Wordbench has built-in modules called "The Outliner" and "The Notetaker" (named for the functions they perform). Create an outline; dash off notes and notions; merge the notes with the outline. The document itself would be written with the module called, oddly enough, "The Writer." You can bring the outline into "The Writer" module, merge it with the document, and have a structure to run with.

Other features worth mentioning are a thesaurus, spell-checker, and "The Viewer," which allows you to see two files at once, a boon for those destined to cut and paste. Contact: Addison-Wesley, One Jacob Way, Reading MA 01867.

Home Office (Tony Stewart Software, $149). Just the name alone makes this computer program worth mentioning. Fortunately, there's more to the program than its name. The *New York Times* said that "for anyone doing free-lance or consulting work . . . [it's] Heaven-sent." It keeps records on contacts; assignments, projects, or just plain jobs; and expenses. It prepares invoices and tracks responses to these. It interconnects in a delightfully timesaving way. Here's how it works. Let us say a good client demands you do a project for many dollars. (If you like, I'll say that again. A good client demands you do a project for many dollars.) You create a file for this job, complete with job number. The client's name and address already are in your contact list. Just a couple of keystrokes and the name, address, and phone number are added to this job's file. You describe the job. You enter the terms. Again, you can bring the terms in from a previous job. You enter expenses as incurred, and assign to the appropriate job number. Come invoice time, by entering the job number (easy to find) and answering "yes" or "no" to a series of questions, you are able to enter the customer's name and address, the terms, the fee, the description, and an itemized list of billable expenses as well as the total sum of expenses. The program is excellent for those who provide professional services. The program is less helpful to those who sell products, especially if you want to keep track of inventory. Contact: Tony Stewart Software, 309 W. 109th St., 2E, New York NY 10025; (212) 222-4332. (Recently, Spinnaker Software began to distribute this program [retitled "The BetterWorking One-Person Office"] for $69.95. Contact: Spinnaker Software, One Kendall Sq., Cambridge MA 02139; [800] 826-0706.)

Works (Microsoft, $149). Works is an effective general-purpose integrated package that helps you keep records of people, places, and things; numbers; and letters, reports, and other written material. Its particular strength is its ability to join these different kinds of information. Works is an integrated program, and as such combines spreadsheet, word processor, data base, and communications. A chart maker in the spreadsheet module adds dramatic flair to the otherwise crunched numbers. Each of the modules rewards with a decent degree of flexibility. It displays the classic virtues of integrated programs: Data can be shipped between the various modules and commands are consistent throughout. It comes with a tutorial disk and a booklet of sample applications. Contact: Microsoft, 1 Microsoft Way, Redmond WA 98052-6399; (206) 882-8080 or 16011 N.E. 36th Way, Box 97107, Redmond WA 98073-9717.

1-2-3 (Lotus Development Corporation, $395, $495). Although this program is integrated, its spreadsheet component is considered to be its greatest asset. It is a Super-Pac-Man when set free among numbers. Its other features are graphics and data base. The resulting achievement is excellent recording, analysis, and achievement of numerical information. Release 3.0 is designed to work with PC/MS/DOS computers that are built around the powerful 386 chip. The less expensive Release 2.2 works with other IBM-style computers. Contact: Lotus Development Corp., 55 Cambridge Parkway, Cambridge MA 02142; (617) 577-8500.

Reflex 2.0 (Borland International, $249.95). This is a heavily upgraded data base that now exploits, we are told, a new approach to programming. Could be. It is powerful. Files can be huge, and in fact can exceed the size of the computer's internal memory. (When in use, the information can go back and forth between the computer and the disk—floppy or hard.) Desired information can be tracked down easily without resorting to rigid, complicated commands (a welcome trend in data bases). The ability to create graphs provides another way of analyzing the data. You can work with several different ways of looking at the data at one time. A change in one view will change that same piece of information in the other views. Whether you examine piles of data at a time or just one entry, you can customize the way the material is presented on the screen. It is not a petty power trip. It enables you to look for what you want in a way that most makes sense to you. A "crosstabbing" feature helps you easily compare and summarize number-related entries. Contact: Borland, 1800 Green Hills Rd., PO Box 660001, Scotts Valley CA 95066-0001.

Grammatik IV (Reference Software, $99). This software program helps you write more clearly. It detects such unpleasantries as grammatical errors, fogginess, poor sentence structure, redundancies, and jargon. It can detect forty different types of bad phrasing. The program does not abandon you. It explains why the word or phrase is inappropriate and it suggest improvements. In all, Grammatik IV can find 10,000 writing errors, a capability that I personally look upon as a significant challenge. You can correct on the spot, rather than return to the word processing program before correcting. Sometimes the error detector is in error. The software cannot be as sensitive to the English language's subtleties as we are. The program has features that make it You-ser friendly. You can grammar-check your document without getting out of the word processing program. You can include your own writing style and grammar rules as part of the program's criteria. You can correct the goof instantly. Anyway, regardless of whatever else is wrong with what you write, use of this program will help make your words grammatical. Contact: Reference Software, 330 Townsend St., Suite 123, San Francisco CA 94107; (800) 872-9933; in CA (415) 541-0222.

Datalife Plus Factory-Formatted Disks (Verbatim). Those who are not yet with computers should know that disk-formatting is one of those little mindless chores that gets in the way of hunkering down to compute. When a disk is first used, it must be processed so that it and the machine understand each other. Verbatim is doing this formatting process in the factory. Otherwise, according to the company's press release, a person could spend fifteen minutes to a half-hour just formatting a box of ten diskettes. The DataLife Plus diskettes also are Teflon-coated to protect them against spills, smudges, and fingerprints. Both 5¼" and 3½" disks are formatted for PC/MS-DOS 3.0 and above. Contact: Verbatim Corp, 1200 W. T. Harris Blvd., Charlotte NC 28210.

Eye Relief Word Processing Program (Ski-Soft Publishing, $295). Relief definitely is the operative word. The program works well both for people with vision problems and for those who use laptop computers in poorly lit areas (as well as any combination thereof). The characters can be enlarged up to five times their normal screen size. You also can adjust the spaces between lines, as well as the spaces between characters. The result is something on the screen that fits your vision needs. It's a workhorse program that does not bother with the bells and whistles of fancy formatting. If you need a finished document that's a bit gaudier, just finish the formatting with a more sophisticated word processor. Ken Skier developed Eye Relief as a follow-up to his "No-Squint Laptop Cursor" program ($39.95). As its name suggests, "No-Squint" allows the laptop user to see the cursor more clearly. Users wrote to Ski and said, "Fine, we can see the cursor; now can you tell us how we can see the characters?" His research revealed that the desired program didn't exist, so he created one. Contact: Ski-Soft

Publishing Corp., 1644 Massachusetts Ave., Suite 79, Lexington MA 02173; (800) 456-8465.

Color-Coded Diskettes (KAO). You can express your urge to color-code through the diskettes themselves. KAO offers 3½″ and 5¼″ diskettes in red, yellow, blue, and green, and orange. They come both in a pack of assorted colors (two per hue) and single colors. You might want to use different colors for different applications (e.g., red for word processing, green for spreadsheet, yellow for data base) or divvy up the colors according to the kinds of documents (letters, reports, invoices) or who and what the files are about (vendors, customers, promotion). Contact: KAO Corporation of America, 2065 Landings Dr., Mountain View CA 94043; (415) 657-8425.

Magellan (Lotus Development, $195). Sometimes computer users will emit a plaintive, "Come out, come out wherever you are." They hope to snare a few errant files from their hard disks. They have an urgent need, but unfortunately, they can't remember the file names. Now there is Magellan. By entering a phrase, concept, or key words, the user can quickly locate all the likely files. Specifically, you can use Magellan to find files, examine files, and work with the information in the files. Magellan is of particular note because it works very quickly, and there are no messy commands to clean. You state the search criteria in English. Magellan displays a list of files in descending order. (The closest matches are on top, and yes, for this, it's okay to play with matches.) It also shows the files. Even though files may be sired by different applications (e.g., word processing, spreadsheet, or data base), you can gather the related information from each and put the new data in their own file. In addition, Magellan has some respectable disk management utilities. Contact: Lotus Development, 55 Cambridge Parkway, Cambridge MA 02142; (617) 577-8500.

Letters On Line (Power Up, $59.95). To paraphrase Henny Youngman, take a letter please. This piece of software contains 800 letters covering all sorts of situations, from professional to personal. You load one of those letters into your computer's memory. Using your own word processing program, you add the appropriate specifics (such as date, name of the person to whom letter is addressed, particular item or situation you're discussing) and you tinker with the wording, if you like. It's a shortcut to creating those touchy grown-up letters that we rarely write. Contact: Power Up Software, P.O. Box 7600, San Mateo CA 94403-7600; (800) 851-2917; in CA (800) 223-1479.

Primavera Project Planner (Primavera Systems, $2,500). This program, known familiarly as P3, is for people who have to plan and direct massive projects that tend to require observations of deadlines, as well as the use of copious amounts of money, resources, and personnel. P3 helps the planner make a coherent campaign out of all the intricacies and variables. As the project proceeds, P3 gives the planner a clear look at how everything really is working. As you might imagine, a prime target consists of that brave brigade known as corporate managers ("Half a league, Half a League, Half a League Onward . . ."): And that's reflected in its price. However, some home officers are appropriate users—for example, an outside consultant brought in by a corporation to make the installation of some new, expensive technology work. Engineers and contractors overseeing heavy megabuck construction also use P3. Primavera offers a free booklet, "Making It Happen," that gives some good insight into project management. Contact: Primavera Systems, Two Bala Plaza, Bala Cynwyd PA 19004.

Soft Breeze (Soft Shell Systems, $169). Soft Breeze helps your operating system to be a shell of its former self. The program helps arrange and manage your files, and helps you retrieve files. In fact, it helps you to do all those necessary little computer chores with that panache usually associated with people who know what they're doing. Soft Breeze is the perfect translator. It talks to you in English and talks to your computer in MS/DOS. Contact: Soft Shell Systems, 1163 Triton Dr., Foster City CA 94494; (800) 322-SOFT.

Mavis Bacon Teaches Typing (Software Toolworks, $49.95). So you've got a computer, and it's got a keyboard, and you think, maybe I should learn how to type because that would save me a lot of time. Then you imagine yourself subjected to the tedium of typing tutorials, and you shrug and return to your cocoa and Ritz crackers. Welcome to the world of Mavis Bacon. Of course, this project has the major computer benefit of giving you feedback and teaching at your speed of learning. This program spices the trip with graphics, jokes, riddles, and quotes from the *Guinness Book of Records*. Progress reports are given. Graphics show the placement of hands. Mistakes are explained in English. There are timed tests. There's even a "Road Racer" typing game, which we, of course, are too dignified to play. Contact: Software Toolworks, 19808 Nordhoff Pl., Chatsworth CA 91311.

The Secretary Bird (Software Toolworks, $59.95). This is the perfect integrated program (word processor, spreadsheet, data-base filer, and spelling checker) for people who are just getting their feet wet, figuratively speaking. Not only does it come with a good amount of useful features but it is easy to use. Contact: Software Toolworks, 19808 Nordhoff Pl., Chatsworth CA 91311.

Microsoft Word 5.0 (Microsoft, $450). Word is one of the handful of heavy-hitting word processing packages that have attracted large swarms of fannish users. It makes it easy for you to have all kinds of formats (letters, memos, reports, etc.) look exactly the way you want them to look. Its macro feature enables you to do a series of steps just by entering one command. This is great when you have to keep writing the same thing over and over. This is great when you have to keep writing the same thing over and over. This is great when you . . . Word is a whiz when it comes to keeping the amount of keystrokes for commands to a minimum. Version 5.0, the latest enhancement, acknowledges desktop publishing with a lot of good visual aids, including good handling of graphics that you put in a document, multiple columns on the screen, and a preview of what your words will look like on paper. Contact: Microsoft Corporation, One Microsoft Way, Redmond WA 98052-6399; (206) 882-8080.

HARDWARE

Computer Tool Sets (Curtis, $29.95, $79.95). Are you comfortable with doing computer maintenance, upgrades, and possibly even repairs by yourself? If so, it probably would help to have tools designed specifically for the tasks, as well as for the internal landscape of your computer. Curtis offers two sets. The eleven-piece set is good for basic surgery. The fifty-two-piece set offers wider and more intricate options. Contact: Curtis Manufacturing, 30 Fitzgerald Dr., Jaffrey NH 03452; (603) 532-4123.

Data-Vac (Metro Data-Vac, $67.50). It's designed to clean computer equipment; you know, get into those hard-to-reach corners that your ordinary dust mop can't handle. The Data-Vac has hose and air pinpoint attachments. They help get into slots on the disk drive and keys on the keyboard. I'm told that a Data-Vac is four times more powerful than a Dustbuster. The device not only has a vacuum to suck that *schmutz* out, but a blower port. When you encounter a hard-to-vac area, just like Dirty Harry, you can blow the dust away and then vacuum. You should know that there's a Data-Vac 2, which is four times more powerful than the Data-Vac, and is particularly good for laser printers and copiers. It seems that the toner in those two types

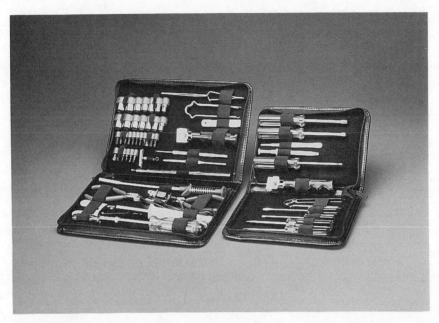

Curtis Tool Sets

of machines leaves particles so fine that they slip through the vacuum's filtration bag. Data-Vac is $67.50; Data-Vac 2 is $140. Contact: Metro Data-Vac, P.O. Box 149, Suffern NY 10901; (800) 822-1602.

Universal Printer Stand (Fellowes Manufacturing, $23.95). Made of high-impact polystyrene, this accessory holds your printer. In the process, it saves space. A paper tray is attached. The printout drops onto the tray in a neat, aligned stack of up to 200 sheets. The stand is "universal" because it holds 80- or 132-column printers. Although it can withstand up to 1,000 pounds, it's not really recommended for laser printers. The stand's adjustable legs allow three positions: horizontal and two angles. The tilts are for those who want to get a better look at what's being printed. Space beneath the stand holds blank, continuous paper (250 sheets at an extreme angle to 600 sheets horizontally). To avoid collisions between cables, and the paper that's chugging along, the stand has a hook around which the power cord or cable gets wrapped, and a paper guide that leads the paper directly into the printer. Contact: Customer Service, Fellowes Manufacturing, 1789 Norwood Ave., Itasca IL 60143; (708) 893-1700.

Clean-A-Printer (Lee Manufacturing, $6.95). Clean the print elements on dot matrix and daisy wheel printers without harming the other parts, plastic or metal. It comes in an aerosol can, and the fluid goes onto an attached brush. It banishes the buildup of dust, dirt, and carbon. Contact: Lee Products, 800 E. 80th St., Minneapolis MN 55420; (800) 356-8969.

Compu-Glo (Miami Paper, $14/box of 124 sheets). Continuous-form paper in screaming fluorescent colors for computer messages that de-

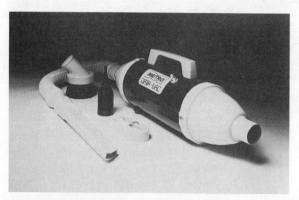

MODEL MDV-1 METRO DATA-VAC

Data-Vac

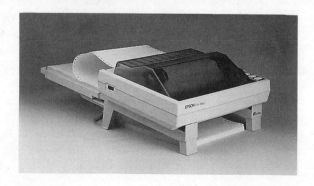

Universal Printer Stand

Keyboard SpaceSaver

mand attention. Available in red, green, orange, pink, and canary, Compu-Glo paper can be used in impact printers (dot matrix and daisy wheel). Fluorescence (which is used to coat the paper) does not make color more intense. Rather, it bends the light so that the light waves bounce around. It's sort of like a visual echo effect. Use Compu-Glo to print out price lists and dramatic announcements. Do not use in laser printers or copiers. Contact: Miami Paper (800) 543-7905.

Keyboard SpaceSaver (Curtis Manufacturing, $39.95). Essentially a housing, it holds your detachable keyboard. The keyboard slides in and out. You can put the SpaceSaver on top of your desk, and then pile the whole computer and kaboodle on top of it, or the accessory can be mounted beneath the desk. What about a desk with a central drawer where the SpaceSaver should go? You can deep-six the drawer if you really don't need it. Contact: Curtis Manufacturing, 30 Fitzgerald Dr., Jaffrey NH 03452.

KX-P1124 24-Pin Printer (Panasonic, $529). Home office needs were taken into account when designing the KX-P1124. Paper can be loaded through the front, rear, or bottom. Single sheets and no. 10 envelopes can be placed easily in the printer through the front. The flat-belt tractor (which moves paper along) swivels so that it either can push from the rear or pull from the bottom or front. Press a button and rear-fed continuous-form paper can be released to make a path for front-fed single sheets or envelopes. The print quality deserves notice. The variety of fonts and enhancements (e.g., italics, boldface, underlining, subscripts) plus the pitch selections allow for the creation of

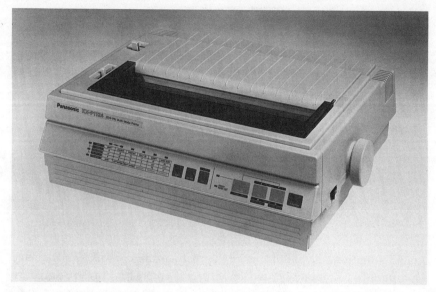

Panasonic KX-P1124

more than 5,000 type styles. The KX-P1124 prints at 192 characters per second in draft mode and 63 cps in letter-quality mode. Print features can be set with an easy-to-use front panel. Its Macro Mode stores up to three different print settings. Contact: Panasonic Industrial, One Panasonic Way, Secaucus, NJ 07094.

LQ-2550 24-Pin Printer (Epson, $1,499). This is a high-quality, high-speed, high-ticket impact printer. The draft speed is 333–500 cps, depending on which type is used. Letter quality is a correspondingly high 111–167 cps. Paper parking allows for the loading of single sheets without having to remove the continuous-feed paper. In addition to the eight resident fonts, other type styles created at our computer can be loaded. Also, the 2550 can work well with a color ribbon. Contact: Epson America, 23530 Hawthorne Blvd., Torrance CA 90505; (213) 539-9511.

Computer Furniture (Bretford). The centerpiece in Bretford's "Trademark" collection is a 48″-wide work surface. A wide bookshelf underneath is very accessible, especially when you let your arms hang down. The furniture becomes more powerful when you add any or all of the other components. The deluxe hutch has a lockable storage cabinet, or get the low hutch just to hold the monitor. The printer stand holds the printer. It has a shelf for the paper. The corner connector

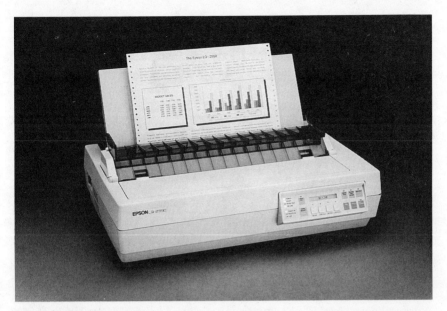

Epson LQ-2550

adds more surface and makes everything one. The individual pieces are made of oak solids and veneers, and assemble easily. It has a hand-rubbed lacquer finish, and you get your choice of medium or dark oak color. Contact: Bretford Manufacturing, 9715 Soreng Ave., Schiller Park IL 60176; (312) 678-2545.

Wesystem Copy Hinge (D. L. West Manufacturing, $14.95–$17.95). Attached to the computer monitor by a foam adhesive tape, this product is a copy holder. It holds material that you might need to consult, such as correspondence, invoices, and magazine articles. Otherwise you would look first at the monitor, then at the material at your desk, then at your monitor, and so on. A copy holder reduces the possibility of suffering whiplash in your home office. The Copy Hinge is an interesting variation on the genre. Instead of securing reference material with a plastic clip or clipboard-type spring, the Copy Hinge uses friction grip rollers. The material slips under the rollers and stays fast. To remove a page, you either hold it by the bottom and lift it upward or slide it out horizontally. When through with the Copy Hinge, swing it closed as if it were a gate. Putty-colored and made of plastic, it is available in the 6″ width (for 8½″ by 11″ or smaller pages) or 12″ for wider pages. Contact: D. L. West Manufacturing, 5170 S. Julian, Suite 318, Tucson AZ 85706; (602) 889-2301.

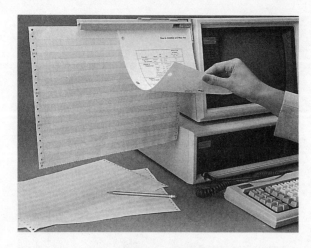

Copy Hinge

Silhouette Copy Holder (Fellowes, $10.95–$24.95). A stylish copy holder, it is made of plastic and stands on your desk. The Silhouette works like an easel. The copy sits in a slot. There are four sizes: steno, letter, legal, and data processing. The latter is appropriate for magazines, looseleaf binders, and books. Contact: Customer Service, Fellowes Manufacturing, 1789 Norwood Ave., Itasca IL 60143; (708) 893-1700.

PC Pillow (Tech-Cessories, $19.95). When you want to lean back in your chair and keep your keyboard on your lap, this accessory is useful. Essentially, we're talking bean bag here. The rigid top is a good base on which to rest the keyboard. The soft bottom—well, who can argue with soft bottoms. Contact: Tech-Cessories, 990 East Rogers Circle #2, Boca Raton FL 33487; (800) 637-0909.

CableManager (Microcomputer Accessories, $39.95). All those power cords from the computer, printer, modem, and electronic phones conjure visions of a bad sci-fi movie *(The Return of the Octopi!)* (Not my favorite pastry). This product consists of a 36″ channel attached to the back of your work surface and an 18″ vertical channel that goes to the floor. There's no need to thread the cables because the cover doesn't go on until the cords and cables are installed. The Cable-Manager itself attaches to the back of the desk with thoughtfully provided industrial-strength double-stick tape. Contact: Microcomputer Accessories, 5405 Jandy Pl., Los Angeles CA 90066-0911; (213) 301-9400.

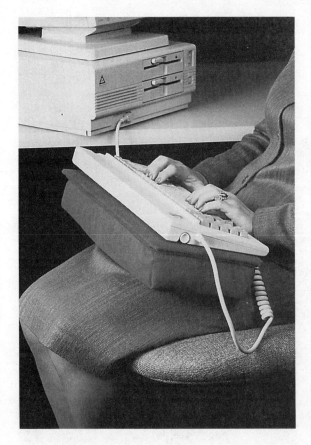

PC Pillow

Printer Stand with Multiple Forms Rack (BALT, Inc., $159). The Tuffy-1 helps those who need more than one kind of paper to go through their printer. For example, in addition to standard white paper, you might find yourself a frequent user of mailing labels, continuous-form stationery, continuous-form invoices, and/or check forms. The Tuffy-1 is a sturdy printer stand. It's got two slide-through paper trays so that four kinds of paper forms can be held with ease. Casters are optional ($30). Contact: BALT, Inc., P.O. Box 713, Cameron TX 76520; (817) 697-6528.

Laser Printer Stand (BALT, Inc., $189). Known alternately as the LB-1 and the Lazer Blazer printer stand, this baby was bred for strength. In addition to sturdiness, it's designed to be stable (i.e., not wobble). The 18″ by 24″ by 27″ stand has two storage shelves (useful for paper and toner). Contact: BALT, Inc., P.O. Box 713, Cameron TX 76520; (817) 697-6528.

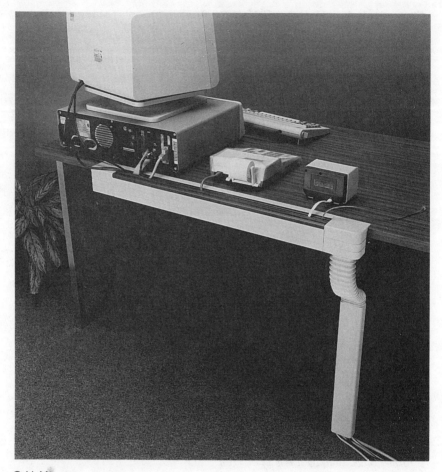

CableManager

Oak Computer Accessories (OfficeTech). Sometimes plastic just isn't enough. For this reason, OfficeTech has created two lines of accessories: one in solid oak, and the other in oak finish. The clean-lined styling is the same for both materials. The disk files have roll-tops. Available products include 80-column printer stand, 132-column printer stand, computer stand (with tray for keyboard), and disk files for either 3½″ or 5¼″ disks. The oak finish 3½″ and 5¼″ disk files hold 50 and 70 disks, respectively. The solid oak line offers these sizes as well as files that accommodate twice the amount. Contact: OfficeTech, P.O. Box 97015, Redmond WA 98073-9715; (206) 881-1000.

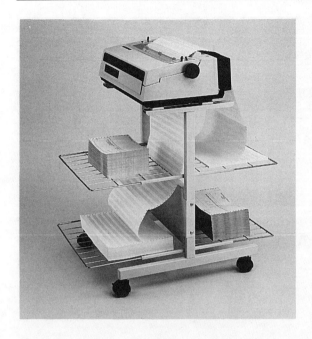

BALT Printer Stand with
Multiple Forms Rack

Survivor Floppy Disk Sleeves (International Envelope, $1.90–$2.20). Made of rough, tough Tyvek, the Survivor Disk Sleeves bring a bit of protection to your floppies. Moreover, they come in different colors so that you can easily categorize and quickly find disks. For example, you can put all your word processing files in red sleeves, all your data-base files in blue sleeves, and all your programs in white sleeves. The floppy survivor disk sleeves are available in red, white, blue, orange, yellow, and green. Survivor products are available only through office products dealers and stationers.

Keyboard Cover (CompuCover, $25.95). The plastic cover adheres to your keyboard. The idea is to protect the keyboard innards from dust, spills, and such little metal objects as staples and paper clips that fall between the cracks. The cover just stays on and the keys are fully responsive when you type. Contact: CompuCover, 2104 Lewis Turner Blvd., Fort Walton Beach FL 32548; (800) 874-6391; in FL (800) 342-9008.

Surge Protectors (Curtis Manufacturing, $39.95–$119.95). This New England–based manufacturer of quality computer accessories offers a range of products to help you spurn that spike. The *Filtered Safe-Strip* ($39.95) provides hot to neutral protection and an EMI-RFI filter.

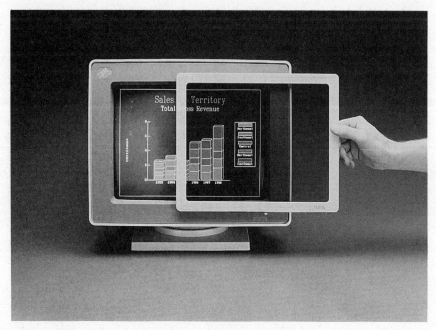

Curtis Anti-Glare Filter

Diamond Plus ($79.95) is a wall-mounted surge protector that has hot to neutral, hot to ground, and neutral to ground protection as well as phone line protection. The *Ruby Plus* ($119.95) strip offers line protection in all the key areas: hot to neutral, hot to ground, neutral to ground, phone line protection, and EMI-RFI filtration. Contact: Curtis Manufacturing, 30 Fitzgerald Dr., Jaffrey NH 03452; (603) 532-4123.

Anti-Glare Filter (Curtis, $59.95). Remember all that glare we told you about in the Executive Suite chapter? Upon reflection, computer monitors are prime culprits because of their glassy facades. The Curtis filter sits in front of the screen. You attach it with Velcro, and it's available in seven standard sizes. The filter helps your peepers in three important ways: It absorbs 95 percent of the reflected light; it does not distort what you see on the screen; and it increases the contrast, sharpening the clarity of the characters. Contact: Curtis Manufacturing, 30 Fitzgerald Dr., Jaffrey NH 03452; (603) 532-4123.

The Box Handler (Tech-Cessories, $29.95). Every new opportunity presents a new problem that presents a new opportunity. Computer printers and copiers gave us the chance to have large, heavy boxes of paper to shift around. The aptly named box handler is a pair of han-

Certron Disk Storage Files with Locks

dles, each of which attaches to (and can be removed from) an end of a box, making the box easier to maneuver. Contact: Tech-Cessories, 990 East Rogers Circle #2, Boca Raton FL 33487; (800) 637-0909.

Disk Storage Files with Locks (Certron). The locks calm those who desire security. You may want to withhold access to your disks from people you work with. You may just want to discourage your progenies from exercising their crayon creativity upon your disks. You may just be anal retentive. No matter. Certron locking disk storage files are available for 3½" (holding 40 or 80 diskettes) and 5¼" (holding 50, 100, or 130 diskettes) diskettes. Contact: Certron Corporation, 1651 S. State College Blvd., Anaheim CA 92806; (714) 634-4280.

Laser Printer (Ricoh Corporation, $1,895). This company's PC Laser 6000/EX exploits a neat new development. All laser printing requires some sort of chip intelligence that tells the printer how to get the effect that you want to achieve. Conventionally (if we can use that word for such a new technology) the controller is built into the laser printer. The computer sends its secret messages to the controller. The controller translates, and the printing commences. When graphics are involved, up to eight minutes can elapse before the first page is printed. (Subsequent pages fly out swiftly.) Ricoh's PC Laser 6000/EX can use a controller card that's installed in the computer. Less time is required to "explain" your instructions to the printer. Also, computer resident controllers provide the possibility of greater flexibility in the printer's

Ricoh Laser 6000/EX

useful life. The PC Laser 6000/EX prints at the rate of six pages per minute. Contact: Ricoh Corporation, 5 Dedrick Pl., West Caldwell NJ 07006; (201) 882-2000.

9-Pin Printer (Star Micronics, $299). Unlike the 9-pound hammer, this 9-pin printer (NX-1000) isn't too heavy for your size. It produces a clear, well-defined printout, especially at its NLQ (near-letter-quality) setting. When operating at NLQ, the NX-1000 prints at 36 characters per second. Draft speed is 144 cps. The printer has a ''paper parking'' feature for the printing of individual sheets as opposed to continuous paper. You can select any of four type styles by pressing buttons on the front panel. Contact: Star Micronics, 200 Park Ave., Suite 3510, New York NY 10166; (212) 966-6770.

Headstart III 286 Computer (HeadStart Technologies). This subsidiary of North American Phillips believes very strongly in the home office trend. This computer gives novices the tools to wade into sophisticated uses, which are accomplished with the computer's hardware. Lots of nice touches are built in. These include a 32-megabyte (MB) hard disk drive and the flexibility afforded by having both 5¼″ and 3½″ disk drives. The Headstart III comes bundled with a good supply of popular useful software (including programs for word processing, data base, graphics, and desktop publishing). In the interest of full disclosure, I should mention that HeadStart lent me a computer to use in the evaluation of software. Contact: HeadStart Technologies, 40 Cutter Mill Rd., Suite 438, Great Neck NY 11021.

HeadStart III 286 Computer

Bernoulli Box (Iomega Corporation, $1,450–$2,350). The Bernoulli Box on page 118 is an attractive alternative to the hard disk drive. The machine is a drive that holds a removable cartridge, a plastic-encased disk. The Bernoulli Principle (something about fluids and gases) is hard at work and creates an environment where megabytes can be stored. Because of the ease with which you can insert and remove cartridges, you have the illusion of unlimited storage. Iomega has a 20-megabyte drive; a double drive, each with 20-MB cartridges (one could be used for backup) and a 44-MB drive. Fill a cartridge to the brim and then you just pop in another cartridge. It's as easy as making toast. Iomega's cartridges, at under $100 each, represent a classic half-empty-glass/half-filled-glass situation. Each cartridge costs much more than a floppy disk, but much less than a new hard drive. Also the engineering is such that the drive can operate effectively under unstable conditions. I know of one person who tested the system by flinging a cartridge against the wall. It kept on ticking. Contact: Iomega Corporation, 1821 West 4000 South, Roy UT 84067; (800) 456-5522.

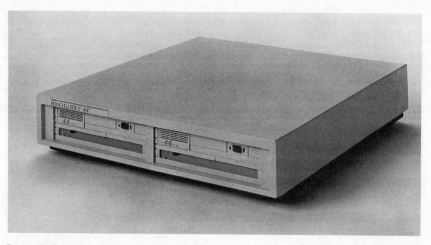

Bernoulli Box

RESOURCES

PUBLICATIONS/VIDEOS

Express Order Software Buyer's Guide (Tandy, free). The Radio Shack folks have put together a mail order (actually phone order) catalog of more than 800 computer software programs, most of which are for MS/DOS computer systems. (Some are for Xenix and OS/2.) It's loaded with business-oriented applications (e.g., word processing, data base, integrated, spreadsheets, productivity, accounting). One does not need a degree in computer science to read this catalog. It is written in clear English and offers fairly detailed descriptions of what the programs do. The copy does accentuate the positive. This is a catalog designed to sell—not a collection of nit-picking reviews. Many of the offerings are discounted from 10 to 30 percent. Delivery is usually UPS ground service (four to seven days), but Tandy knows that computer users tend to be instant gratification freaks, so overnight or two-day delivery can be arranged at an additional charge. Contact: Tandy (800) 321-3133.

How to Buy a Personal Computer (Electronic Industries Association). This forty-eight-page booklet helps you grapple with your computer-buying decision. The Electronic Industries Association definitely is a trade association, so never is heard a discouraging word. Even so, this slim volume is a helpful hand-holder. With clear and simple prose, it describes and clarifies all those issues and little terms that lurk in the computer store. Sections cover such topics as "How Do the Computers Compare?" "What Software Do I Want?" "What Kind of Printer Do I Want?" and "What Other Peripherals Should I Consider?" It has a workbook format with appropriate checklists. It also discusses the important issues of maintenance and retail practices. Contact: EIA, Consumer Electronics Group, P.O. Box 19100, Washington DC 20036.

Mail Order Hit Parade. In its February 1989 issue, *Personal Computing* magazine spotlighted mail-order computer vendors with "award winning . . . strategies." The editors carefully and properly pointed out that, "These are not necessarily the only companies you should deal with, but each offers qualities to recommend it." A couple of the categories may be a bit esoteric, but what the heck. Let's look at those desirable qualities and the companies that were honored. By the way, the article's explanation of how these various companies came to be identified is a good primer on buying by mail order and is worth checking out. You can get a copy by sending $2 to "Stories," *Personal Computing,* 999 Riverview Rd., Totowa NJ 07512. Be sure to specify the article by name.

PRICE
The New Computer Network
625 Academy Dr.
Northbrook IL 60062
(800) 621-SAVE; in IL
  (312) 205-1300

VARIETY OF HARDWARE
Advanced Computer Products
1310 E. Edinger
Santa Ana CA 92705
(800) FONE ACP; in CA
  (714) 558-8813

CORPORATE SUPPORT AND SERVICE
Compuadd
12303 Technology Blvd.
Austin TX 78727
(800) 666-1872; in TX
  (512) 250-1489

VARIETY OF SOFTWARE
PC Exchange
7 Vel Plaza
Spring Valley NY 10977
(800) DIAL PCX; in NY
  (914) 426-2400

CUSTOMER SERVICE AND SUPPORT
P. C. Brand Inc.
95 W. Washington St.
Chicago, IL 60607
(800) PC BRAND; in IL
  (312) 226-3500

NETWORK SUPPLIES
707 Computer Wholesales
707 Dartmouth Dr.
Buffalo Grove IL 60089
(800) 426-2487; in IL
  (312) 537-3600

PRINTER EXPERTISE
Printers Plus
P.O. Box 3069
Chesterfield MO 63006
(800) 562-2727; in MO
 (314) 532-6977

HARD DISK SUPPLIER
Hard Drives International
1208 E. Broadway, #10
Tempe AZ 85282
(800) 234-DISK; in AZ
 (602) 967-4999

CAD SUPPLIES
CAD Express
4315 Lakeshore Dr.
Waco TX 76710
(817) 776-7399

ALL-AROUND PERFORMERS
Priority One Electronics
21622 Plummer St.
Chatsworth CA 91311
(800) 423-5922; in CA
 (818) 709-6789

National Shop-by-Mail Directory for Personal Computer Users (Pilot Books, $4.95, including postage and handling). Clearly written and easy to use, this thirty-eight page softcover book puts sources at your fingertips or at least on your bookshelf. The four key sections are Computers, Supplies, and Accessories; Software; Electronic Kits, Components, Tools, and Assemblies; and Office Products. Sixty-nine sources are listed. Contact: Pilot Books, 103 Cooper St., Babylon NY 11702.

Learning Computers on the Computer (American Training International, $29.95 and up). Perhaps ATI's approach should be subtitled "Zen and the Art of Computer Fluency." The focus is on absorbing skills first, and then learning what it's all about. A typical procedure would be to have you do something, verify that you did it, and then tell you the significance of what you did. Both new and advanced users have the opportunity to quickly learn the subtleties of a software package new to them. They can do it at their own pace and, according to ATI, graduate within a couple of hours. At the time of this writing, ATI has forty-three tutorial programs. Most are for specific software. A few are designed to help you stroll through specific computers. A few are for general skills. ATI offers training programs for Ventura Publisher ($129), Microsoft Word 5.0 ($75), and PC Tools ($29.95). Contact: American Training International, 12638 Beatrice St., Los Angeles CA 90066; (800) 421-4827; in CA (213) 823-1129.

Learning the Computer through Video (Jaz & Associates, $129.95). The complete Jaz package for each of its (currently) three tutorials includes two videotapes and a workbook/reference guide. For each package, the book and each of the tapes (beginning and advanced) can be purchased separately. The California Department of Justice wanted its minions to learn computers through video instruction and conducted a tape test, comparing video instructional tapes from eight vendors. The criteria included "production qualities, organization, clarity of explanation, thoroughness, interest, and suitability to our needs." The envelope, please. Jaz was selected. The three tutorial offerings are "Lotus 1-2-3," "Introduction to Computers/DOS," and "WordPerfect 5.0." Contact: Jaz & Associates, 6951 Warner Ave., Huntington Beach CA 92647; (714) 557-8620.

CompuServe (CompuServe Information Service, Inc.). This information utility with the largest list of subscribers is, I believe, the largest of services. Probably best known for its leisure and hobbyist features, CompuServe offers many perks to the business user. It's got industry and professional forums where you check to see what's going on in your area; news and specialized journal data base; and heavy financial information services and programs to download. Some CompuServe services, ostensibly for the taking-it-easy moments, offer much to the home officer. These include forums devoted to specific computer hardware or software or computer magazine articles. Also, there are the travel data bases to find out what's going on where, when the plane leaves, and how little it may cost. Shopping services ("the electronic mall") allow you to buy such items as books, cars, computing supplies, and airline reservations. And certainly, let's not forget the CompuServe Working at Home Forum, administered by Paul and Sarah Edwards (co-authors of *Working at Home).* The forum functions well as an information exchange. There are questions, answers, and maybe a few cries and whispers. It even serves as a vehicle for networking. Contact: CompuServe, 5000 Arlington Centre Blvd., P.O. Box 20212, Columbus OH 43220; (800) 848-8199; in OH (614) 457-0802.

GEnie (GE Information Services). This deceptively looks like a scaled-down version of CompuServe. GEnie (which stands for GE Network for Information Exchange) is a somewhat different animal. Although there are news, games, encyclopedia entries, and travel service entries, the emphasis is on communication (at a lower price). GEnie's forums seem quite attractive. A forum is an online conversation among interested individuals. Sometimes there are guest "speakers." In each issue GEnie's magazine *Live Wire* lists the forums with the same reverence usually associated with TV listings. This information utility also has something just for us: the Home Office/Small

Business Roundtable. Obviously, the distinction between "home" and "small" business is not sacred here. A random look at the several files in this section shows such titles as "Collecting from Business Accounts," "How a New Potato Chip Was Born," "Jeff Lant Text on Mental Selling," and "Insurance in the Home Office." Contact: GE Consumer Services, Department 2B, 401 N. Washington St., Rockville MD 20850; (800) 638-9636.

Personal Computing magazine ($22.50/year). Month in and month out this magazine presents balanced material that serves the sophisticated user as well as the rookie. It's got lots of overviews and round-ups, as well as frequent buyers' guides. Read and save the guides. They give insights to a category of hardware or software. They explain the criteria applied by the reviewers. They also name the preferred products. The regular review section consistently sparkles. There are delicious helpings of leading edge and blue sky material. In the aggregate, it is a publication about computer ideas you can use or think about now. The target reader does seem to be mired in the corporation. Still, there is the sense that the reader has gone home and changed from suit to jeans before picking up a copy of the magazine. Contact: Personal Computing, 999 Riverview Rd., Totowa NJ 07512.

Home Office Computing magazine (Scholastic, Inc. $19.97/year). First, the considerable pluses. The editors have gathered an extremely knowledgeable, even stellar, bunch of regular contributors. The information particularly shines in the computing section. These reviews and features inform and assist. Furthermore, they're written in English for humans who have very few if any hacker bones in their bodies. But the home office information is of mixed quality. Some of it is sharp, and a lot of it isn't. Also I don't like the magazine's terms and payment policies for free-lance contributors. The magazine is worth checking out, but try to find it in the library if you can. Contact: Scholastic, Inc., 730 Broadway, New York NY 10003.

Encyclopedia of Shareware (PC-SIG, $17.95). Shareware is one of the great ideas of computer culture. Individuals around the country create programs that accomplish specific tasks. Others try their hand at creating their own versions of classic applications. The program developers are so pleased with their software that they want to share the applications with others. The software writers offer a copy of the program at a nominal price. If you like the program and intend to use it, you send an additional registration fee. (It varies, depending on the programs, but tends to be less expensive than conventionally distributed programs.) PC-SIG has established itself as the leading archive and clearinghouse for shareware. *The PC-SIG Encyclopedia of Shareware* is a hybrid. It's part reference work and part catalog. It contains salient data on more than 1,500 programs, any of which you can order from PC-SIG. Price definitely is one attractive shareware attribute. Moreover, many of the programs were designed for a specific profession or to handle a certain business requirement. So, you may find a program that matches your exact needs. Some of the categories are accounting (billing, inventory control, payroll, job costing, agriculture, auto/vehicle management, chemistry and physics, engineering, health management, math, personnel management, project management, and real estate and property management. There also are many programs designed to make your computer and programs work more effectively. The encyclopedia also has some good basic information on how to use your computer. Any of the programs can be ordered from PC-SIG for $6 apiece. The registration fees vary. PC-SIG also offers *Shareware* magazine, $20, six issues. The magazine contains news, reviews, and how-to articles. Contact: PC-SIG, 1030-D East Duane Ave., Sunnyvale CA 94086; (800) 245-6717.

Recap: PC (Recap Publications, $60/year). This thirty-page monthly magazine, printed on newsprint, is a useful resource for people who are heavy computer users but who don't have the time to be heavy computer press readers. Its raison d'être in the sun is its extensive listing of articles that appeared in the previous calendar month's computer press. Each listing is a paragraph summarizing the article. Each issue, according to *Recap PC,* reports on "almost 4,000 pages of news and product evaluation in the IBM PC and compatible world from the major trade and newsstand publications." This publication is primarily targeted toward computer professionals. It also runs a couple of its own reviews and articles. Contact: Recap, 201 W. 92nd St., New York NY 10025.

Dow Jones News/Retrieval (Dow Jones, $29.95). Now we're talking business. This utility is built around the corporation's news-gathering services, as in *Wall Street Journal* and *Barron's.* There are data bases covering capital market reports; investors' reports; daily Japanese business news; news, sports, and weather reports. Also available are data bases with full texts of articles from regional business publications, McGraw-Hill business publications, *Wall Street Journal, Barron's, Forbes, Fortune, Money, American Demographics, Inc.,* plus plenty of statistics, forecasts, and market quotes. Retrieval also provides access to corporate press releases that are distributed electronically.

Dow Jones also offers a searching aid called DowQuest. It works by giving a starter list of articles that deal with various aspects of the topic being searched. When you select the articles that are on the money, DowQuest revisits its archives and presents you with another bunch of even more pertinent articles, and so on. Contact: Dow Jones & Company, P.O. Box 300, Princeton NJ 08543-0300; (609) 520-4000.

Computer Books (Brady Books, various prices). Brady, a division of Prentice-Hall, which is a division of Simon & Schuster, which is a division of Gulf & Western, has a pretty good list of computer books. I'd like to point out three that can prove to be particularly helpful. *InfoWorld Computer Product Guide* edited by Jeff Angus ($26.95) is distilled from a year's worth of hardware and software reviews, all of which first ran in *InfoWorld* magazine. Although geared toward the corporate user, the book assists in two ways. First, it tells you what some pretty judgmental people really think of products you are looking at. The comments that accompany the product categories describe the pertinent features examined, and just what procedures were used to test. *The Brady Guide to Microcomputer Troubleshooting and Maintenance* by Henry F. Beechhold ($14.95) helps with simple repairs and maintenance, and has a very important troubleshooting section. Professor Beechhold, chairman of the Trenton State College English department's linguistic program, has painstakingly prepared a fairly painless guide to maintaining your computer. This guide won't launch you on a computer repair career, but it will give you the technical chops to upgrade your computer. *The Winn Rosch Hardware Bible* by Winn Rosch ($29.95) takes your hand and leads you on a trek that goes under the hood of your IBM and IBM compatible. Rosch delves into the hows and the whys of the whats and the watts. With this book at your side, you probably not only will know what you want for your computer but why and which one. Contact: Brady Books (800) 223-2336.

ORGANIZATIONS/SERVICES

Independent Computer Consultants Association. ICCA President Evans Bruner says that the national organization will put you in touch with a local chapter. Tell the regional folks as much as you can, particularly what business you're in, the specific challenges you're trying to cope with, and how much you've allocated for software and hardware. The local administrative office will look at the skill profiles of its various members and refer you to the appropriate firms. Contact: ICCA, 933 Gardenview Office Parkway, St. Louis MO 63141; (800) GET-ICCA.

Computer Consultants (McMullen & McMullen). John and Barbara McMullen and staff offer full-service consulting. The firm's client roster includes both corporations and individuals. Although the McMullens are generalists, they are best known for their work in desktop publishing services, database programming management, and education (both individual instruction and groups). They are proficient in MS-DOS, OS2, and Macintosh. They are active in computer clubs and teach at the New School. Although most McMullen & McMullen clients are in the New York area, the firm has had clients as far south as Mexico City and as far west as Los Angeles. Contact: McMullen & McMullen, MCM Plaza, Jefferson Valley NY 10535.

CHAPTER 7

Switchboard Central

What do big-time corporations do when it's time to make some change in their phones? They don't send a messenger to K Mart to buy a bunch of phones. They hire a consultant to design a phone *system*. They understand that if a telephone is a weapon, a telephone system is an arsenal.

Yes, at its most basic level, we're talking about tin cans strung together so that two kids can say, "I can hear you, can you hear me?" Today's cans and strings do marvelous tricks that help carry useful messages between us and our customers, vendors, advisors, and critics. Hiring a consultant is too costly for most of us, but still we can think in terms of a system rather than a phone. When you plan your telephone system, think about how it will get those messages through. Watch for ways that you might inadvertently block communication. Artful development of your telephone system has the effect of adding hands, voices, and, in some cases, branch offices to your business.

A home office telephone system has three parts: (1) equipment, (2) services, (3) you.

BUYING THE EQUIPMENT

When it comes to buying telephones, a dazzling number of choices are available, especially now that telephones are electronic. (They can do all sorts of acrobatics, thanks to built-in microchips and touch-tone technology.) You can take your pick of manufacturers, styles, and built-in features. You can buy phones just about anywhere, ranging from a street vendor to an official phone company store.

When you get beyond the cans-and-string approach, you'll find that each feature in today's electronic phones is designed to make it easier to get that message through.

Telemarketing consultant George Walther notices that people make a major phone error when they don't "take advantage of the fantastic features built into the most inexpensive phones today." He says this happens too often, and could be avoided if more people "picked up the instruction book and really read it." Let's look at some of the features.

Last-number redial. Lolling in the phone's memory is the last number you called. Press a single button and you can call it again. The feature saves time when you receive a busy signal or no answer and want to call again. Similarly, it's handy if you want to add a P.S. to a recent phone conversation.

Auto redial. This is industrial-strength last-number redial. The phone automatically dials the last number called, over and over again, until you get an answer or for a predetermined while. It's great for compulsives.

Memory dialing. You can store numbers that you expect to call frequently. The amount of stored numbers can range from 3 to more than 150. Don't pay for more storage than you will really use.

Hold. We all know what the hold button does. It puts the person on the other end of the line in his or her place. Actually it spares them the indignity of listening to you turn your attention to something or someone else. It's an especially important feature for people with small children and other living things.

Music on hold. The phrase "adding insult to injury" popped into my head. Music on hold is a way of letting the other person know that the lines of communication are still open. Perhaps it's more comforting than hearing no sound at all while on hold. Still, the collected works of Neil Diamond as performed by the Lite FM Orchestra never did much for me.

Adjustable volume. The hearing impaired should not forget about this feature. It adjusts the volume of sound that the handset puts into your ear. If it doesn't come with the telephone, it can be added.

Intercom. This may come in handy when your home office occupies two or more areas of your home (e.g., den and garage). Also, it helps when you are called away from active duty to wash the dishes and a dry-handed family member wants you to know a call has come in.

Clock. Yes, the telephone is one more place for a timepiece, but it's a good place. Phones with built-in clocks have alarm and call-timing features. They even let you know what time it is.

Multiline phone. These phones accommodate two and sometimes more phone lines. The planning-for-growth contingent might want to think about multiline phones and the intercom feature. Since the call waiting service allows you to deal with more than one incoming call at a time, when do multiline phones and/or more than one business line definitely help you?

- You might have someone working in your office who needs to use a phone while you need to use the phone.
- A multiline system allows you to make an outgoing call while a phone line is in use. This way you can concentrate on sales calls while incoming calls get picked up by an answering machine.
- A line can be dedicated to computer modem or fax machine. Dedicated lines serve two purposes: They permit us to chatter on the phone while the machines commune with their brethren. Since call waiting tends to bump fax and modem calls out of the way, a dedicated line avoids this problem by not having call waiting.
- Two-line phones are commonly used to keep both home and business lines in handy reach. No matter where you are in your house, you can pick up your business calls.

Many people start with one business line. Some find they want a line just for their computer modem and/or fax machine. Even at this point, two lines may not be necessary. You can clumsily switch between voice and machine, and there are also switching devices to make the transit convenient. Some decide they need a second line plus answering machine just to better handle the incoming calls. People also might want to add a private line.

In electronics (and that includes phones) today's features usually cost less tomorrow. On the other hand, today's features can be pretty helpful today.

When installing telephone equipment, make sure your phone jacks are accessible and remain accessible. The upgrading of equipment will be much easier. Also, try to get a phone that has letters you can read. The all-digit telephone numbers prompted phone manufacturers to design instruments with large numerals and tiny letters. Now, all of a sudden, businesses flaunt telephone numbers that are words.

There are steps to follow before going to the phone company, according to Dr. Ward Deutschmann of the New York Institute of Technology. "The first thing people should do is an analysis of what they need. You can do that with a pencil and a piece of paper. Sit down and imagine what you would like to have in your wildest dreams. Then the question is how much of that, first, is available. Second, what does it cost, and, third, how much of it do you really need. What you then do is bracket in on what you really need. For example, do you need an intercom? If so, do you have it as part of the phone system or do you have a separate one? Do you, in fact, have a multiline phone? Be careful not to have too many lines coming in because most people can't talk on more than one or two lines at any one time.''

In addition to meditating on the types of equipment, it is wise to mull over the twin towers of reliability and service. Dr. Deutschmann suggests a number of questions to ponder:

1. How reliable is it? For information, you go to people who already own one.
2. How much does it cost to maintain?
3. What happens if it breaks? Will you come out and fix it? Do I have to bring it back? Can I bring it back?
4. Is there a maintenance contract, and, if so, how much does it cost?
5. Does the contract cover only one instrument or all of the instruments?
6. Can the service coverage be extended to more than one instrument, and, if so, how much would it cost?
7. If the equipment lasts for more than one year, does it pay to have a maintenance contract?

Not every piece of phone equipment needs to be plugged into the wall or, for that matter, is included in a phone equipment catalog. Take a look at Robert ''Tiger'' Beaudoin's two favorite phone accessories. Beaudoin is one of the three partners who run Bull & Bear Marketing Group, and he does a lot of phonework.

''I have,'' says ''Tiger'' Beaudoin, ''what must be a 30-foot phone cord on the phone. It allows me to walk and talk which creates a much better projection.''

Beaudoin's other accessory provides plenty of opportunity for reflection. ''Facing my phone,'' says Beaudoin, ''are six panels of floor-to-ceiling mirrors. It looks almost like a ballerina's studio. It's set up like that so I can see myself speak, and respond physically in addition to verbally.''

ANSWERING THE CALL

The industry calls telephone answering machines TADs (for telephone answering devices). I find this a tad exotic, although TADs are anything but exotic. In fact, answering machines easily predate computers, faxes, and copiers in the home office hall of fame. Answering machines made it possible for the home office to have a telephone receptionist—someone to answer the phone, and, yes, even to screen your calls.

Naturally, today's answering machines shine with features:

One-cassette machines. Both outgoing and incoming messages squeeze onto the same tape. At the end of each usage, the tape returns to the reel's beginning so that the outgoing message is poised and ready to go. The same thing happens when the playback of calls is finished, which may add a bit of extra wear and tear on the machine's otherwise joyful existence.

Two-cassette machines. One cassette croons your outgoing message. The other cassette takes the incoming calls. Two-cassetters generally provide more room for messages than the solo machines. There's generally a faster response to every function.

Remote. You can phone your machine and listen to any messages it recorded. Some machines require beepers. These are hand-held devices that, when held to the phone's mouthpiece and pressed, emit a tone recognized by your machine. The artful emitting of tones allows you to play back your messages.

Beeperless remote. When calling from a touch-tone phone, you make the TAD do its tricks by pressing a button on the telephone, which eliminates the hand-held beeper and is easier to operate. Beware of the machines that require only a one-digit code. The easier it is to crack the code, the easier it is for a business rival or spurned lover to discover who has been calling you. Of course, even in this enlightened age, we still encounter rotary or pulse phones. To overcome this problem, beeperless phone owners sometimes carry touch-tone emulators. These are no larger than remote beepers.

Call monitoring. This useful but standard characteristic is disguised as a special feature. When the machine takes a call, if the TAD's volume is turned up, you can hear the caller.

Memo record. You can use the answering device's tape recorder soul to capture any memos you choose to utter in its presence. I always wonder what would happen if you're issuing a deathless memo and the phone rings, and you want to monitor the call.

Toll saver. When you call in and there are no messages you can avoid paying for the call.

Showtime

The song "Another Opening, Another Show" well may apply to the razzle-dazzle world of answering machines. What should your outgoing message be? Many philosophies prevail. Unfortunately, all are correct.

There's the bare-bones method that one friend calls the Rockford approach: "Hi, this is Jim Rockford. When you hear the tone, just leave your name and number."

Then there's the nearly Busby Berkeley approach, super production values with just about everything but choreography: Opening bars of the "Theme from 2001 Space Odyssey." VOICE fades in over tympani thuds. "Greetings mortal, you have reached . . ."

Others favor the just plain folks method: (MALE VOICE) "Hi, this is Bob." (FEMALE VOICE) "And this is Cindy Lou." (UNISON) "Gosharoony, we're darned sorry we missed your call, but tell you what . . ."

Comedy has its boosters. "Man walks into a psychiatrist's office and says, 'My brother thinks he's a telephone.' 'Explain to him that he's a person,' says the psychiatrist. 'What,' said the man, 'and miss my calls?' If you don't want me to miss your call, just . . ."

When concocting an outgoing message you should consider several factors:

1. *The message represents you.* For people calling you for the first time, your outgoing message is the first impression you get to make. For people who continuously call you, the outgoing message reinforces or detracts from the professional impression you'd like to make. This doesn't mean you have to be somber and boring. It might even advance your standing to be thought of as an off-the-wall lunatic. Just let there be some symmetry between your outgoing message and your desired image.
2. *Think about the sorrow felt by the people who are calling.* They have picked up the phone because of a desire to speak to you at this very second. Now, they have to listen to your outgoing message. Does it give them hope that the next step in the communication process will take place or does it make them feel as if they are being punished?
3. *Respect the eternal verities.* Regardless of the form of your outgoing message, certain standards should be respected. (These truths first were revealed in Aristotle's "Theory of Telephonics.")

    a. *Remind your caller to leave name and telephone number.* Some people think you love them enough to recognize their voices and know their numbers by heart.

b. *Ask them to mention the day and time of calling.* It's a convenient point of reference. (It's not a necessary request if the TAD has a "time/date" stamp.)

c. *Encourage them to leave a brief message about why they are calling.* If you know what's on a person's mind, you can be prepared and work more effectively when you return the call.

d. *Be courteous.* I was grappling with whether or not it was necessary to mention the need for courtesy. I decided that it isn't necessary, but it couldn't hurt.

Some people prefer answering and voice mail services to TADs. We'll look at these in, of all places, the service section a little later in the chapter.

FAX

In 1988, a University of Virginia program placed facsimile machines in thirty-two medical libraries. Doctors, hospitals, and other librarians needing information were able to fax questions to appropriate libraries, which made the process of asking and answering easier and faster. It may even have saved a few lives. Fax machines have enhanced the way we can communicate with each other. When selecting a fax, here are the variables to consider:

How large are the largest documents you will send? One size does not fit all. It helps if the machine you get accommodates the pieces of paper you send.

Are you receiving drawings or other graphic materials that require extremely faithful reproduction? Machines that give better resolution tend to cost more. Resolution categories are "normal" (for plain text), "fine" (some gradation of tone), and "super fine" (for detailed gradation). The ability to control the gray scale is a useful feature when graphics are involved.

How much work will you tolerate? Labor-saving features cost money. Your needs determine whether these features are windowdressing or vital to your mental health.

The amount of pages that can be automatically fed differs among the various fax machines. It ranges from only one, which is not terribly automatic, to fifty. Consider the length of the documents you're likely to send and how willing you are to stand there and feed the hungry fax.

How many pages will you receive at one time, as well as throughout the day and night? A fax machine equipped with an automatic paper cutter cuts the tedium of separating lots of pages from each other. An automatic paper cutter demands extra vigilance in getting the paper thickness recommended by the manufacturer. Otherwise the paper may jam.

What is the compatibility of fax machines you will deal with? This is an easier question to deal with than technology usually permits. Fax machines fall into one of four categories: group I, group II, group III, and group IV. Group I is least expensive and least useful; it's not compatible with groups II, III, and IV. Group IV is the most expensive and is compatible with the other three, but its features are most suited for big corporate-type applications. Groups I and IV should be ignored by most people. Group II is incompatible with III, but group III generally is compatible with group II. Thus, group III currently is the wisest choice.

Do you want thermal or plain paper? Well of course everybody wants plain paper, but the fax machines that go with it tend to be noticeably more expensive. If you have a thermal paper fax machine and you have to hang on to the document sent to you, it might be a good idea to use a copier to make a plain-paper duplicate.

Fax machines need some upkeep. Tiny particles can get scraped off the paper and find lodging in fax roller mechanisms. These particles include iotas of ink, graphite, correction fluid, and the paper itself. And dust from the paper and room dust that's decided to settle. At some point there may be problems. Possible mishaps include interrupted transmissions. *Shmutz* can cause a misfeed, which can lead to a paper jam, which can cause the fax to end the phone call. It's also possible that the original document can be stained or damaged. Although not as serious a social gaffe as drops that spot in your dishwasher, a dirty roller is to be deplored. Cleaning the rollers on a regular basis can help you sidestep these problems, and avoid the expense of a service call.

Just Say No to Junk

"When the director of the State Consumer Protection Board needed to get an urgent memo on the Shoreham nuclear power plant to the governor a month ago," writes *New York Newsday* reporter Alvin E. Bessent, "he couldn't use the facsimile machine in his Manhattan office. The machine was busily receiving an unsolicited, three-page sandwich shop menu."

The article went on to describe anti-junk fax legislation that was being prepared in New York State. By the time this book is published, the bill may have been passed, signed, and ignored. Still, it illustrates two problems built into the fax machine. Some jerk may be willing to tie up your paper, toner, time, and fax to tell you something you really don't need to know at a time you don't need to know it.

Treat your fax machine phone number as if it were an unlisted line. Instead of printing it on your card, give it out only to those who have legitimate reason to use it. Scrawl it on the card, if you must. Dispense the number as if it were an award that you are conferring upon worthy candidates.

Second, if you think of your fax as a way to contact people who never heard of you, then you will have hit upon a new, modern, electronic way to generate bad will.

SERVICES

Call Waiting

I once wrote that the world is made up of two kinds of people: those who hate answering machines, and those who have them. That sentiment is even truer for call waiting. This service, a phone company dream, allows you to know that somebody is calling while you're busy blabbing to somebody else.

Before I added call waiting, I absolutely despised the concept. Here, I would be chirping away and saying all sorts of very important things, when all of a sudden I'd hear a rude click. I sheepishly introduced call waiting into my life when I was writing a column for a weekly travel magazine. I had to make and receive lots of calls. I was faced with the dynamic of either willing myself to stay off the phone so certain calls could get through, or making certain calls I had to make and thereby inflicting busy signals on those who were trying to reach me (some of whom would just give up).

Now I love call waiting. It enables every call to get through to me. Since those calls can actually mean money and good wishes, my life has been brightened. I also am more tolerant toward other people and their rude clicks.

And now, for an opposing point of view we present a different experience. Call waiting can be horror, as Tony Stewart, developer of the "Home Office" computer program discovered. Stewart, who had the call waiting service, was away from his office a lot and relied on his answering machine to take the calls. One day a wonderful thing happened. The *New York Times* gave "Home Office" an emphatically positive review.

"The day the *New York Times* review hit," recalls Stewart, "I had fifty-seven messages on my phone answering machine when I came back that afternoon. Many of the messages had been cut off by call waiting service which caused the machine to hang up when the second call came in. It was a nightmare.

"Since then, I have gotten two lines with a rollover and no call waiting as a business phone. With rollover, if one number is busy, the other rings. I got a $10 device from Radio Shack which allows your phone machine to pick up whichever line is ringing."

Another call waiting ex-user abandoned the service because she felt it misrepresented her company's image. "If you're on the phone and a second call comes in," she says, "but you can't get off the first call you've got a big problem. All the second caller hears is the phone continuing to ring. There's no busy signal, so it sounds like nobody's watching the office."

Some people consider call waiting to be an assault on civility. In Judith Martin's "Miss Manners" column, she likens call waiting to "a child screaming for attention while one is on the telephone," and cites its nonemergency use as "the rude policy of 'last come, first served.' " She may have been directing her disapproval of use of the service on a personal line as opposed to a business line. Still the notion of etiquette is worth noting when considering the feelings of people with whom you talk on the phone.

Here are some obvious but useful call-waiting tips:

1. Jot a little note about who was saying what before you check to see who the second caller is. When you get back on line with the first caller, you can say "you were in the middle of telling me . . ."
2. Depart from the first caller gracefully, as in "Excuse me, it looks like I have another call. Hold on just a second please and I'll be right back with you. Or would you like me to call you back?"
3. Find out what the second caller wants. If you can settle it quickly, and on the spot, do so. Otherwise call back.
4. Make note of who you are supposed to get back to. Sometimes we get so engrossed in the first call that we forget to return the second.
5. Incoming long-distance calls have the right of way. It's a miserly but useful traffic rule. For some silly selfless reason, most everyone respects it, even the person with whom you're speaking.

Call Forwarding

Touch-tone technology makes this service possible. A phone call to your telephone gets routed to another number that you specify. The other telephone can be in another office, which in fact can be in another state. You pick a receiver and enter a code that includes the phone number your calls are sent to. You pay the charges incurred when the calls go from your phone to the designated phone. It's probably helpful to cancel the forwarding when leaving the other office. Otherwise, you'll be sitting in your office wistfully waiting for the phone to ring.

1-800-Y-O-U

According to the Direct Marketing Association, AT&T introduced 800 numbers in 1967, but it wasn't until 1969 that a company (Sheraton Corporation) offered and promoted the service. Two years is a long time to be temporarily disconnected. Although mostly associated with megacorps that have acres of operators wired into switchboards, the 800 service may be of value to us. AT&T's readyline makes 800 numbers available for home officers. No special equipment is required, and the calls get routed right into your very own working phone. There's a one-time installation charge (under $100 when last checked). There's a monthly service charge of $20 (at the time of this writing). Then there are the charges for the calls that come in on your 800 line. These charges are based on distance and the length of your call. Volume usage and calls received during off-peak hours invite discounts.

Are the charges worth it? That can be answered only in the privacy of your own phone booth, but here are two positive situations to consider.

The service could be useful if you sell something to people who live in other states. The 800 number makes it easier for them to call and order.

If you are a consultant you may be getting phone calls from out-of-state clients who seek advice. They may appreciate the service of an 800 number. Remember to bill them for your time. Unless you are collecting hefty fees, it probably is poor business judgment to give free long-distance advice while paying for the phone call. You may want to be a little selective about giving out your 800 number to anyone but current or potential clients. You'll notice that some catalog houses accompany the listing of their 800 numbers with the phrase, "for credit card orders."

I've come across two shrewd ploys that give a scaled-down 800-number effect for less money. Some businesses send AT&T long-distance gift certificates to customers. It's like keeping track of bonus miles. Clients that spend a certain amount of money in the course of a month get long-distance gift certificates. In effect, their long-distance calls to the home officer are free.

The "Call Me" card also has been put to work. It's a credit card that can be used only when calling a specific telephone number. It's been touted as a way of making sure the dear progenies call. Home officers have given the "Call Me" card to certain key customers.

Long-Distance Teleconferencing

AT&T's Alliance teleconferencing service enables you to call people at up to fifty-seven other telephones throughout the country. The calls actually get routed to their destinations through one of four "junctions": White Plains, Chicago, Dallas, and Los Angeles. There's no cover or minimum, but you do get charged for the individual hookups. The charges are for calls between the junction and the various locations on the call (including your own).

Instead of you calling everybody to get them online, you can have your conference attendees call at a designated time. In either event, setting up a teleconference is similar to running a conference at a hotel. Of course, you don't have to provide weak coffee and stale Danish. You do have to hire a "room." That is, you have to reserve a spot on the "bridge" where everybody will meet. Then, you can send out invitations to register. To schedule a teleconference, call AT&T at (800) 544-6363.

Answering Services

This is the old-fashioned way of getting your calls answered when you're not around. Depending on the service, the caller dials your number or the service number, and the person who answers takes the message. When you call in, you get your messages. Adherents to this approach feel (and perhaps rightly so) that their customers prefer talking to people rather than machines. When checking out answering services, talk to users about reliability. Will you get the messages that are left for you? Also, find out if the service customarily is able to take elaborate messages. You might be helped by something more than name, phone number, and time of call. Some answering services provide voice mail. It's an automated system wherein your phone is answered in your voice. With many voice-mail systems, callers get to review their messages before leaving them, and you can route specific messages to specific people who call in.

When you use an answering service (voice mail and otherwise), your callers can phone your number or a number provided by the service. If you prefer that your own number be used, then you will need the call-forwarding service on your line.

YOU

The *you* component of your phone system is probably the most valuable part (even if it's the cheapest). All of these glittering, beeping devices exist so that you can communicate your message to some lucky person. George Walther, whose firm TelExcel tells customers how to use "Phone Power," has some definite ideas about how to make the phone a powerful tool in projecting your business image.

"Regard the ringing of the phone," says Walther, "as a kind of Pavlovian cue that says that for the next three, five, or twenty minutes that call is the most important thing in the world to me. I'm going to make sure this call is the very best possible ten or so minutes of communication I can manage. By doing that with all telephone calls, you convey a consistent image of excellence."

Your personal search for excellence becomes easier when you know what you're going to say on the phone and how you're going to say it. Walther suggests you try to arrange "phone appointments," scheduled meetings that happen to be phone-to-phone rather than face-to-face. He says it's better to be the caller than the callee, and that phone bill charges are "inconsequential" compared to the value of the call.

"When you're in the position of the one who calls," says Walther, "that means you're prepared; you've made your outline; you have your notes at hand; you've cleared away distractions; you know exactly what you're out to accomplish. It also means you should literally write out what you want to achieve during the call."

The phone appointment concept is a weapon with which you can exorcise "phone tag." "Step one," says Walther, "is to reach further. If you call somebody and the secretary says, 'he's not there would you like to leave a message,' and if you say, 'yes,' phone tag has just begun. Instead you ask a *now* question: 'Is there another extension where I can reach him *now?* Is he in another part of the building where you can have him paged for me *now?* Can we set a telephone appointment *now?*'

"The second point is to leave a thorough and detailed message. Let the party you intend to talk with know exactly what the call is about; what he or she must do to be prepared for it; what reference materials he or she should have at hand. The third step is to schedule a specific phone appointment.''

One home officer has learned to add a neat touch to the phone appointment approach. He sets aside a certain time each day for outgoing calls. His partner picks up the incoming calls.

''He is with a client at the moment,'' she says. ''Would you like me to interrupt?''

Invariably the answer is no.

''He'll be returning calls between three and five,'' she continues. ''Would it be convenient to have him call you then?''

The appointment is made and life goes on. This business feels that the ''he's with a client'' response is more palatable and better for the image than the perhaps more accurate ''he's out of the office'' or ''he's on the other line.''

''The most important thing about projecting a positive image,'' says Walther, ''is to have a positive language coupled with a positive voice so the person with whom you are speaking realizes that you are a follow-through get-things-done person and that your intention is clear with your words. 'I'll try and see if I can get to that maybe next week' compared with 'I will complete that project by Wednesday' conveys a completely different image of professionalism.''

Mark Twain said that ''The difference between the right word and the wrong word is the difference between lightning and a lightning bug.''

Mary Pekas, president of the Telemarketing Institute, Inc., would probably add that this is particularly true when you're on the phone. ''When something enters the mind via our interconnectors, the mind forms an opinion, based on the word or phrase that goes in, as to whether they like or dislike the idea, whether it's negative or positive.'' Pekas favors words that don't create pressure or induce a negative reaction.

Another telephone edge comes from the act of listening and learning from what you're hearing. Be alert not only to what the people at the other end say but to how they say it. George Walther says, ''Make the other person feel comfortable in communicating with you. That is best accomplished by adjusting your voice variables: your rate of speech, for example, your volume and your vocabulary. These should not be used at the level you feel comfortable, but rather at the level with which the person you are speaking feels comfortable. If you are conducting a business telephone call with someone who speaks rapidly, and has a highly educated vocabulary, and you speak slowly with a basic vocabulary, you will not be establishing peer-level respect. The reverse is also true.

"If you talk with somebody who has a more basic education, whose personal communication style is such that they speak very slowly and you go rattling away with a very complex vocabulary, you push the other person away. The best, most important, part of communicating is first dealing with the emotional agenda. Get comfortable with each other and then you can get down to exchanging facts."

Walther adds that you needn't worry about doing hasty computations of words spoken per minute, or average amount of syllables per word. Just listen, get a feel, and intuitively fall into step.

Through their respective companies, Mary Pekas and George Walther package and sell telemarketing insights to major corporations. That's where the money is. Moreover that's where they truly are needed.

I just received a phone call from a business magazine. It seems my subscription is expiring. Mercy me! The call was reassuring, in that it was a mini-textbook of what not to do. It's great to know that a major corporation can spend trainloads of money on research, personnel, and installation and still fall on its fat belly.

The telemarketer began by saying that she was calling long distance for the magazine. Apparently the term *long distance* is supposed to suggest that this call is important. Stop everything—it's a long-distance call. She pointed out that my subscription was expiring and then detailed the wonderful offer. She unreeled her rap in that singsong cue-card style that borders on the onanistic. I even was given the opportunity to recite my credit card number right there on the spot so that the mags would keep on coming. I explained that I was letting the subscription drop on purpose.

She asked why.

"The magazine doesn't interest me," I explained.

"Oh," she said, "well I'm sure you won't want to miss the regular news features and . . ."

At this point I cut her off, explained I was willing to take the risk, and suggested she continue with her calls. If I indeed valued the magazine, and happened to disregard the many renewal notices I received prior to the calls, I probably would be singing a different song. I'd be praising the publisher for keeping me informed despite my sloth. Also I have no problem with the woman who phoned me. Her style reflected her training which, in my opinion, was inadequate.

This episode shows that resources are no substitute for good sense.

The telephone pitch used phrases that rubbed me the wrong way (particularly *long-distance*). The caller was not talking to me or paying attention to me.

Interestingly enough, home officers are the ideal practitioners of phonenastics. To our customers, clients, vendors, and contacts we are the voices at the other end of the phone. However, there are no bloated layers of telephonic bureaucracy between them and us. When they talk with us, they are talking with someone who is alert, committed, and vitally interested in their concerns. They are not talking with an employee who draws a check whether or not anything happens on this phone call. Consequently, regardless of how much we use our phones and for what purposes, we can learn from the telemarketing world. Let's take an even closer look.

Telemarketing, as defined by Eugene B. Kordahl (president of National Telemarketing, Inc.) is "the planned use of the telephone in conjunction with traditional marketing methods and techniques." Corporations set aside floors or at least rooms filled with people armed with telephones and computer terminals. This is the universe inhabited by (among others) those famous operators who are standing by. The successful people in this field have refined a set of guidelines that enable them to deal effectively on the telephone.

It may come as a shock, but telemarketers know what they are going to say before they even ring you. Each uses a carefully polished appeal or pitch or series of statements known as a script. It contains key words and concepts. Often, it encourages the prospective customer to say yes. Built into the script are ways to exist if the person being called is not a prospect after all. Also built into the script are effective challenges to objections.

Whenever we make a phone call, we're really following a script. We may have given little thought to what kind of a script we use.

Mary D. Pekas, president of the Telemarketing Institute in Sioux Falls, South Dakota, has compiled a list of thirty-one different telemarketing activities. These include getting appointments, reactivating old accounts, answering questions from customers, doing market research, collecting past due moneys, offering a new service, and selling.

You might associate telemarketing with that annoying phone call that comes just when you sit down to a well-deserved dinner. It's usually about a magazine subscription or that great real estate opportunity in Florida or your wonderful chance to get in the precious metals market.

Telemarketing doesn't have to be rude. At least, that's the firm belief of Mary D. Pekas. Her Telemarketing Institute runs seminars and sets up telemarketing operations around the country. Corporations pay respectful sums to learn the intricacies of the approach she calls conversational soft sell (CSS). The CSS basics include talking in a low-key friendly manner, and giving an opportunity to choose to accept what's offered without feeling pressured. The method also emphasizes a positive service-oriented attitude.

There's a lot more to CSS than meets the ear. When intelligently followed, it turns prospects into first-time customers, and first-time customers into repeat customers. It identifies definite noncustomers and gives you the opportunity to pull them from your list.

The CSS way actually does not begin with a phone call. First, you send a handwritten note that lets the prospect know a phone call is coming about such and such a subject. You also tell them they can call you and say they do not wish to receive any such calls. This courtesy is intended to reduce the feeling of pressure, and it also has a benignly self-serving component. Everyone's time is valuable—even your own.

If all systems are go, you then make a phone call. Attitudes of genuine service and respect permeate the telephone dialog. "We go right into the flow of the call," says Mary Pekas. "We always ask for time. We ask them if this is a good time to talk. If they say 'yes,' we ask if they prefer we call them by their first or last name.

"We give them an initial benefit statement to see if they have an interest in going forth. After the initial benefit we ask permission to ask questions. We never would assume asking questions without asking permission first. We give them a reason why we would ask the questions. 'Based on this benefit I have just gone over, would you mind if I asked you a few questions to see if this whatever works for you?' If they say they don't mind we go ahead; if they do mind, we don't.

"We move through the four steps of the sale: opening, fact finding, persuasion, and closing. Each time before we move into the next step we ask permission."

Isn't that taking a chance? What if the folks at the other end inconsiderately put their own interests first and tell you to go away? Not to worry! You just ask permission to call again.

"We say, 'yes the timing isn't always right; however, since things do have a way of changing would you mind if we gave you a call in three months just to touch base?' "

Embodied within that simple response are hundreds of hours of intense research. Consider first an alternative reply: Can I give you a call in one month to see if you might be interested then?

Mary Pekas finds that *interested* is an assumptive word, and, as such, is a turnoff. *Touch base,* on the other hand, is one of the neutral non-threatening vocabulary choices that Pekas loves to collect and use.

Moreover, she reports fascinating conclusions as to when people are open to being called again.

"We've done research on the time line," says Pekas. "Only 41 percent will say yes if you ask them if you can call in one month; 72 percent will say yes if you ask to call in two months; in three months it's 80 to 85 percent. In four months that number doesn't change so we decided that three months is the time with which people are comfortable in being recontacted."

These statistics first appeared in *Sales & Marketing Management* magazine. They become more important when pinned to another statistic: 75 to 80 percent of all new business happens after the fifth contact, or the fifth no. The CSS technique is one way to keep the momentum going, and give those probable customers an opportunity to choose you.

CATALOG

Two-Line Telephone (Northwestern Bell, $100). The Techline 2702S is a well-designed compact two-line phone. It can mount on your desk or your wall. It's got automatic redial, twenty-seven phone-number capacity memory (three are grouped as emergency numbers), speaker, and mute control. You can control the ringer volume for each line separately. Contact: Northwestern Bell, 9394 West Dodge Rd., Suite 100, Omaha NE 68114; (800) 822-1000.

Telephone Answering Machine (Panasonic, $89.95). A reliable TAD for the budget-minded, Panasonic's KX-T1450 uses two standard cas-

Northwestern Bell Two-Line Telephone

Panasonic KX-T1450 Telephone Answering Machine

settes. Favored callers can be spared the ritual of hearing your outgoing message. They just press a code (which you've thoughtfully provided) and get straight to the important part, namely, leaving their messages. Other features include automatic interrupt, memo recording, ability to record the outgoing message from a remote location, and indicators to tell you how many calls you've received. Contact: Panasonic, One Panasonic Way, Secaucus NJ 07094; (201) 348-7000.

Two-Line Telephone Answering Machine (Panasonic, $189.95). The KX-T1470 juggles both your phones. You can have two different outgoing messages on this dual, standard cassette system. It's got a time/date stamp, beeperless remote, and the wherewithal to allow certain callers to skip the outgoing message. When you call in for your messages you'll find a digitized voice telling you how many calls there were and what time each call came. You can record memos as well as both sides of your phone conversations. Contact: Panasonic, One Panasonic Way, Secaucus NJ 07094; (201) 348-7000.

Combination Telephone Answering Machine (Code-a-Phone, $279.95). The Code-a-Phone 5890, a combination phone/answering machine, has its outgoing announcement recorded directly onto a microchip. Incoming messages get recorded on a microcassette. The 5890 has a toll-saver, memo recorder, phone conversation recorder, and time/day stamp. There's a little bonus to the time/day stamp. You can press a button and hear the machine enunciate the time and date. Its message-forwarding feature allows the phone to call you at a preprogrammed number to let you know about and/or hear your message(s). You can leave a private message for a specified caller who enters the right code on his or her touch-tone phone. The auto/disconnect feature turns off the system when you pick up the phone extension. The beeperless

Panasonic KX-T1470
Two-Line Telephone
Answering Machine

Code-a-Phone 5890 Combination Telephone Answering Machine

remote has a security plus in that you select your own three-digit code. As a telephone, the 5890 has a twenty-four-number auto-dial memory, a speakerphone, last-number redial, and an autoredial. Contact: Code-a-Phone, P.O. Box 5678; Portland OR 97228; (503) 655-0132.

Combination Answering Machine/Telephone (AT&T, $159.95). As a phone, the 1510 has a ten-number memory and adjustable receiver and ringer volume controls. The answering machine is a beeperless remote and has a one-button playback system. If the call is answered on an extension, the machine resets itself. Contact: AT&T (800) 222-3111.

MCI Fax Dedicated Network (MCI, nominal switch fee). The established upstart, MCI, announced that it was the first long-distance company to offer a telephone line network especially for fax transmission. Actually, you can use the network for voice messages, but what a waste. The network has lots of amenities built in for facsimile machine users. They lend extra sophistication and power to fax machines of humble origins. The network features include high-speed quality transmission from fax to fax; the ability to store messages at one time and have them go out at another; redial when there's a busy signal; reports that include pertinent billing details for every fax sent through the network; and storage of phone number lists for mass distribution. You also can get an 800 fax number, so that people can send you vital information, toll-free.

As a built-in money-saver, after the first thirty seconds of transmission a call is billed at six-second increments. You order the network the way you order any long-distance service. You just call MCI and tell them which of your phone lines should be connected to the MCI Fax Dedicated Network. This service probably is not cost-effective if most of your fax transmissions are within your city or state. Contact: MCI (800) 950-4FAX.

MCI Calling Plans (MCI). The company's Premier calling plans ("PrimeTime" and "SuperSaver") are not geared toward business needs. The exception would be if you are in the eastern time zone and making lots of calls to people in the West. It would also help if you make a lot of weekend interstate business calls. MCI says its "Dial 1 Long Distance Service" is cheaper than AT&T's "standard state-to-state rates." Contact: MCI (800) 444-3333.

Electronic Controller (Panasonic, $169.95). VA-9210 is a nice little black box that allows the phone system perks of intercom, door phones,

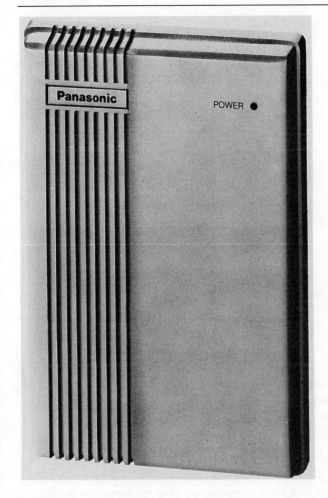

Panasonic Electronic
Controller

sufficiently powered extensions, and paging. The intercom feature also is useful for parents who want to keep an eye—or rather an ear—on their children. The controller works with one- or two-line phones and accommodates up to eight extensions and three door phones. It is designed to work in conjunction with Panasonic 9230 phones. Contact: Panasonic, One Panasonic Way, Secaucus NJ 07094; (201) 348-7000.

Two-Line Telephone (Panasonic, $169.95). The VA-9230 phone is designed to work with the 9210. This phone has a door-phone selector, speakerphone, twenty-three-number memory, hold, volume control, and redial. A conference call button simplifies use of the service. The two-color LED line status indicator lets you know what lines are being used—a useful piece of information. (A 9210 controller plus two 9230 phones come packaged as a 9200 kit for $509.95.) Contact: Panasonic, One Panasonic Way, Secaucus NJ 07094; (201) 348-7000.

Panasonic Two-Line Telephone

Speakerphone for the Disabled (AT&T, $325). Even sitting in a wheel-chair, a motion-impaired person can do business with the outside world. With a mouth stick, the user can answer AT&T's RC-3000 and make calls. The memory holds eighteen numbers. Instead of using a mouth stick, the user can operate the phone with a touch switch, a foot switch, or a puff-and-sip switch. Contact: AT&T (800) 233-1222.

Fax and Voice Phone on One Line (VSI Telecommunications, Inc., $225). The Faxswitch II shares a single phone line with a voice phone or answering machine. This product is suitable for people who like the idea of a fax machine, but are saddened by the additional installation and monthly expense caused by another business phone line. If you answer the phone and hear the telltale fax sound coming from the other end, you press a phone button and the call gets routed to your fax. If the answering machine is on, the Faxswitch II will help the TAD either answer a voice call or send the fax call to the fax machines. VSI President William Gavitt, Jr., says, "Our approach to line-sharing assumes most of your calls are voice calls from people who want to talk to you. We feel you should not put those callers through an exercise or delay to get to you." VSI has prepared a question and answer fact sheet. Contact: VSI Telecommunications, 9329 Douglas Dr., Riverside CA 92053-5618; (800) 999-8232.

Fax Machine (Citizen, $1,399). An economy-priced machine (as fax economies go), the Citizen FX-3000 offers some modest strengths. It

AT&T Speakerphone for the Disabled

has a document feeder (five pages), an automatic paper cutter, and an ability to transmit halftones. Its memory holds seventy-two phone numbers. Contact: Citizen Business Machines (800) 421-6516.

Cordless Phone (Southwestern Bell, $189). The Southwestern Bell cordless Freedom Phone allows you to follow that old saying, "When at home do what the roamin's do." Signals carry 900 feet and the phone's sound is quite good. The base can double as a speakerphone. It has its own keyboard, ringer, and volume control. Intercom buttons allow for meaningful messages to be exchanged between base and handset locations. There's a storage capacity of eighteen phone numbers, and there's a redial feature. Freedom Phone, 7486 Shadeland Station Way, Indianapolis IN 46256; (800) 558-7347.

Cardwear (Izer International, $3). Peel and reveal the adhesive on this artfully notched strip. Place a business card (yours or somebody else's) on the sticky part, and that card can now go in a Rolodex tray.

Faxswitch II

Fifty strips cost about $3. It's a great way to make sure your business card gets filed in the active confines of someone's Rolodex. It's also a great way to keep track of other people's cards. Izer International, the manufacturer, also makes products (Cardwear Hardware) to store cards and carry strips. Contact: Izer International, 8467 Melrose Pl., Los Angeles CA 90069.

2254D Rotary Card File (Rolodex, $36.70). This is the designer version of the classic telephone number rotary file. Made of heavy-gauge steel, it has a roll-top cover and an easy-to-grip knob. Cards turn fluidly. When you stop turning the knob, a ball-bearing clutch assures that the cards will stay put. Alphabetical tabs are placed on heavy, transparent acetate guides that are inserted between Rolodex cards, rather than affixed to the cards. The 2254D can hold 500 2¼″ by 4″ cards. It measures 7″ by 7½″ by 7¼″. It has walnut accents and comes in gray, tan, or black. Some people use color coding to find entries more quickly in their rotary card files. The idea is to assign colors to categories that they want to locate or bypass easily. In addition to white cards, Rolodex offers canary, salmon, blue, pink, and green cards. Rolodex also makes plastic card protectors that are useful for the heavily thumbed files. These are transparent as well as (for the color-coders) orange, pink, yellow, and blue. Contact: Rolodex, 245 Secaucus Rd., Secaucus NJ 07094.

Cityfiles (Metrofiles, $39.95). Each Cityfiles set of 4,000 preprinted Rolodex cards essentially is a telephone directory for a specific city. The entries are of particular interest to business. Obviously, it's more expensive than the yellow pages. It's also much less bulky and easier

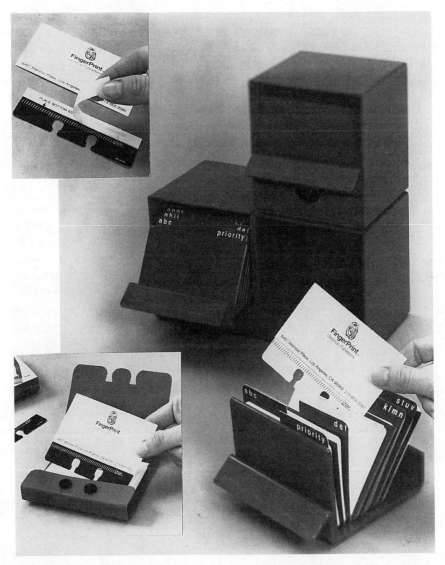

Cardwear

to use. Currently, twenty-two cities are covered in this series: Atlanta, Baltimore, Boston, Chicago, Cleveland, Dallas, Denver, Houston, Los Angeles, Miami, Minneapolis, New York, Orange County (CA), Peninsula (CA), Philadelphia, Phoenix, Pittsburgh, St. Louis, San Diego, San Francisco, Seattle, and Washington DC. Metrofiles also offers a Rolodex directory of toll-free 800 numbers ($9.95). Contact: Metrofiles (800) 426-5564.

The Fax Mill. An energetic marketer of competitively priced Fax paper, this firm is affiliated with Better Methods, Inc., a major paper manufacturer. The Fax Mill sells its paper directly to the end user. Minimum order is one case. Contact: The Fax Mill Ltd., 1200 Madison Ave., Paterson NJ 07503; (800) THE FAX MILL.

SP2 Headset (Plantronics, $79.95). A comfortable metal band fits over your head. A foam-cushioned earpiece and microphone are attached to the band. With a headset you'll look like one of those famous operators standing by. Better than the fashion statement is the fact that your hands are free. You don't have to clutch a phone to your ear. You can use your hands for things like taking notes, running numbers through a calculator, and making entries on your computer, or even gesturing dramatically to boost your adrenaline level. If you do a lot of phone work, you might just want to wear the headset all or most of the time. Then, instead of picking up and putting down the handset, you get on and off the phone just by pressing buttons. The SP-2's sound is clear, and the headset is compatible with all single-line electronic and standard telephones. There's a mute/hold switch, and also a "flash" key for such custom services as call waiting. Contact: Plantronics, 345 Encinal St., Santa Cruz CA 95060.

Cleaning Kit (Fax Care, $34.95). To prevent dirt buildup from mucking up the works, a bit of fax machine housecleaning is in order. The Fax Care Cleaning Kit was specifically designed to clean the paper feed mechanisms. The kit consists of a bottle of nonflammable, nonconductive cleaning solution; a special aluminum applicator tool; cleaning pads; head-cleaning swabs; and cabinet cleaner wipes. Clean the rollers (document feed and thermal feed) with the pads, and use the swabs on the print heads. The long slim applicator helps get the fluid into cramped hard-to-reach spaces. It carefully regulates the amount of cleaning solution that will go onto the pad. The cleaning kit also can be used on computer printer platen rollers. Fax Care reminds us that a cleaning pad should be used only once. Replacements for every single part can be purchased separately. Contact: Fax Care, 100 Wilmot Dr., Suite 347, Deerfield IL 60015.

Act! (Contact Software, $395). Act bills itself as contact software, as in telephone contact. It helps you reign supreme over all the activities that radiate from your phone conversations. There are several basic information building blocks with which you work: your contact's

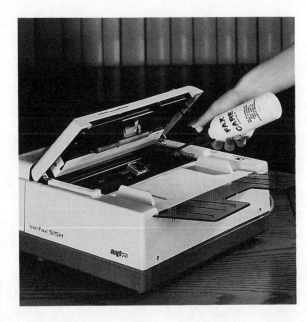

Fax Care

name, company, address, and phone number; relevant notes about contact; time and date of call; and action taken because of call. Other ACT! components are calendar, word processor, calculator, and modem communications program. You summon your contact name to the screen. You'll see all pertinent information you've entered, including what happened the last time you spoke. You press a button to let the computer make the phone call. As you talk, you make appropriate notes and/or calculations. If you need to set an appointment or deadline, you check the calendar and make an entry. You also might hear, "Send us a bill on such and such a date." That too goes on the calendar. Presumably you and the other party will reach a conclusion by the end of the call. For example, if you're asked to send a letter, the program's word processor helps you write the letter immediately. Any of the contact information (name, company, address, etc.) can be used in formulating the letter. Form letters are easily generated. All results—even the vague ones—are significant. They help give a fuller profile of our history with the contact. So, if no action is to be taken, or if you weren't even able to talk to the contact, you should enter that information. The calendar plus the entered information enables you to generate "to do" lists, schedules, and tickler files. You also can use the contact information for creating mailing lists. In addition to all that phone call stuff, ACT! is an instant, centralized source for data about the status of your various contacts. Contact: Contact Software, Inc., 9208 W. Royal La., Irving TX 75063; (214) 929-4749.

Handset Amplifier (Hello Direct, $29.95–$44.95). What's that? I can't hear you. I have a phone in my ear. Whether you have a hearing problem or just work in a noisy environment, an amplifier that steps up the sound might be the right connection for you. You don't have to keep telling the parties on the other end to speak up. And you can even hear what they're saying, which usually is an asset rather than a liability. Contact: Hello Direct (800) 444-3556.

RESOURCES

PUBLICATIONS/VIDEOS

The Book of Fax by Daniel Fishman and Elliot King (Ventana Press, $12.95). Accurately subtitled "An Impartial Guide to Buying and Using Facsimile Machines," this book delves into the scenery of life in the fax lane. It's filled with rules and checklists and definitions. A lot of information clearly is intended for megaperson offices. For example, we needn't care if the fax machine is located in the mailroom or near the copier. Still *The Book of Fax* has many nuggets for the home officer. There's solid advice on selecting the fax machine features best suited to you, where and how to buy, and strategies for use. Contact: Ventana Press, P.O. Box 2468, Chapel Hill NC 27515; (919) 942-0220.

Chilton's Guide to Telephone Installation and Repair by John T. Martin (Chilton). A comprehensive and useful book, this volume was written by a telephone technician with a good background in repair and installation. It's perfect for those who want to take advantage of the wire-it-yourself option. There also is excellent material of a less technical nature. Major topics include a general description of a telephone system, telephone instruments, available phone services, installations for a single-unit dwelling, installations for a multiunit dwelling, telephone repair, and getting along with the local telephone company. Contact: Chilton Book Company, Radnor PA 19089.

Phone Power by George Walther (Berkley Books, $3.50). This paperback book details effective ways to get your call and message through on the phone. Among topics covered are ending phone tag, accomplishing more in less time, Power Talking for great phone impressions, and improving your public image. Contact: Berkley Books, 200 Madison Ave., New York NY 10016.

Hello Direct. This mail-order catalog is devoted strictly to telephone products for business. The company really markets to large and medium-size businesses. Still, it is a handy source for all sorts of problem-solving telephones and accessories. Hello Direct is proud of its same-day shipping and good customer service record. Although it's more geared toward larger customers with larger problems, it will provide some knowledgeable advice about products as well as technical support. Contact: Hello Direct (800) 444-3556.

Do It Yourself Telephone Accessories and Wiring Products (AT&T, free). This thirty-two-page booklet describes every type of wire, cord, jack, plug converter, and so on that you might possibly need. These are the little hardware miscellanea that help you expand, upgrade, or some-how modify your phone system. The booklet tells you in simple language how to install these various items. Contact: AT&T (800) 222-3111.

Telephone Mastery by Mary Pekas (Paradigm Press). This handbook, from the developer of the Conversational Soft Sell method, lights the path to professional telephone technique. The publisher says it's intended for secretaries and other such corporate infantry. You'll learn the skills that can make you a good phone talker and a good listener. The book also gives insights into projecting a positive image and handling stressful calls. Contact: Telemarketing Institute, Inc., P.O. Box 1632, Sioux Falls SD 57101; (605) 335-3970.

Organizations/Services

TelExcel. This is George Walther's company. You might not hire him to run a seminar for you, but you might glean some nuggets from his audiotapes and videotapes. He has assembled a bunch of Phone Power programs ("for effective communication," "for the accounts receivable collector," "for Dealing with Difficult People," and so on). The easiest way to get an overview of Walther's products is to ask for a free copy of his newsletter *Phone PowerLine.* Contact: TelExcel, 401 Second Ave., Seattle WA 98104; (800) 843-8353.

The American Facsimile Association. Also known as AFaxA, its members include manufacturers and users of fax equipment. A spokesperson called AFaxA a rah-rah association. It gives members the lowdown on new fax uses, products, and players. It also hooks up members with problem-solving consultants (done at no charge unless in-depth study required). It stages FaxExpos and exhibits around the country. There's a weekly newspaper ($80 for members, $100 for non-members) and a monthly newsletter, both sent out by fax of course. Contact: American Facsimile Association, 1701 Arch St., Philadelphia PA 19103; (215) 496-9250.

Voice Mail (Mail Boxes Etc. USA, $12.95 and up). This franchise chain includes voice mail as one of the office services it delivers to small businesses. MBE provides three tiers of service, starting with "Answer Max," which holds ten thirty-second messages for five days. Contact: Mail Boxes Etc. USA (800) 356-5324.

CHAPTER 8

The Mailroom

Repeat the following words: "Neither rain, nor snow, nor gloom of night will stay the courier from the swift completion of his appointed rounds."

I'll let other more patient souls devote their time to why the U.S. Postal Service doesn't work, or works better than it's given credit for, or will work wonderfully as soon as simple reforms take place, or . . .

THE ABCS OF OCR

Getting mail delivered promptly and accurately is not as easy as ABC, but it can be helped with OCR. The initials stand for optical character recognition. These machines look at ink marks on paper, and accurately decipher the letters and numbers that the ink marks represent (no Rorschach fantasies for them). The principle is similar to scanners that many computer owners now have.

The U.S. Postal Service uses highly sophisticated OCR machines that can read 36,000 pieces of mail an hour. After reading the address, the OCR prints a bar code version of zip code or zip plus four code of that address. Bar code sorters (BCS) further sort the mail. The OCRs churn away at post offices in really big cities, the kind that have fast lights and bright women. Ultimately there will be 450 optical character readers around the country. Even if there's no such machine in your local post office, it's likely that your mail will be sent along the yellow brick road to a larger station that does have an OCR. If the OCR cannot read the address, the piece gets tossed to a multiple-position letter sorter (MPLS).

Although still heavily automated, the MPLS requires a flesh-and-blood person to quickly make out the address as the letter zooms through at the rate of forty pieces a minute. Getting bumped from the OCR express can delay a piece of mail by a few hours to a full day.

Addressing your mail so that it is OCR-readable will help your letters work with the system. It's like sailing with the wind behind you instead of in front.

On each piece of mail the OCR operates within a rectangular area. Anything outside the area is not read, but there's plenty of room. Just imagine a 2⅛″ high and 6″ wide block that starts a little bit more than ½″ from the envelope's bottom edge. Then give it 1″ margins.

The OCR has tunnel vision. The OCR reads from bottom to top and left to right. It only cares about three lines of the address.

Recipient line. This line states whatever the post office ultimately surrenders the piece to. If you were sending a letter to me, the line would read "Norman Schreiber." If, heaven help me, I were working for a corporation, that corporation's name would be on the recipient line. My name would be on the line above. It would be up to the corporate mailroom to get the letter to me. The recipient line is the top line the OCR cares about. The post office way of looking at it is that it's the third line from the bottom.

Delivery address line. This line is fairly straightforward. It's the street address and it's the second line from the bottom. For example, it could read "1600 Pennsylvania Avenue." If you include a suite, room, or apartment number in the address, it goes on this line, *after* the street address: 1600 Pennsylvania Avenue, The Basement. Do not use an intersection (e.g., 12th Street & Vine) unless it's actually designated as an authorized delivery address.

Post office, state, and zip code line. This is the famous bottom line. The post office is the city. If there's no room for the zip code on this line, or if you want the zip code to stand out, it should go on the line below. Interestingly enough, I'm one of many people who thoughtfully put the zip on its own line and to the right. It should be placed on the left.

There can be a bottomer line. If you send the mail to another country, that destination goes below the post office, state, and zip code line.

The very bottom of the envelope gets used. Somewhere in a space measuring ⅝″ high and 4½″ long (starting from the envelope's right edge), the OCR prints a barcode that represents the address. Anything else that you might have put in the space (such as printing, markings, or attractive borders) bars the use of a barcode.

The OCR needs help from you in the following ways:

• Space must separate each character from the next.
There must be space above and below each line.

There must be space between each character on a line.

Each character must be separate and distinct.

- The characters must be clearly defined.

Script, italic, and other stylized letterings cannot be read.

Dot matrix characters are a problem, unless the dots touch each other.

- Print quality must be sharp and clear.

Faded, broken, or smudged characters are a no-no.

Dark ink against a light background (preferably black on white) is required.

- It helps if the address appears in a particular form.

Capital letters are easier to read.

Sans serif types are easier to read.

Forget everything you learned in school and avoid punctuation (except for the hyphen in the ZIP + 4 code).

Use standard two-letter state abbreviations (e.g., NY for New York).

When abbreviating street names, use standard post office form. (See resources section of this chapter.)

If you want to be a good citizen, you can follow certain formats that help the OCR read your envelopes. Without them, the OCR suffers a microsecond loss. It is of negligible consequence to your own mail, still the loss of 36,000 microseconds per hour can add up in the course of a year.

There's more to what the post office can do for you (or to you, as the case may be). The USPS has developed a number of useful services. For example, we've heard of laundering money, but now we know the USPS will launder your mailing list. It is a free service that helps both you and the post office. The USPS would love for everybody's mail to be processed by the OCRs and barcode printers and readers without ever being sullied by human hands. To help your mail zip right through the system, the post office will take your mailing list and make your entries kosher in the following ways:

1. It will put your addresses into standard form.
2. It will make sure you have the right five-digit zip code.
3. It will add the four extra digits of the ZIP + 4 codes.
4. It will let you know about any addresses that just can't be coded.

The turnaround time on this service is about ten days. Naturally, the USPS prefers to launder mailing lists that are on computer floppy disks. I am told, however, that it is willing to do the same for lists that are on paper. Contact your local post office for this service.

STAMPS

The USPS sells stamps by mail. You can get stamps by mail order form from the post office or your letter carrier. It even has a postpaid envelope. You can order sheets, booklets, and/or coils. State your desires, drop in your check, seal, and mail or give to your letter carrier. You can expect the stamps by return mail. If your letter carrier is the go-between, you'll probably get your stamps the day after you order them. It's also possible to order stamps by phone. Just call (800) STAMP-24.

THE BETTER WEIGH

To the uneducated eye, a postal scale is a device with which you weigh outgoing mail. To the experienced mailer, a scale controls costs. Knowing how much an envelope or parcel weighs means knowing the exact amount of postage. There's no need to give the post office the benefit of the doubt, let alone the benefit of an extra stamp or two. It helps if the scale is accurate.

Which Scale?

If you're only going to send out letters and other materials that fit in standard number 10 business-size envelopes, a scale that is calibrated up to one pound is fine. If you're mailing books, pamphlets, catalogs, and the like, a two-pound scale is in order.

Better-quality scales show not only the weight on their dials but the amount of postage, according to the type of mail you're using. Usually the greater the scale's capacity, the smaller the print on the dial. You would be kinder to your eyes if you picked a scale that does not out-weigh your needs.

Electronic scales give a digital readout of weight and rates. It's easier to read the digital numbers than it is to see the lines on the dial of a conventional scale. Bob Fisher, president of Pelouze Scale Co., says you needn't bother with electronic scales, unless your outgoing volume is twenty pieces a day. He notes that twenty is an arbitrary number, and if the same kind of mailing is sent out over and over again, only one piece would need to be weighed.

Scale Update

What happens to the listing of rates on the scale when the post office ups the dues? "We work twenty-four hours a day to get out new dials for conventional scales and chips for electronic scales," says Pelouze's Fisher. "The dials on it are removable and snap out a little. The chip is like an old radio tube. You plug it in."

Treat your scale well. Place the stuff to be weighed gently on the scale. Don't drop or slap anything onto its platform. Don't do what I have done, which is to treat the scale as if it were one more flat surface on which things can be stored indefinitely.

PAGING LOVELY RITA

A number of home officers have postage meters in their "mail rooms." Meters are not sold; they are leased. The USPS allows four companies (Friden-Alcatel, IMS/Hasler, Pitney Bowes, and Postalia) to rent out meters. I got a lot of my information from Pitney Bowes, the company that originated the process. The barebones Pitney Bowes rental charge is $15 a month, and the minimum leasing period is twelve months.

There's no magic level at which the postage meter suddenly becomes more economical than using stamps. With a meter, your expenses will always be the cost of the postage used plus the cost of renting the meter. Still, the postage meter offers a number of advantages that might appeal to your sense of how business should be done.

- Metered mail reinforces a professional image. The very look of metered postage suggests that you are a full-fledged card-carrying member of the business community. This helps those who feel that working at home deprives them of a certain credibility.
- You pay for only the postage that you actually use. Thus, you can avoid the stockpiling of different denominations of stamps for the one-ounce first-class letters, promotional postcards, and parcels requiring additional postage.
- Use of a postage meter can reduce trips to the post office, which is especially true when you use Pitney Bowes' "Postage by Phone" service. If you have a touch-tone phone, you can set the meter just by making a phone call to a Pitney Bowes computer. This service costs $6 per month. The post office will want to check out your meter only two times a year.
- Some find postage meters easier to use than stamps. When one Pitney Bowes marketing man uses the term "licking stamps," he

seems to say it with an immense amount of revulsion and pity. Most number 10 envelopes containing one ounce or less just get slipped through the meter where they emerge stamped. For pieces that do not slip through the meter, you just stamp a self-adhesive label, peel it from its backing, and place it on the package to be mailed.

- The meter is neater than stamping mail, particularly when you send a bulky piece or something in a tube. The single strip of metered postage appeals more to some people than the multistamp collage that otherwise would be there.

- Pitney Bowes gives its customers free mail consultation. For example, if you plan to do a large mailing, Pitney Bowes will tell you the ins and outs of how to save money and/or time.

- Meter vendors will tell you that metered mail generally moves a little faster through the postal system. When you meter, they say, you actually save the post office the task of postmarking the mail. However, the post office has to know mail is metered *before* it gets processed. Thus, the mail has to be taken to the post office and dropped into a slot for metered mail or given to a human who will put it with the other metered mail. It also can go into a street mail box that is specifically labeled "Metered Mail."

- Metering lets you make a statement to your clients, the public, or the post office by adding an advertising or public service message to the envelope. It gets imprinted along with your postage. You can use an off-the-shelf Pitney Bowes message or design your own. With the latter, you supply the artwork. (PB is willing to make the stamp for you at an additional fee.) The Pitney Bowes collection of messages ranges from "At your service twenty-four hours a day" to "Use your library" to "Zip + 4." The ads cost $19 (for public service messages) and $24 for all others. Pitney Bowes will set four lines of type at no charge.

Postal meter users should remember to change the date stamp. (It's a simple push-button process.) Your mail still would go through even with the wrong date on it, but it gets treated like common stamped mail and goes through the postmarking mill. Thus, you would lose the time-saving perk. Also, remember to renew your postage in time. Running on empty is a no-no. Here are some additional metering tips from the post office.

- The stamped date tells your lucky recipients (some of whom are surely customers) just when you sent out the mail.

- Make sure the meter is making a clear impression. When testing set the meter at no postage.
- Face the metered mail in the same direction. You save the post office a step, and help the mail on its way.
- Package five or more metered pieces securely, and the mail gets handled more efficiently. You may be able to mooch some rubber bands from the post office.
- When putting together a large volume of letter mail, place it in trays from the post office.
- It's also worth knowing that you can get a postal service employee to come to your home office to set the meter. It's done by appointment only. It costs $5 to start and $5 to close an account. The per visit charge is $25. Coupled with the "postage by phone" service, this service makes it possible to avoid post office trips altogether, except perhaps for nostalgia's sake. I would think this service is useful for disabled people who work in their own home offices.

EXPRESS YOURSELF

The USPS express mail service at its most basic is a good deal. Furthermore, it has a few helpful wrinkles. For $8.75 you can send an overnight package that weighs up to one-half pound. The cost is $12 for a package that weighs between one-half and two pounds. The postal fee on a two- to five-pound package is $15.25. From there, the price increases at various increments until you reach the maximum of seventy pounds.

There may be an occasion when you'll appreciate express mail reshipping. With this service, you rent a post office box in some other city. (If the boxes are all spoken for, you can get "caller" service, which means they hold your mail at the post office and you pick it up.) At specified intervals (one, two, or three days, whatever), the mail is stashed into a sack and sent to you overnight via express mail at express mail rates. (For example, a sack of mail weighing fifty pounds would cost about $35.) I'm told that photo processors have developed an interest in express mail reshipping. All the baggies of exposed film go to a post office box, and then get sent quickly to processing central. The service also is useful if you want to receive orders from a targeted city where you happen not to live.

Express mail dropshipping is sort of the same thing. With this service, you can bombard a particular city with a large volume of mail (e.g., advertisements, newsletters, questionnaires). The mail (regardless of class) gets stuffed into an express mail sack that gets sent overnight to a post office management sectional center in the designated city. There it essentially is dropped into the local mail box. Express mail reshipping is particularly helpful if you want to spread the gospel of your product or service in a faraway city and shave a couple of days or more off the delivery time.

Those individuals crazed beyond mere hysteria because time pressure is about to flatten them should know about airport to airport express mail service. It's not convenient, but it's fast.

You take your parcel to an airport that has an express mail office. There it grabs a flight on the next plane going to its destination: an airport that also has an express mail office. The post office is not involved in getting the parcels to or from the airports. Allow an hour each way for the package to move between airplane and express mail office, plus, of course, the flight time. The result tends to be same-day service at normal USPS express mail fees (plus whatever it costs to get the parcel to and from the airports). It's a good idea to call first for flight schedules.

You can get an account with the express mail division. You pay a deposit and the post office charges your express mail expenses against this account. You arc issued a registration number that you write on your express mail envelope. The post office checks each number. To arrange for an express mail account, contact your local post office.

OTHER POSTAL SERVICES

You also may want your mail to enjoy the benefits of third-class bulk mail citizenship. If you don't mind waiting up to three weeks for people to get your valuable message, you can save a lot on the postage costs (compared to first-class mail). There's a whole slew of requirements and cost incentives based on such variables as quantity of pieces being mailed, use of zip plus four codes, presorting according to zip, and imprinting of barcodes on the envelopes. The first step in taking advantage of this category is getting a bulk mail permit. Apply at your local post office. It's not a complicated process, but you'll probably have to discuss what you're doing with your local postmaster or postal employee operating the information window.

Prepaid business reply cards and envelopes are the pieces that allow your prospect to respond to your offer without even risking a stamp. Again a permit is required. Again, you had better be prepared to chat about the ins and outs of it all at your local post office. You are charged only for those pieces that are mailed back to you. You can pay on a cash-on-delivery (COD) basis or set up an account. The amount you are charged per piece can be as little as five cents. We're talking variable city here. The costs depend on the degree to which your card or envelope conforms to all the many standards that make for automated mail from the contrast caused by the colors of the ink and the envelope to the use of various codes. Before setting fees, your local postal people will want to examine samples.

To get a better grasp of these and other postal regulations, you'll want to do two things. Get a copy of the *Domestic Mail Manual*. It's got every USPS mailing regulation you never wanted to know. The book costs $19 and it's available from the Superintendent of Documents, Government Printing Office, Washington, DC 20402. After scrupulously studying pertinent sections of the book, drop in on your local post office and ask them to explain it to you.

YOUR MAIL'S APPEARANCE

The mail you send starts to make an impression the moment it is received. People touch, sniff, taste, and even look at the envelope for all sorts of signs. Heavy-duty direct mail mavens know this and design a complete package to satisfy the senses and the mind. They're not only concerned with what the pitch letter says but with what it looks like in terms of its shape, size, and design. What enticing enclosures are sent? What kind of envelope does it go into? What is printed on the outside of the envelope that will make people open the envelope even though they know such action might result in their giving money to some undeserving wretch?

We can't all bear the cost of custom-printing envelopes. However, Tension Envelopes assures us that we can get extra promo mileage out of stock envelopes. The company is a major supplier of custom-printed envelopes for mass mailers, as well as a manufacturer of stock envelopes. Here are some ideas that Tension has shared with us:

- If your enclosure is trumpeting a special offer, deadline, or sale, flag it. Use a rubber stamp or a pressure-sensitive stick-on label on each envelope.
- Even if there is no special offer, you can go crazy with labels. There are all kinds of labels with designs, words, colors (pastel and fluorescent) that you can stick onto the envelopes.
- Try putting an enclosure in an "interoffice memo" envelope. These envelopes have holes. People will see the material through the holes and wonder what it is.
- Get real radical and put the address and stamp on the back rather

than on the front of the envelope. You also can put some sort of provocative message on the front.

- Experiment with envelope sizes. There's more to heaven and earth than the number 10 business envelope. For example—

   A greeting-card-size (Baronial) envelope carries with it the aura of good feelings and maybe even an invitation.

   The monarch style accommodates a larger letterhead and conveys a sense of importance.

   Oversize envelopes (nos. 11, 12, 14, or 16) command respect. These have bankers' flaps (the standard way of sealing a business envelope). A broadside can be inserted.

- A number 10 envelope may be more appropriate, but it doesn't have to be white. Brown Kraft paper is available as are blue, canary, green, or pink.

Another way to cut corners when doing a mailing is to involve, as early as possible, the company that will print your envelopes and/or enclosures. Review with them the dimensions and weight of the paper you plan to use. Maybe the printer can suggest cost-cutting alternatives. Maybe the printer has some paper at a sale price. Can your job be printed with someone else's as part of a gang run? Finally, does the format of the paper or envelope you plan to use demand extra costs that the printer will pass on to you? Is there an approximately similar format that would be less expensive?

COURIER SERVICES

"I don't see why the post office has to make a profit," I told my letter carrier a few years ago. "After all, the army doesn't have to make a profit." The observation always delighted him.

It seems that in the post office's search for the black ink road two things have happened. Services such as list cleaning and stamps by mail that aid the productivity of both the USPS and its patrons have been added. Services that contribute to the timely delivery and special handling of mail have been affected by what I view as productivity triage. For example, special delivery has become not so special delivery. Overnight delivery is guaranteed only when a premium price is paid.

Private competitors have seen a chance to supplement the post office's efforts. Before we discuss alternatives, let's get a bit of perspective.

I called Federal Express to get some information for this book.

They promptly sent a package of press releases, annual and quarterly reports, rate descriptions, backgrounders, and other assorted educating pieces of paper. Still the most instructive piece was the envelope containing the enclosures. It was your run-of-the-mill classy red, white, and blue Federal Express envelope. It had just one extra feature: the metered postage on the upper right-hand quarter. That's right, Federal Express used USPS. The lesson for me is that there's no one way to send anything. See? Even the philosophy of mail can be cosmic.

Courier services find they can profit by giving us the one thing the post office generally cannot: relative certainty. They will take our parcels from our hands and deliver them to the hands of the people with whom we do business. And they'll do it within a specified period of time. And, oh yes, they charge for this. The charges are worth it (depending on what's being sent) when the courier services deliver on the certainty they promise (generally the case) and when that certainty is important.

Which courier service is right for you? The major players seem to be engaged in a highly visible drag race. In their earnest competition, they modify rate structures, add destinations, and develop new services for particular markets. The motto seems to be "a niche in time . . ." Rather than list what these companies are offering at the time of this writing, I probably would serve you better by detailing the questions you should ask when selecting a courier. Ask to speak to an account executive. Otherwise, you'll probably talk to someone who arranges for the pickup and delivery of your parcel, and who may not know answers to all of your questions.

1. Do you pick up from and deliver to my community? Most likely, the answer is yes, especially if you happen to live in a major city. It doesn't hurt to ask, especially if you don't happen to live in a major city.
2. Do you pick up from and deliver to the places where people with whom I do business are located? Again, it may not be a problem in the United States, but it particularly requires exploration when your parcels become international jet-setters.
3. How much do you charge? If you're sending packages that weigh pretty much the same to only a few destinations, this question probably could be answered on the phone. Otherwise, you had better request a rate schedule. These listings of rates in all their variety are to railroad schedules as calculus is to long division. Still they should help with the big "how much" question.

4. What do I have to do to open an account? Generally, you are required to have a pulse. You can get by without an account, but getting on the roll makes it easier for you to take advantage of whatever special services or perks might be open to account holders.
5. Would I be entitled to any discounts based on the volume or frequency of packages I send out? If the answer is anything but "no, never," try to pin down the account executive into explaining when discounts can be earned.
6. Based on the volume or frequency of packages I send out, are there any services to which I'm entitled? For example, can you get computer software or hardware that helps you fill out forms and/or ties you into the courier's system?
7. Do you offer any services that are particularly appropriate for my industry?
8. Can you bill third parties? For example, if I want something picked up from a supplier and delivered to a customer, can you bill me instead of either of the other two?
9. What are your liability policies? How much can my packages be insured for?

When talking with the account executive, try to supply certain basic information. It will help both of you. What business are you in? What are the weights and sizes of the packages you send? Where do you send them? Do you have special handling or timing requirements? Between the answers to the questions you ask and the responses to the information you supply, you should get some sense of which courier service is for you.

In the very last days of writing this book, I learned of a courier company, Express Courier Centers, that offers discounts. ECC arranges to send daily bundles of parcels with various established shippers. In return, ECC gets an excellent discount. It reaches its quota by rounding up parcels from individuals and businesses who, in turn, get a lower price than they would otherwise. Sounds great, and it sort of is. At the time of this writing, the Birmingham, Michigan-based ECC provides its services to only three cities: Chicago, Dallas, and Detroit. Washington, D.C., is being contemplated. I have no idea as to how to help you identify a local consolidator, short of calling up every express and courier in your yellow pages to ask if they are consolidators.

BLIP MAIL

"When do you need it?"

"Yesterday?"

Now it's almost possible to fulfill this timely request. In recent years, a small corner of the world of mail has provided a kind of instant gratification. I refer to electronic mail, known to savants as "E-mail," and facsimile machines.

E-mail requires computers and modems. You use a service such as MCI Mail or one of the information utilities such as CompuServe. Each user is provided with an electronic mailbox, a code number to which messages are directed and stored.

You write your letter on the computer. Without printing it out, you send it via modem to the recipient's mailbox. The addressee checks his or her mailbox and reads your message. Similarly, if you want to see if there's any mail for you, you just check into your own mailbox. When you read your electronic mail, you have the options of storing it in the mailbox, erasing it from the mailbox, storing it on your disk, or sending a return message. You also can print it out.

Publicist Wes Thomas, who specializes in leading-edge computer industry clients, is an MCI Mail user. He feels E-mail is a home office essential. He contrasts its use with the way things were when he had an office downtown.

"In the past," says Thomas, "I would write a letter by hand, and somebody would type it. I would correct all the typos, and that would go through about three different drafts until the secretary got it straight. The envelope would be addressed, and the letter inserted. Postage would be applied. All of these steps are extremely expensive. Three or four days later, somebody would get the letter and by then, of course, the world has changed."

Thomas believes that E-mail fits well with the independence of working at home. In fact, he gets absolutely technorhapsodic over the subject: "When you find yourself with the flexibility and freedom you have with a home office, you don't want to be stuck in the old paradigm of working nine to five, particularly if you have a business where you don't necessarily have to be in front of the phone all day long.

"I frequently find myself working at three in the morning because a lot of my work involves thinking and writing out backgrounders, press releases, and so forth. I'll find that I have an idea I want to communicate with a particular person. Almost 90 percent of the people I want to talk to (including most of the key press and a lot of the influential industry leaders) are among the 75,000 people on MCI

Mail. I type out the thought, pop a few keys, and upload the file onto MCI.''

Wes Thomas sends the message at his convenience. He's at the computer. The thought is singing loudly in his head. With scarcely more effort than it takes to write down the thought, he has sent it on its way to the recipient. The addressee, in turn, reads the letter at his or her own convenience.

"Increasingly," observes Thomas, "the kind of people with whom I want to work, work asynchronously. They communicate with people not in real time but in delayed time. They send you a message. You pick it up in an hour or two. You send them a message. There is the added benefit that you're not stuck with the normal social obligation to engage in a longwinded ten-minute conversation when all you want to do is communicate one sentence. Furthermore, the asynchronous communication lets people receive your messages at the optimum time for them. There's none of the phone tag of repeated calls or catching somebody at a bad time.''

When getting messages through electronic mail, a helpful strategy is to save the message on your disk as it is coming into your computer. You then read the letter after you disconnect from the system, thus saving a bit of time and money. Obviously, both you and the people you communicate with this way must be customers of the same system. Actually, you can use a form of E-mail to communicate with people who are not on the system.

MCI Mail has provisions for sending hard copy, which is a fancy way of saying that a letter ultimately gets delivered by the USPS. For example, if you wanted to send hard copy from Los Angeles to New York, first you would move to Los Angeles. Having solved that problem, you would log on to MCI Mail, specify that you were sending hard copy, and the missive would take a few seconds to travel the first 3,000 miles from your home to the system's branch office in New York City. There, it would be printed out on a laser printer, stuck in an envelope, and mailed. It would take a bit more than a few seconds to get from the post office to the final destination. You even can keep your letterhead on file so that your sterling words can be printed on your own (reproduced) letterhead.

E-mail has been around for a while, and although not all that hard to work with, it has not captured the imagination of the technically timid. Fax machines fill that vacuum. There's no computer choreography to mess with. Essentially, you just insert the item to be copied, dial a number, and away it goes. In addition to simplicity, the fax has another advantage over E-mail. Electronic mail generally is better suited for sending and receiving of text rather than graphics. The facsimile machine does not care if it's sending text or graphics.

Fax is right on the money when people in one location need or deserve to have and examine a piece of paper in possession of people in another location, and they need to see it today. Most obvious candidates include visual material such as blueprints, drawings, photographs, and thumbnail sketches. Often when public relations counselor Alan Caruba phones prospective clients, he faxes background information during the phone call. Then, there's deadline textual material such as reports, memos, and legal papers. The fax machine has proven to be a wonderful antidote to invoice-losing.

"Gee, I guess we misplaced your invoice. Would you mind sending us another?"

"No problem. I'll fax it to you right now."

The fax is also useful for doing an end run around international mail. Photographer Bob Rattner negotiated by fax with a British publisher over the use of his photos of manatees. Terms were sent and studied instantly. They saved the time that otherwise would be spent by the British and American post offices. They also sidestepped the constraints of a five-hour time difference by sending fax messages at their respective conveniences.

A hybrid form of communication that combines elements of fax and E-mail is emerging. With computer and modem you send a message to an electronic mailbox. The message then gets relayed to the designated fax machine. MCI Mail subscribers enjoy this perk.

Xpedite Systems make itinerary between personal computers and fax a two-way street. A message can go from someone's fax machine to your electronic mailbox to your computer. You are hooked up to fax machines without having to part with the bread it takes to buy one. Its cost-effectiveness is reduced when receiving graphics, as visual material uses up a lot of computer memory and takes longer to squeeze through the phone line. In addition to phone charges, you would be paying the service for either the size of the document as measured in computer-k's or the amount of time you're on the phone.

Another hybrid is the fax board. This computer accessory allows the computer with modem to send directly to and receive directly from fax machines. Again, you are saved the tasks of printing out a document and then inserting it into a fax machine. The fax board cannot send a picture unless you first use a scanner to enter the visual material into the computer's memory.

The effect of all these electronic words sidestepping the limitations of the post office, telephones, and time itself is wondrous. Wes Thomas calls the linking gained through E-mail and fax a "virtual network." In fact, he will only accept clients who become MCI Mail subscribers or who at least have fax machines. Part of his argument is that since they are in the computer industry, they should show technology smarts to the press. His argument is instructive to any of us who have clients and or vendors. It's an effective way to communicate and make thoughtful decisions.

CATALOG

One-Pound Scale (Pelouze). The Petite PAA1 scale has a dial that shows rates for first class, priority, third class, air, and Europe–Asia. The platform is 2″ by 2⅛″. Contact: Pelouze Scales, P.O. Box 1058, Evanston IL 60204.

Two-Pound Scale (Pelouze). The Duchess X-2 accepts up to two pounds. Rates shown are parcel post, first class, priority, third class, air, and Europe–Asia. Use of colors makes the rates easier to read. The platform is 3¾″ by 3¼″. Contact: Pelouze Scales, P.O. Box 1058, Evanston IL 60204.

Electronic Scale (Pelouze). The PS6R1 measures up to six pounds. It gives the weight and rates for first class, priority, third class, express mail, parcel post, Canada, Mexico, air mail, international air mail, and UPS (ground, next-day air, second-day air, ground Canada, and air Canada). An optional feature will convert zip code to zone. Contact: Pelouze Scales, P.O. Box 1058, Evanston IL 60204.

Execufold (ADI Machines for Business, $295). The machine is for those moments when neatness counts. It mechanically folds a piece of

Pelouze One-Pound Scale

paper (8½″ by 11″ or less) to fit into a standard number 10 business envelope. Just slip the paper in, and out comes a sharply creased document, unsmudged by human hands. The easy operation takes a few seconds. It's ideal for invoices, newsletters (up to three pages), and other sorts of business mail. The manufacturer says it's not appropriate for mass mailings (meaning that it doesn't make sense to do more than

Pelouze Six-Pound
Electronic Scale

Execufold

USPS Stamp Applicator

"somewhere between 300 to 500 foldings a day"). It can accommodate up to three sheets of twenty-four-pound bond paper (or one thicker sheet) at a time. You can staple the multiple sheets together, but do not use paper clips. Contact: ADI (800) 255-3713.

Stamp Applicator (U.S. Post Office, $24.95). Avoid the old glue on the tongue syndrome. Just load a roll of stamps inside the applicator and press on. It's a neat way of affixing stamps to envelopes. Contact: your local post office.

The Original Personal Message Center (Spin-Rite). Designed to hold those pink while-you-were-out telephone messages, this 6¼"-high, 8½"-long sorter is a convenient way to hold and arrange mail, bills, receipts, and other maddeningly miscellaneous pieces of paper. It's got eight removable partitions, as well as a bunch of exactly sized labels that you can stick onto the partitions. Contact: Spin-Rite, P.O. Box 8474, Waco TX 76714; (800) 327-7845.

Expansion Envelopes (International Envelope). Part of International's Survivor line, these are designed to mail bulky items such as catalogs, books, and printouts. An accordion pleat affords the ex-

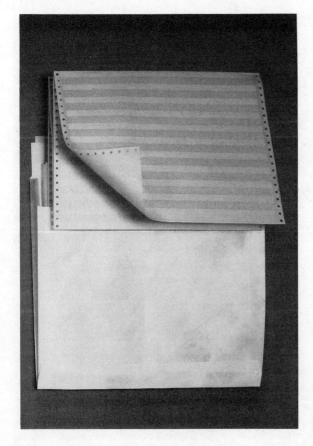

Expansion Envelopes

pandability that gives each envelope a 2″ width. Measurements range from 9″ by 12″ by 2″ to 12″ by 16″ by 2″. The envelopes are made of lightweight, sturdy Tyvek. To seal, just remove the paper liner from the flap, and the envelope's pressure-sensitive stickum does the job. Survivor products are available only through office products dealers and stationers.

FAX Forms (Visual Organizers, $1.95–$2.95). You can use these forms to flag your fax transmission to a particular person's attention; to indicate that you want a return transmission by phone or fax (check one); and to note that it was you who sent the message. The FAX and Figures form allows you to enumerate items and can be used as a purchase order, sales order, quotation request, quotation, or proposal. There also is a form specifically for purchase orders. Other forms include Faxogram, Fax Bax Reply Message, and Fax Receipt. The FAX

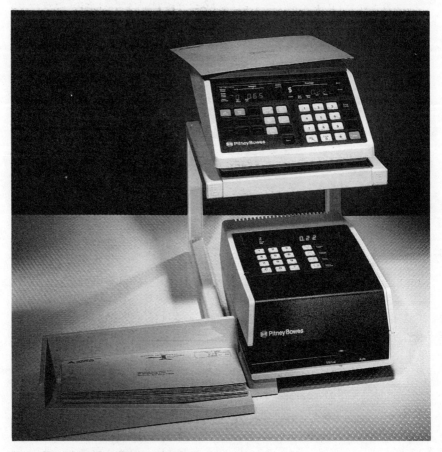

Pitney Bowes Postage Meter with Scale

Form is sent as the first sheet of a transmission. In some cases, it is the transmission. The FAX Forms come fifty to a pad. Contact: Visual Organizers, 355 Beinoris, Wood Dale IL 60191.

Postage Meters (Pitney Bowes, $15/month and up). Four different meters seem most appropriate for the home office. Two are mechanical and two are electronic. The electronic postage meters make postage by phone possible. They also can interface with a Pitney Bowes electronic scale so that the weighing of an item sets the postage for that item. The 5707 costs $15 per month. Its electronic counterpart, the 6900, rents for $20.75 per month. The 5380 mechanical meter is heavy artillery for frequent and copious mailings. The meter sits atop a mailing machine base that automatically seals and feeds. The electronic heavy mailer is the 6500 and it costs $34.25 a month. Again, the prices cited for meters specifically refer to lease costs. Contact: Pitney Bowes (800) 243-2300.

Strapping Tape (Fidelity, $35.88 for twelve rolls). This strong tape is polyester-backed and reinforced with glass strands. It's for sealing cartons so that they stay sealed. It also is used to bundle odd-shaped items that otherwise would shift around. Fidelity includes a free metal dispenser with every twelve rolls sold. Contact: Fidelity Products (800) 328-3034; in MN (800) 862-3765.

Precut Packaging Tape (3M, $6.50). Some thoughtful elves went into the 3M factory and cut heavy-duty packaging tape into 2″ by 6″ strips. It's a good size for envelopes and small packages. The product, which comes in boxes of 100, makes particular sense for those who don't want to mess with dispensers or don't have many packages to send. Available in transparent or tan. Contact: 3M Commercial Office Supply Division, Building 223-3S-03, 3M Center, St. Paul MN 55144-1000.

Label Protection Tape Dispenser (3M, $60). Broad waterproof tape is used to laminate shipping labels. The tape keeps the label on and protects it from the elements. The dispenser makes applying the tape easy. You place the label face-down on the dispenser's tray, tear the tape, and slap the tape on the package. A second reel on the side holds other tape for the all-around adhesion opportunities. If you ship a lot, this dispenser may be useful. Contact: 3M Commercial Office Supply Division, Building 223-3S-03, 3M Center, St. Paul MN 55144-1000.

Precut Label Protection Tape (3M, $6.50). For those who would like to dispense with the dispenser, these 4″ by 6″ individual sheets come on a pad. You'll find 100 sheets in a package. Contact: 3M Commercial Office Supply Division, Building 223-3S-03, 3M Center, St. Paul MN 55144-1000.

Tension Envelope Corporation. This manufacturer of custom and stock envelopes provided us with that creative list of suggestions about how to get more mileage out of stock envelopes. Contact: Tension Envelopes, 819 East 19th St., Kansas City MO 64108-1781; (816) 471-3800.

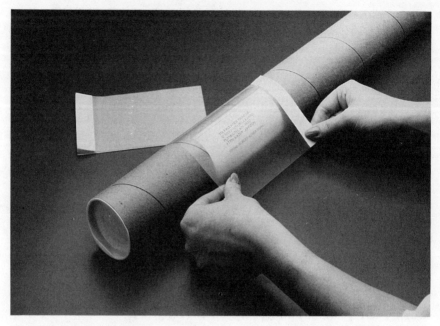

Precut Label Protection Tape

Packing Your Mail (Tape, Inc., various prices). How do I pack thee? Let me count the ways. Tape Inc.'s Mail-Away line has postal packaging for likely ship-it-out needs. Its padded mailing bags come in seven sizes (4″ by 8″ to 10″ by 16″). You seal them by folding over the top and taping or stapling the newfound flap. The recipient opens by gripping a tab and pulling. The Mail-Away mailing boxes are easy to assemble. They have fold-over panels, and the cover just gets tucked in. They are made of strong white corrugated cardboard, and they come packaged with reinforced sealing tape. In case you're not using shipping labels, spaces to write "TO" and "FROM" are clearly designated. Three sizes are available (9″ by 6″ by 3¾″; 11″ by 8⅝″ by 4″; 14″ by 10″ by 5″). Use mailing tubes when you're sending out those documents or artworks or other pieces of paper that can't be folded. They're made of fiberboard, wrapped with blue Kraft paper. The range of sizes will accommodate enclosures ranging from 1″ by 15″ to 3″ by 42″. The sixty-pound Kraft postal wrapping paper comes in three sizes: 2 feet by 50 feet; 2.5 feet by 20 feet; 2.5 feet by 15 feet. Contact: Consumer Products Division, Tape, Inc., Green Bay WI 54307-1067; (414) 499-0601.

Smartfax Fax Board (American Data Technology, $499). A board is a tray—filled with a particular technology—that you connect inside your computer. The Smartfax enables your computer to act as a fax machine. As with all fax boards, the Smartfax converts an outbound computer file (text or graphics) into a fax file. An incoming fax document gets converted into a computer graphics file. The software that comes with it is easy to use. The Smartfax exploits the computer's own memory for storage of documents to be sent later. The computer also assists with storage of telephone numbers. Smartfax operates in the background, which means you can do other computer work while messages come in or go out. Although fax boards can send and receive graphics, it should be noted that incoming graphics use up a lot of memory. Contact: American Data Technology (818) 578-1339.

RESOURCES

PUBLICATIONS/VIDEOS

ZIP Code Directory (U.S. Postal Service, $49). The post office annually publishes a great big directory of every five-digit zip code in the country. You can look up a street address and find its zip code. Contact: your local post office or the superintendent of documents.

ZIP + 4 Directory (U.S. Postal Service, $12 each). This directory actually is a series of books. Usually each volume in the series gives access to the ZIP + 4 codes in one state. Some volumes include more than one state. Contact: your local post office or the superintendent of documents.

Memo to Mailers (U.S. Postal Service, free). Published monthly, this newsletter is intended for postal patrons "originating significant quantities of mail" (not necessarily quantities of significant mail). Its contents appropriately deal with matters more likely to concern heavy mailers. These range from regulatory changes to tips on using the service. Contact: *Memo to Mailers,* P.O. Box 999, Springfield VA 22150-0999.

The Complete MCI Mail Handbook by Stephen Manes (Bantam, $22.95). Veteran users of the system praise this book, as do MCI Mail personnel. It explains the ins and outs of MCI Mail with a decent clarity. While describing how to get the most out of MCI Mail, Manes includes a number of details that just don't appear in the MCI Mail documentation. Contact: Bantam Books, 666 Fifth Ave., New York NY 10103.

ORGANIZATIONS/SERVICES

MCI Mail (MCI, $25 plus). An electronic mail system to which many businesspeople subscribe, MCI Mail is very easy to use. The biggest challenge I faced was learning my eight-letter password. (Writing it down helped a lot.) MCI Mail messages can be sent blippingly to the mailboxes of other MCI Mail subscribers. You can also send the message to somebody's telex or fax machine. (If MCI's fax encounters a busy signal, it will keep trying to connect for four hours, unless you tell it to take longer. Meanwhile, you and your computer already will have galloped off into the sunset.) MCI Mail subscribers can send messages to CompuServe subscribers. MCI Mail subscribers can delve into Dow Jones/Retrieval (at the usual DJ charges). Speaking of charges, you can get MCI Mail either a la carte (charge per message sent with a minimum of 45 cents per message, depending on length) or combo dinner ($10 a month, which allows up to forty messages plus a 25 cents minimum rate for additional messages). Contact: MCI (800) 444-MAIL.

MCI Mail Plus (Oppenheimer Software). Just as there are independent insurance agents, there are independent MCI Mail agents. Gary Oppenheimer is one such agent. He works from his home office in his houseboat docked in Manhattan, although he has clients nationwide. In addition to signing up and servicing MCI Mail customers, he sells software. He also writes and sends out (electronically, of course) a newsletter on an irregular basis. The publication gives advice on how best to use MCI Mail and also offers relevant news. His background as a software developer and computer consultant can be useful. Contact: Gary Oppenheimer, Oppenheimer Software, 79th St. Boat Basin #39, New York NY 10024.

Fax Network (Xpedite Systems, $49 plus). The system uses the E-mail to fax route. The $49 you spend pays for the software. You also get charged for each message sent or received. For outgoing messages, you pay for both time and size of the document, measured in 5K increments. (The 17K document currently in my computer is four single-spaced pages long.) Incoming messages are $2 each (regardless of size) plus time costs (at least 13 cents a minute). Several nice features are built into the Xpedite System. You can store your letterhead so that your messages are transmitted with all the trappings. You can get confirmation that the document has been delivered. You can specify that the document be sent overnight at the cheaper rates rather than the priority do-it-now rate. Billing codes allow you to allocate the costs to different clients if appropriate. Subscribers can use the system to send E-mail to each other. Contact: Xpedite Systems, 446 Highway 35, Eatontown NJ 07724; (800) 227-9379.

Courier Services. DHL (800) 225-5345; Emory Worldwide (800) 443-6379; Federal Express (800) 238-5355; United Parcel Service. UPS has no national 800 number. A spokesperson suggested you check the phone directory for the number of your local office.

Private Post Offices (Mailboxes, Etc.). How about postal service with the personal touch, with conveniences? This network of franchised alternate postal centers provides twenty-six services that cluster around the notion of communications. They rent out their post office boxes. Customers have twenty-four-hour access to the boxes. Before you go to a Mailbox, Etc., to get the day's mail, you can give a call and see if anything is in the box. I'm told that if your Mailboxes, Etc., postmaster isn't too busy, he or she will tell you who your mail is from when you call. You can send parcels via UPS, Federal Express, and overnight mail. They provide an answering service through the Voice Boxes USA system. They also offer fax, Western Union, and telex services. When talking with someone from the corporate office of the parent company, I asked the unasked question that people are too polite to ask: What happens if I rent a post office box and the franchisee goes belly up? How will I get my mail? It hardly happens these days I was told, but in the rare event that it does, the USPS will forward the mail. Contact: Mailboxes, Etc. (800) 356-5324.

CHAPTER 9

The Traveling Home Office

For a while I wanted to name this book in honor of one of the most endearing home office perks: *The One-Minute Commuter*. Still, even we find occasions when we are reduced to braving the elements and going out to do business. There are the little trips that one does within one's own borders such as going out on sales calls or doing errands. Then there are the all-day, two-day, and longer trips to alien cities where people speak funny and cabdrivers are polite.

Even though we journey forth, our home office is still with us. In addition to whatever lured us to faraway glittering ports, we've got to deal with the everydays of our business: phone, correspondence, paperwork, background reading, and deadlines.

The first step is the most elusive: have foresight. (It sounds a little like the Steve Martin secret of being rich: "First get a million dollars.") Train yourself to make lists for travel.

Jefferson D. Bates, coauthor with Stewart F. Crump, Jr., of *The Portable Office* (Acropolis Books), speaks well of list-making. In his book, he writes, "My first and most important advice is to make a master checklist of clothing, toiletries, and any other necessities. Always keep the checklist handy, and consult it before leaving your hotel to make sure you've left nothing behind. You may want to make several different lists."

For example, who are you going to see? What materials should you have when you see these people? Do you have to make phone calls while you're away from the office? Who do you have to ring and what are their numbers? Do you have to send any letters? To whom? What are their addresses? How much stationery will you need? Do you have any correction fluid in case you have to white out something on a letter?

182

What should you know about the city where you are spending time? What's the phone number of a taxicab dispatcher? What are some good restaurants? (Good might mean something very specific such as fancy, ethnic, or vegetarian.) Does the hotel provide a courtesy bus from the airport? How should you pack for the weather? A call to the city's convention, or tourist, bureau, or possibly its chamber of commerce, can yield much useful information including maps, restaurant guides, business services, and special events.

"Very often when people travel outside the country for the first time," says Myron S. Silverman of Traveler's Checklist (a mail-order marketer), "they discover that the foreign electrical systems are different. There's twice as much voltage and the wall outlets are different. Their shaver or hair dryer doesn't work, if they're lucky, or it burns out because twice as much juice is going through."

The voltage converter and adapter plugs are perennial Traveler's Checklist sellers. Other popular "be prepared" items are moneybelts and shoulder pouches to protect valuables, and electronic calculators that instantly answer the major question of our times: "How much is this in dollars?"

What can you do to make yourself feel as comfortable as possible? Wes Thomas uses an inflatable headrest (actually neckrest) to make his air voyages more comfortable. He also listens to environmental tapes on his Walkman (making sure to listen with really good stereo headphones). He arrives rested and ready. Sometimes I'll bring a box of dry cereal along because I want something cheap and good to snack on during the nonprime-time hours when I'm in the hotel room.

When packing, think light. Heed the parental voice that says, "You can have it but you're going to have to carry it." Jefferson Bates recommends that the exercise-minded forget the golf clubs and instead pack a swimsuit. Speaking of hotel facilities and exercise, some hotels will be happy to deliver a stationary bicycle to your room.

The personal computer often is credited with opening the home office floodgates. I hold the revisionist view that the telephone answering machine really ignited this revolution. For the first time, it gave the home office the equivalent of an employee—in this case, a receptionist. Even when you're out of town, your "receptionist" will continue to answer your phone. Is it necessary to mention that, when used this way, the TAD should have a remote feature?

Periodically checking with your answering machine or answering service is fine as far as it goes. It's also wise to return the calls on a timely basis. You may know that what caller Jones wanted simply is not pressing, but the call should be returned the same day or the following morning, at the very latest. Having someone else return the calls is perfectly fine. We just don't want Jones or any other caller to think that when you are out of the office everything stops (especially if the observation is accurate). Jones & Co. need to be trained to the comforting idea that when they call, you will respond.

All too often when people leave an incoming message on an answering machine they omit their phone numbers. Is it hostility? Is it arrogance? Is it short-term memory deficit? Who knows? Just as tantalizing are those who recite their phone numbers too quickly for the untrained ear to catch. Then there are the word swallowers, mumblers, and soft talkers. It would be wise to carry a small address book that has the phone numbers of all or most of your contacts. At the very least, it would help to have a list of those most likely to call.

Pagers offer quick access. Now that some vendors are using satellite technology, the same paging service can work in most of the country's metro areas. You discover who wants to contact you just about as soon as they make the call. Your pager number can be on your business card, or you can leave it on your answering machine. Again, it's important to respond swiftly.

For the normal corporate crowd, cellular phones are marvelous productivity tools. They keep people hooked in to what's happening during the many daily hours of car-incarcerated commuting. Otherwise they'll have to listen to radio traffic reports or motivational tapes. Traveling home officers have identified the cellular phone as one more instrument of freedom. It's another tool that lets you be where you want to be.

Incoming mail is a bit trickier to handle if you're away for more than two days. You'll want to have somebody gather your mail and review it with you over the phone. The best solution is to have an employee. Otherwise, ask someone—family member, friend, peer—to collect your mail for you and be in touch every couple of days. Urgent, vital messages can be sent back and forth by fax. You can have a portable fax machine with you or use the services of a business center in or near the hotel.

If time allows, you can have important letters, documents, checks, and so forth sent to you by express mail. In fact, if you're going to be away for a while you might want to arrange for express mail reshipping (see Chapter Eight, ''The Mailroom'').

Your ability to do the paperwork, read background materials, and meet deadlines depends on what you take with you. Some people take laptop computers; some prefer legal pads. If you need office support such as typing, mailing, or photocopying, the aforementioned business centers can help you. A look at the yellow pages reveals the where-abouts of secretarial services. Many of the Mailboxes, Etc. storefronts include secretarial services as one of their products. When preparing for the trip, you might want to call the Mailboxes, Etc. headquarters at (800) 456-0414 and ask if there is a franchise near the hotel at which you'll be staying.

Whether you're away for four hours or four months, you'll want to keep track of what's been going on in your travels. What happened when you visited Ms. Brown's office? Did she give you an order? Did she ask for information? Did she tell you to get lost? Who are the people who sat next to you during lunch? They gave you their cards, and you're supposed to get back to them about something or other.

Make a note about what happened. You have several choices, de-pending on your personal style and how you care to live your life. Some people like to dictate notes into a small battery-operated tape recorder. Others turn to an organizer, such as the Day Runner, as an orderly way to keep track of such information. If you're a Post-it per-son, you can attach the notes you've written to a pad or to your Day-Runner organizer. When I first started working on this book, there was an organizer just for Post-its. It was called the Noteport. I can't seem to locate the company, but if you find a Noteport at your local office supplier, check it out.

Some home officers carry the files of people and organizations they are going to call on. Last-minute cramming never hurts. Also results of the meeting would be dropped into the file. (When transporting files, it's probably a good idea to keep original documents or sensitive in-formation in your home office. Why tempt the gods of theft, loss, and coffee stains?) You could even write notes in a notebook. I prefer to stay away from any system that generates loose pieces of paper.

Then there is the expense record. You should have one. You could use any of those note-holding items we referred to above. Also, you can find a little book that says "Expenses" on the cover so you know what it is for. I have a friend who carries a piece of plain 8½″ by 11″ paper, folded into quarters. When the space is used, he just slips a clean piece of paper into his pocket. It's also good to keep a 6″ by 9″ catalog envelope with you as a safe place for stashing receipts.

In recent years we've seen the arrival of the hand-held electronic organizers. They combine a number of record-keeping and informa-tional capabilities in one small battery-operated package.

Let's look at two very different but very productive approaches to the traveling home office. Wes Thomas of East Northport, Long Is-land, does public relations for leading-edge companies in the computer industry. As a result, he generally spends two or three days a month at trade shows.

Thomas is likely to stroll into a client's office and slap a magnetic-mount car antenna onto a file cabinet. The antenna is for his cellular phone. The file cabinet is for better reception. When Thomas is on the road, his telephone answering machine outgoing message gives callers the cellular phone number. Callers have the option of leaving their message on the TAD or going to the next plateau and ringing his wandering phone. Shades of Maxwell Smart!

What do people do when Thomas pauses in the middle of a conference to answer his phone? "First of all, people don't seem to mind," says Thomas. "They find it kind of funny when you're in a meeting and get a call on the cellular phone, especially if you pull it out of your bag. I usually just say, 'I'll call you back.' I've never had any real problems with people misusing the cellular phone. Generally they leave a message on the machine unless the situation really is urgent. The point is you want to give people as many options as possible."

In addition to the telephone, Wes Thomas has another traveling home office option: his portable laptop computer, a Zenith 183 with an internal modem and a built-in 20-megabyte hard disk. The computer flows with keep-in-touch power because of Thomas's status as an MCI Mail subscriber. He can plug into his virtual network of clients and press contacts no matter where he is. If he spots a trend before his very eyes at the trade show, he need not languish on the pay phone or worry about time-zone differences. He just shoots the message into the other person's mailbox.

"I never have had the need of a printer while away," says Thomas. "Generally everything I do is electronic. For those renegades stuck in the paper mentality I send a fax via MCI Mail."

Thomas says that taking the computer is like carrying his whole office with him. "I have all my current files, my contacts, press materials, client information online in the form of disks, and all my files are backed up. When I come back home I just transfer the modifications to the desktop computer."

To make this whole operation work, Wes Thomas needs to have the hotel supply one little item: an RJ-11 phone adapter so he can plug in the computer's modem. He makes this request of the hotel at check-in time, and he's never been disappointed. It should be noted that he stays at the kind of hotel that leaves chocolate mints on the pillow. The budget cinder-block crash pads may be a bit slow in getting their business centers off and running.

Some home officers opt for low-tech logistics. Telemarketing consultant Mary Pekas of Sioux Falls, South Dakota, also travels. In addition to the couple of days that she might spend consulting on a new telemarketing system or training the employees of various clients, she now is putting in ten or more days a month in New Jersey. She is setting up a second household there and hence a second home office. When she goes on the road, Pekas makes sure that she keeps all the paperwork, memo-taking, and report writing flowing. It's likely that during the day she will be training a client's employees, and at night writing reports or manuals. She makes sure that she has everything to support these activities with her and ready to use.

"Whether I fly or drive," says Mary Pekas, "I have a mini-version of everything I need from stapler to 6″ ruler to correction fluid. It's very easy to analyze just what you use on a daily basis. You should always have a duplicate all ready to go. If you don't have it ready you don't take it with you."

When she drives, her office sits in a skinny portable file box. In the air she relies on the time-honored salesperson's sample case. "They're sturdy and have a hard surface," says Pekas. "You can put files in there. I have a supply of my stationery, travel forms in case I need to get airplane reservations. I carry overnight mail prepayments and already addressed overnight mail envelopes. Hotels will send overnight mail for you, but a great deal of time can be wasted if they go through the whole process. If you have everything done they can just take it."

Mary Pekas also carries a binder portfolio. Resembling a small briefcase, it opens to reveal a three-ring binder. There she keeps paperclips, pens, pencils, refills, date book, phone book, blank sheets of paper, and to-do lists: "I've divided my to-do lists into letters to write, phone calls to make, long-range to-do's, and short range to-do's. I look through my date book and find all the people I'm supposed to be calling while I'm away and pull those files. They go with me also."

Meanwhile, back at the Telemarketing Institute in South Dakota, her office staff keeps on humming. Before she leaves town, Pekas reviews her project schedule and date book. She puts the notes and material for the coming week's work into file folders and leaves them out for her staff. She stays in touch with her office several times a day by phone. They use voice mail. If the results of her day's work have to be returned to her office, she uses one of the overnight mail envelopes she brought with her. If she needs on-the-spot office support, she finds a nearby secretarial service.

The options are many for a home away from the home and an office away from the office. So, a little traveling music, maestro, if you please.

CATALOG

One-Pound 512K Computer (Poqet Computer Corp., $1,995). This remarkable MS/DOS computer, the Poqet PC, is a marvel of compactness and utility. Its traveling credentials alone (it weighs one pound, is less than 9″ long and less than 1″ thick, and runs for about 100 hours on two AA batteries) merit applause. The Poqet is not too shabby in the how-it-works and what-you-can-do-with-it departments. It's got a black-on-silver LCD screen that displays twenty-four lines of eighty characters each. Instead of floppy disks, you use credit-card-size Poqet Memory Cards that slip into slots. These function almost as if they were part of the computer itself; consequently, little of the computer's internal memory is used by the programs. Thus, the Poqet can run very sophisticated software and still have room for lots of data. Some programs being put into Poqet Memory Card format are ACT!, Lotus 1-2-3-, Wordperfect 5.0, and Xywrite III Plus. Five useful programs are built in: word processing, an appointment calendar, an address and phone book, a calculator, and a modem communications program. It also has a program and cable for transferring files from the Poqet to a desktop computer. You also can purchase a peripheral 3.5″ disk drive (powered by four AA batteries). Contact: Poqet Computer Corp., 650 North Mary Ave., Sunnyvale CA 94086; (408) 737-8100.

Poqet One-Pound 512K Computer

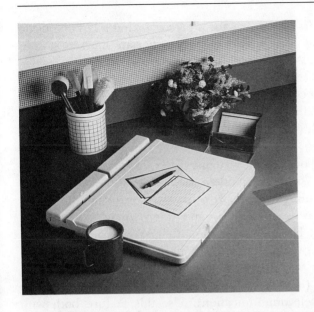

Rubbermaid Portable Desk

Portable Desk (Rubbermaid). Essentially, this is a compact, light-weight writing table. It's got two exterior compartments for pens, pencils, and so forth. The desk opens to reveal three inside compartments—divisions that can hold notebooks, pads, calculators, small reference books, and other items (e.g., scissors, stapler, tape, clips). It measures 18¾″ by 15″ by 2″. Contact: Rubbermaid, 3124 Valley Ave., Winchester VA 22601.

LapLink III (Traveling Software, $139.95). When you return from your travels, it's time to take off your laptop sneakers. Put all that data you've accumulated during your wanderings where it belongs. Transfer it from your laptop to your desktop computer. LapLink III makes the drop, and does it with a couple of fancy flourishes. It is most swift. Files get transferred at about one megabyte per minute depending on how many files. (A few large files sent together make the journey seconds faster than a bundle of many small files.) You can send files in batches and bunches. You can stipulate that only data entered within a certain period (as in the dates of your trip) be transferred. In addition, LapLink provides some hard disk management extras, as well as a fast, efficient approach to backup. Contact: Traveling Software, 18702 North Creek Parkway, Bothell WA 98011; (800) 662-2652; in WA (206) 483-8088.

Travel Tech Catalog (Travel Tech, free). Established as a marketing arm of Traveling Software products, this catalog now has a life (and separate division) of its own. "It's for a person taking a laptop out on the road," I was told. As such, it offers appropriate hardware, software, and accessories. About one-fifth to one-third of the catalog (which is issued four times a year) consists of new entries. The *Travel Tech* staff believes in speedy processing of orders. There's two-day delivery, and if the order is received by noon, the product moves out the same day. Contact: Travel Tech (800) 343-8080.

Portable Modem (Touchbase Systems, $199, $359). A petite 4″ long, Touchbase's WorldPort modem is available in the 300/1200 and 300/1200/2400 configurations. It comes with error-handling software and it conforms to both U.S. and international communications standards. A Hayes-compatible, the WorldPort has both autodial and autoanswer features. Although you'd ordinarily connect the modem directly into the wall, it also has a jack that accepts an acoustic coupler (a device into which you place the telephone handset during the telecommunication). Use this feature both with Radio Shack portables and those occasions when you just can't plug the modem into a wall phone jack. The WorldPort comes with an AC adapter, but a 9-volt battery also can be used. Contact: Touchbase Systems, 160 Laurel Ave., Northport NY 11768; (800) 261-0243; in NY (516) 261-0423.

Combination Fax/Modem (Touchbase Systems, $699). The WorldPort 2496 operates both as a 2400 bps modem and a 9600 bps fax machine. As a fax, it's a full-featured group III device. While you do other computing chores, the 2496 can operate in the background for both sending and receiving. It keeps a log of transmissions. Its memory feature allows you to arrange for a message to automatically go out at a later time. Is an incoming message from a fax or a modem? I wouldn't know, but the 2496 automatically figures it out. Contact: Touchbase Systems, 160 Laurel Ave., Northport NY 11768; (800) 261-0243; in NY (516) 261-0423.

SkyPager (SkyTel). This is for just about anywhere in the USA Paging. The person seeking you calls an 800 number. The up-to-twenty-character message in the bottle goes from telephone to uplink to the whirling satellite in space back to downlinks on Earth where the message is decoded and sent to radio transmitters around the country. They all beam it out across their coverage areas, one of which gets it right to your pager. The message flashes across your pager's ribbon screen. As an option, you can receive a message in the form of voice mail. In that case, the other party calls a different 800 number and leaves a message up to thirty seconds long. Then, when you are paged you call an 800 number, and give a listen. A SkyTel spokeswoman told me that some entrepreneurs give out the voice mail number as their own 800 number. The service can be leased on a month-to-month basis. Conceivably you can rent it one month a year or on and off during the year. Lease arrangements accommodate those who want a volume discount as well as those who prefer to pay on a per message basis. (The volume plans begin to make sense when you get fifteen or more calls a month.) Contact: Skytel (800) 456-6477.

Travel Product Catalog (Traveler's Checklist, 50 cents). Herein is a collection of about forty useful items. Many are those things you know you ought to have, but really don't know where to get. Products include voltage converters, plug adapters, toiletry cases, strap-on wheels for luggage, curling irons, electronic translators, and a book of *Travel Safety Tips*. Contact: Traveler's Checklist, Cornwall Bridge Rd., Sharon CT 06069.

The Wizard (Sharp Electronics, $299). Everything you need to know about your life is right in this hand-held instrument. You enter phone numbers, memos, appointments, and expenses. It's got an electronic calendar and a clock (you can check the time around the world). Of course, it has a calculator. You can download information from the Wizard into your computer. The keyboard is arranged in alphabetical order, which I find a bit frustrating because my typewriter-trained fingers have to look carefully for the letters. Because the Wizard uses plug-in modules, you can keep adding functions (at $99 each). I know several people who are quite happy to use it for just one function. (A friend of mine explains, "It's difficult to write expenses down legibly while riding a rocky taxi cab, but it's easy to enter the data into my Wizard.") Contact: Sharp Electronics, Sharp Plaza, Mahwah NJ 07430.

Pocket Correction Pen (Pentel). This pen contains correction fluid. The pen format makes it easy to store, carry with you, and even use. The pinpoint (or is that penpoint) applicator reaches those squeezed-in typos. It's especially good for covering cut lines that show up when you have pasted one or more pieces of paper to another piece of paper for photocopying. Contact: Pentel of America, 2805 Columbia St., Torrance CA 90503; (213) 320-3831.

The Wizard

Portable Fax And (Panasonic). You'll get more than just the fax ma'am with Panasonic's KX-F80. This facsimile machine really is a portable phone center. It also serves as an answering machine and a speaker phone. It plugs into a standard modular phone jack, and gets its juice from an AC outlet. Contact: Panasonic, One Panasonic Way, Secaucus NJ 07094.

Catalog Case (Stebco, $96). At 13.5" wide and 22" long, this carrying case holds lots of stuff. It's made of a vinyl-covered fabric and has a leather look. Two partitions give you compartments. It opens from the top with brass-locked flaps. Available in brown or black. Contact: Stebco Products, 3950 S. Morgan St., Chicago IL 60609.

Portable Filing System   (Fellowes). It's a sturdy varnish-coated corrugated fiberboard box with cover. It's designed to hold letter-size hanging folders, and in fact comes with ten hanging folders, as well as index

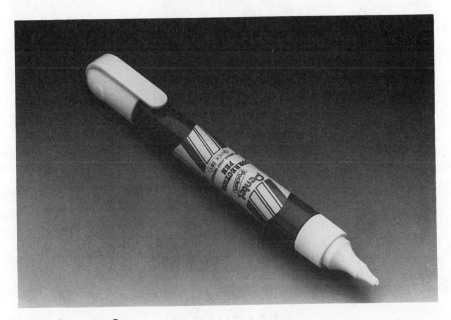

Pocket Correction Pen

Panasonic KX-F80 Portable Fax And

Fellowes Portable Filing
System

tabs and indexes. The strategically placed hand-grip slots make it portable. Officially a traveling file cabinet, the box also can stay at home and hold materials not yet filed or files currently in use. The gray box is 11¾″ by 10¼″ by 13⅜″. Contact: Fellowes, 1789 Norwood Ave., Itasca IL 60143.

RESOURCES

The Portable Office by Jefferson D. Bates and Stewart D. Crump, Jr. (Acropolis, 1989, $16.95). A thorough handbook for business travelers, *The Portable Office* describes in detail all the personal technology that helps those on the go. There are sections on laptops, cellular phones, E-mail, on-line data bases, pagers, and dictation machines. Not to be ignored are the many travel tips, such as what to look for when buying luggage, how to pack, and where to sit on the plane. Contact: Acropolis Books, 2400 17th St., NW, Washington DC 20009-9964; (202) 387-6805.

CHAPTER 10

Administrative Services

Do you provide yourself with the right kind of logistical support? Will you be the most significant thinker in your field as soon as you locate your ballpoint pen? Will you close the best deal of your life as soon as you figure out which pile of papers is concealing your telephone? Do you worship the quicksand upon which you walk?

A large corporation is likely to have a department called administrative services. This section's role is to provide the support—tools, systems, supplies—that enable people to do their jobs. Need a box of Post-its? Need a different filing system? Need something to keep track of expenses? Call administrative services. We home officers quickly learn that Administrative Services R Us.

"When we formed this business," says John McMullen of McMullen and McMullen, "I was director of data processing for Morgan Stanley. I was used to positions of responsibility. I was used to having people around who got the coffee and took care of ordering the pens and so forth. Number one, there are an awful lot of things you immediately have to start doing for yourself."

The more effectively we administer the details of our work, the more energy and concentration we can bring to our work. Administering your office depends a lot on how you organize your space. Just where do you put your work surface, your files, your business machines, and your butt? Are you using your walls? How much storage space do you have and where is it?

Sunny Schlenger says a very logical rule of thumb often gets overlooked. A professional organizer whose function is to bring order to people's homes and offices, Schlenger is the coauthor (with Roberta Roesch) of *How to Be Organized in Spite of Yourself* (NAL, 1989).

"When you're sitting at your work center," says Schlenger, "you really need to make sure that the things you use most frequently are very accessible. The more you can keep yourself central and focused to the task at hand, the better chance you have of finishing it. Have everything that you use frequently—a pencil sharpener, a tape, whatever—as close to you as you possibly can. The stuff that you use less frequently can be further away. It's logical but sometimes people put something down and it sinks roots. I'm not sure that they're all aware of how they may be getting in their own way.''

It's time to get organized. Schlenger has identified five basic styles by which people organize their space: everything out, nothing out, right angular, pack rat, and total slob.

In addition to putting your hands on staplers, paper clips, and other residents in the world of things, you need to put your hands on pieces of paper: invoices, contracts, memos, telephone numbers, client lists, magazines, journals, comic books, catalogs, dictionaries, and so on. Accordingly, you need places to put these pieces of paper.

Schlenger tells of one client, a community college president, who ''just could not file anything.'' He is a classic example of the ''everything out'' style. ''He really felt out of sight was out of mind,'' recalls Schlenger. ''He eventually called me in because he lost something very critical.''

Even so, the president did not want the intrusion of such alien values as clearing up his desk. ''I went out,'' says Schlenger, ''and got fifty plastic filing pockets—those clear ones that attach to the wall. We created a filing system that was organized, neat, and off the desk. Still he felt very much in control because he could look around and see it.''

After you decide where you're going to keep your stuff, you'll want to set up your files. Chances are that you've already established a system. Is the system by which you organize your space working? Sunny Schlenger says just pay attention to a few simple warning signs.

''You tend to lose things,'' observes Schlenger, ''or it takes you a long time to get something accomplished, or you're very distractable, or you're hopping around so much that you're not finishing things. People are all complaining that you don't follow through.''

There are only three basic ways to categorize your files, according to *How to File,* a Pendaflex booklet. You can file by name, subject, or number.

WHO'S ON FIRST

The name game is the most common approach, and no wonder. Just about every person and company we deal with has a name. Suppose you want to know everything about a particular client's history or current status. It would be a lot easier to bring home the info if all pertinent records were filed under that client's name. Otherwise, you might be looking first under "ɪ" for Invoices, then "ᴄᴏɴ" for contracts, "ᴄᴏʀ" for correspondence, and so on.

WHAT'S ON SECOND

With subject filing, you arrange items according to "what" rather than "who." For example, each of the products or services you sell may earn its own file. Sources might be arranged according to what they provide rather than company name. Thus, if you're doing an analysis of widgets, you go straight to the widget file rather than pull out all the separate files that you believe are pertinent to widgets.

I DON'T KNOW'S ON THIRD

Numeric filing provides the kind of privacy and security that probably is too paranoid for the home office. Numeric files are classified by number rather than by any word or phrase that reveals the contents. Crucial to this system is some kind of ledger or index that tells what each number represents.

The system by which you file, according to Sunny Schlenger, "should be a reflection of how you plan to use the system, the way in which you frequently refer to your information, and your style."

New York Times columnist Enid Nemy wrote about the personal approach some bring to filing. The owner of magazines *Rod & Reel* and *Global Finance* entered her publications, respectively, as "fishing" and "business" in her address book and Rolodex. Someone with a "really bad memory for names" files according to subject matter. Otherwise, she'd have to look up something in order to know what to look up. In both cases, the idea was to arrange things so that they could go straight to the spot where the treasure was buried.

If your mind rebels against the cherished conventions by which filing is done, that's okay. Develop guidelines that conform to how your mind works. Just be consistent. When setting up a filing system, remember that you may not be the only person to use it. You might in the future, if not sooner, take on a partner or hire a full- or part-time employee. It is wise to set up some sort of reference to your files. It should describe your system so that strangers to your way of thinking can successfully retrieve materials.

The file folder is the basic filing unit, the building block, the protein, the atom, the essence of all power and strength in your information retrieval system. Moreover, it can be color-coded.

The benefits of color-coding were demonstrated during the unearthing of one of New York City's corruption scandals. (Yes, such things do go on!) It seems that a City Hall Talent Bank, supposedly set up to aid minority hiring, was subverted and used as a good old-fashioned political patronage mill.

Information about applicants was routed into red, pink, and green file folders. The red folders held the names of people who were, according to the *Daily News*, "high-priority political referrals." Pink folders were for those whose sponsors were political, but just not that important. Into the green folders went those who had no political sponsorship whatsoever. In addition, green dots were affixed to resume cover sheets from applicants with political backing. Efficiency in government is very important.

Knowledge of the wild and wacky world of file folders is not without its rewards. The folders you use and how you use them can increase the ease with which you can stash and later triumphantly retrieve filed material. Let us look at the possibilities.

True to its name, the folder is a folded-over piece of heavy paper. You put things, generally pieces of paper, in it. One edge of the folder has a tab, a projecting portion on which you indicate what's inside. Tabs can be on either end of the edge or portions in between, and are classified according to the cut (tab size).

- *Straight cut.* The tab is the same size as the entire width of the folder.
- *Half cut.* The tab is one-half the width of the folder.
- *Third cut.* The tab is one-third the width of the folder.
- *Fifth cut.* The tab is one-fifth the width of the folder.

The larger the tab size, the larger the canvas on which you can describe the folder's contents. If you can find a universe in a grain of sand, just imagine what you can find in a file folder. There is more to say about this enchantingly prosaic topic, but first we must look at hanging folders.

RIDING THE RAILS

You can transform the file folder melody into an orderly symphony with the hanging folder system. These folders have hooks at either end and hang on rails. Some deep desk drawers and file cabinets have built-in rails. You also can buy rail frames to hold hanging folders, and set up these frames in drawers, cabinets, bookcases, storage boxes, and so on. You can even suspend rails from walls and give new meaning to the notion of hanging folders. Being suspended from the hooks keeps the folders even. It's easy to get access to the material because the folders slide along the rails rather drag along the bottom.

Hanging folders plus file folders equal a system with smarts. Dedicate each hanging folder to a specific topic, for example, the Whatsit Company, one of your best and dearest clients. Assign a file folder to each Whatsit subcategory.

Esselte Pendaflex (Garden City, New York), most associated with hanging folders, refers to file folders as interior folders. (They're placed in the interior of the hanging folder.) You can make your filing system more formidable by the use of color coding. For example, all invoices could go in dark blue interior folders. All contracts could go in light green folders. If you wanted to find the Whatsit contract, you'd go straight to the light green interior folder within the Whatsit hanging folder. Oxford colored file folders have a lighter tone on the inside. Turning them inside out gives you a new color to play with, a new hue so to speak.

You also can color code hanging folders. For example, all clients could be assigned red folders; suppliers could be in found in blue folders. Green could be set aside for your products.

There are some very useful specialized folders. The box bottom, for example, is not a dance but a hanging folder designed to hold such bulky items as catalogs, booklets, reports, and periodicals (maybe even magazines). Pendaflex advises that the box bottom width be pretty much equal to the total material going into it. A 2" box bottom should hold about 2" of stuff. Leaving plenty of room in the box bottom is a bad idea. "Two inches of paper," according to Pendaflex's booklet, *How to File,* "will flop over in a 4" box bottom."

Hanging box files have the same flat bottom as box-bottom folders. Unlike the folders, the box bottoms have sides. These are particularly useful for storing different-size documents together with bulky items.

Folders with fasteners keep all the stored pages in place and in order. The fasteners are prongs and can be found either on the top or the side.

Classification folders also have fasteners. In addition, they have tabbed dividers. Thus, you can keep different categories of paperwork in the same folder, yet be assured that they will not get shuffled together. Classification folders also are available in a hanging format.

Folders are most effective when you know what they contain. You can write the folder's contents on its tab cut, or you can write or type it on an adhesive label that you stick on the tab cut. If you use a variety of cuts, the labels then become staggered. Arranging the folders so that you can vary the location of the tab (between left and right) is a good idea. Not only is it esthetically charming but it allows you to identify and locate easily the various files.

Hanging folders use plastic tabs. The plastic tab sits on the top of the folder. (The hanging folder has slots in which to insert the tab.) The contents are defined on a label that slips into the tab. The concept is reminiscent of the name badges you get stuck with at trade shows and seminars. Pendaflex recommends putting the tab on the front of the folder rather than the rear. Again, staggering of the tabs makes it easier to find what you want. The additional touch of alphabetical tabs also may help.

THE MEANING OF PAPER

The most prevalent filing problem, according to Sunny Schlenger, is deciding the significance of each piece of paper.

"Most people," says Schlenger, "ask the wrong question when they file. They say, 'Where should I put this?' The right question is, 'How do I plan to use this?' Deciding how you plan to use it can lead in two directions. If you decide you have no plan, that makes it much easier to get rid of it. If you do have a plan, it gives you a clue as to where to file according to how you plan to use it.

"I find that working in this way gets people more in touch with their plans and objectives and priorities. It's not just a question of putting papers into a drawer which can be a very dreary kind of a task. The papers become alive because they're physical representations of where you're going and what you're trying to achieve and can be very motivating."

The ideal time to propel a piece of paper toward its final file is that moment when you first confront it. When the document plops onto your desk, note on the corner of the page where you're going to put it. You can make that note with a pencil or write it on a Post-it that you stick onto the page. This notation has two effects. It triggers thought about what you're going to do with the paper. It makes it easier for you to plant the page in an intermediate file or its final resting file.

Sunny Schlenger stresses the importance of evaluating what you have, and suggests that this process should take place twice a year. "Ask, 'Does this make sense for me in terms of my current business, my current operations,'" says Schlenger. "It may be that you can use the space more wisely than you already have, but a lot of times people don't think that way; they just keep growing and adding.

"People don't realize that the value of things changes with time. What was really important to you to have displayed on the wall or the bookshelf two or three years ago, may not have the same value today."

Not all folders end up in file cabinets, and for that matter not all home offices require and/or contain file cabinets. There exists a variety of fancified boxes for the effective stashing of files. They go on walls, floors, and desks. They're made of cardboard or plastic or wood. Some have handles for easy portage between car and office. Some are on wheels.

INSIDE INDEX CARDS

Index cards represent a mundane but mighty approach to record-keeping. They're particularly useful for keeping track of things and people. Index cards serve service and agency businesses quite well. Each card represents one something. For example, if you run a house-keeping agency, you can have one index card for each customer and one index card for each employee. A family calls and begs for someone to clean their house next Thursday. Reach for their card. They want Augie Stables to do the job? Check his card to see if he's available that day. Make appropriate notations on both cards.

Some free-lance writers and photographers use index cards to keep track of their submissions. On the card, they write the name of the project, where they've sent it, when, and any appropriate updating material. Author/astrologer Debbi Kempton-Smith keeps track of talk shows on which she's appeared. The information includes addresses, phone numbers, length of shows, names of on-air and production staff. A mail-order purveyor of costume jewelry keeps track of his customers, their orders, shipping dates, and payments on index cards. Yes, you can use a computer to keep track of the same kinds of information. Let me say something a bit blasphemous. When you need to get just one piece of information, an index card filing system tends to be easier than a computer.

An index card system is simple and compact. The cards are organized alphabetically. Individual entries are easy to locate and modify. Cards can be added, and you can take advantage of color-coding.

Now that we've talked about some tools and concepts, let's get real. It's one thing to set up a system. It's quite another to extricate oneself from a self-created paper swamp.

MID-FILE CRISIS

Professional organizer Carol Kropnick of Brooklyn often doesn't get hired until the new clients find themselves knee-deep in mid-file crises. Her approach can instruct those few of us who find a sudden need to bring order to an office gone amok. She first finds out just what the client does. Each activity deserves its own grouping of files.

"I have some clients," says Kropnick, "who are both photographers and inventors. There's no reason for the photography business to mix in with the inventing business. I try to encourage them to start separating that stuff out.

"It doesn't hurt to have separate drawers altogether for separate things. In my own office, I have an art drawer that holds all the stuff that's related to my art career. The very front is things I'm currently working on. I have another drawer for my organizing business."

Rather than impose the way in which files get arranged, Kropnick wants to know how her clients think. "Some people might think of recipes alphabetically. For them apple pie would be in the 'A' section. Somebody else might find the recipe more easily if it were in the pie folder over in the 'P' section."

And then she goes into a sorting frenzy. "I sort ruthlessly," says Carol Kropnick. "I have no personal attachment to these papers which means I can really whip through them."

She tosses likely circular file candidates into one pile. The pile might include junk mail received during the last year, two years, or five years. (For clarity's sake, junk mail is what we receive, not what we send.) Other debris might be time-related material from another era. It's not all glamor. A goodly number of papers must be saved and prepared for storage.

"I'll try to break everything up into categories," says Kropnick, "and I'll make the categories up as I go along."

As Carol Kropnick treads her way through the unsorted pile, she's likely to say, "Oh, I haven't seen one of these before." A new sorting pile gets born.

"In the case of someone who's got years of stuff," says Kropnick, "I separate out the years too. There's no sense in piling something from 1984 with something from 1988."

She is particularly alert to pieces of paper that have dollar signs on them. "Things that are related to money—invoices, bills, etc.—will go into another pile. I do try to encourage clients to keep money things separate from information things. They really are separate issues.

"People have to be serious about those money files. I try to figure out the best ways for them to save their receipts, just to keep tabs on how they're spending their money. Some people like to do it by month or topic. The two are the same in a way. Most people I run into have vendors that they deal with continuously—one messenger service, one processing lab, one place where they buy most of their props. They'll have a folder for each of the vendors. Then for taxis and various petty cash stuff they can have a monthly envelope because they can break it down. That's easy.''

The piles she's created become categories or subcategories. Each gets its own folder. They are arranged according to the logic understood by the home officer (see *Apple Pie v. Pie, Apple;* Supreme Court, 1986). The idea is to find something you need quickly and easily. Kropnick says beware of the category that is too general.

"For example,'' she says, "it might not be a good idea having a file marked 'correspondence 1989.' You might want to break that down into subtopics—perhaps someone you correspond with regularly, or a particular project you're working on, etc.''

She says that some people can err in the other direction and get too specific in their filing. Allocating a separate folder for each piece of paper is tantamount to having no system. You still have to figure out where that piece of paper is.

The hanging folders are set up. The categories and subcategories, placed in file folders, are arranged in the appropriate order. The different facets of your business are separated from each other. Color-coding prevails. Just by looking at your files, you have a sense of where everything is. It's been hard work, a troublesome journey, and now you can relax. But *noooo*.

The jungle will fill in relentlessly, if you allow your machete to get rusty. If it's any consolation, maintaining your filing system is much easier than existing in the gulag of having to set up a new system. The system will work if you remember that paper must flow. There really are only two ways to cause a breakdown. If you've been working with pieces of paper, don't return them to the filing system. When new pieces of paper come into the office, let them bask on your desk.

"People,'' says Kropnick, "get into this vague idea of 'I have to deal with these papers soon so I'm going to keep them out on my desk.' Some more papers come in that also have to be dealt with soon.

"There's that basic rule. You get a piece of paper and you should only handle it one time. You shouldn't keep delegating it to different piles. The more you handle that sheet of paper, the more time you waste and I think the less chance you ever have of dealing with it. I think you're even liable to lose it.

"I advise my clients to ask themselves the basic question: What are you going to do with this? With each piece of paper you have one of three choices: You either file it, deal with it (send a letter back, pay a bill, etc.), or you throw it away."

Filing is like voting. You should do it early and often, or at least regularly. How you schedule it—daily, every few days, weekly, etc.—is a matter of personal inclination and circumstances. The willingness to schedule is what's important. Carol Kropnick suggests that people pencil in filing time right on their calendars. It's like noting in your calendar an important phone call you must make.

What about those papers you really, truly have to deal with soon? Once they're tucked into their file folders in that silent Calvinistic shrine of a file drawer, won't you forget them? Probably—at least if you're anything like me.

But there are two antidotes. The first is to fight paper with paper. You write up a "to do" list on which you note all those tasks that lie ahead of you. State the deadline, if any. Indicate the importance of this task. Must it come ahead of others? Can it wait? How long can it wait? Now that you're thinking about it, do you have to do it at all? That famous piece of paper you were planning to use "soon" goes on the "to do" list. If using that very paper itself is the task, then you can write something like "Follow up on ABC letter (located in XYZ file)." If the piece of paper is to be used in connection with some task, then you might write "Contact ABC; get letter from XYZ file."

The "to do" list's value goes well beyond keeping papery things out of sight but not out of mind. The list helps us keep track of what we have to do. When we prioritize, we have a better chance of preventing big projects from sneaking up and scaring us. We prevent less significant activities from gobbling up our time and energy.

You can administer the second antidote to paper flow jams at mail-opening time. It is the very first opportunity to move the paper along. It is the first chance you get to file the paper, deal with it, or throw it away.

From time to time you might want to remove documents and records from your active files and store them in some out-of-the-way pasture. It might be a good idea to color-code the individual pieces according to the year (and possibly quarter) in which they were first filed. When you winnow your records you can easily identify those you want to throw into the freezer.

Carol Kropnick is not a fire-and-brimstone organizer. She recognizes that some individuals simply do not have the strength of character to instantly file as paper crosses the threshold.

"I think it's okay to have 'in' and 'out' boxes on the desk," says Kropnick, "and maybe a 'bills to pay' box. Some people are very comfortable with a 'bills to pay' folder in a desk drawer. They can just dump the bills in there. I've just seen too many people with those folders that never use them. It seems like an in/out box situation works better. The bills are ready for you on the one or two days a month that you sit down and write the checks. File the bills away when you're done paying them. It's kind of taking the task to completion."

COMPUTERS AGAIN

No chapter on administrative services would be complete without mention of the computer. The focused efficiency of an index card file is indeed a wonder. The computer, however, excels when you want to do tricks and coax extra insights out of the kind of information scrawled across index cards. If you want a list of who owes you money, you could go through your customer index cards, scan each one for outstanding receivables, and jot down the appropriate information. With the computer you get the information in a zip or two. Similarly, you can use the computer to find many phone numbers and many addresses at one time. Free-lancers can use the computer to see quickly where all their manuscripts, proposals, and photographs have been sent.

You can achieve these and related computer acrobatics with a filing or data base program. It's easy and nearly accurate to think of these programs as electronic index card files. This software's three basic components are records, fields, and labels. The record can be likened to the individual index card. All the kinds of info entered on a card (e.g., name, address, dates, phone number, current order) get entered on a single record. A field is the individual category of information. Company name, date of order, date that order is fulfilled, item ordered, and quantity of item are the kinds of categories that people use as fields. The label is an identifying word or phrase that tells you what the field is. The word *name* is a label. The field is the actual space where somebody's name gets entered.

Creating a data base takes a bit of thought. First, you decide what fields you will need. Then you consider where you will want these fields to show up on your monitor screen. Using the index card analogy, you are deciding what information you want on the card and how you want the card to look. Together, the fields you have selected are called the data base's structure. The way the fields and their accompanying labels all show up on the screen is called the data base's form.

When you're ready to use the data base, the form pops up on the screen, and you just fill it in. If you used a data base program to track all your sales, each record might have fields for customer name, contact, address (this actually would be broken into separate components—street, city, state, zip), phone number, item(s) ordered, quantity of each, cost of each item, total cost, date order received, status, date order fulfilled, date invoiced, date of second invoice, and date payment received. The information for this order would be entered onto this record at the appropriate times. A new order is a new event that calls for a new record. With most programs, you don't retype the constants such as company name and address.

Lest we get too complacent with the index card analogy, let's note a difference. Each new event relating to the subject of a particular index card gets noted on that card. There can be a whole string of dates when orders were received or shipped.

OTHER ORGANIZING SOLUTIONS

The Bull & Bear folks use Post-its for project management. Bob Beaudoin has created a graph-like chart that hangs above his desk. He's divided the vertical line into four segments: marketing, systems, production, and administration. The horizontal axis is divided into weeks.

Instead of writing directly on the chart, he uses a Post-it. A project or task is written on a small Post-it, and the wonder paper is affixed to the appropriate spot.

"The beauty," says Beaudoin, "is that you can move these around as your time line changes and/or just take them off and throw them away when you finish the task. You get a sense of progress moving them to the left from week four to week one."

Instead of stuffing like-minded pieces of paper into a designated file folder, you might want to use a looseleaf ring binder. The binder is particularly useful when you want to keep a collection of related papers at a location closer to you than the file cabinet. If the pages do not have holes for the rings, a simple surgical procedure with a hole punch will do the trick. The binder can sit on a nearby shelf for quick and frequent reference. In addition to such paperwork as invoices, binders easily store thin catalogs, newsletters, and chronological material such as diaries or expense accounts.

TIME IN

Somehow the mention of chronological material reminds me of time. Strange how the mind works. We cannot talk of self-organizing and omit the subject of managing our time.

When Alan Lakein chose to emphasize the importance of time management, he entitled his book on the subject *How to Get Control of Time and Your Life* (NAL, 1973). Two species of time toss mud across our schedules: those we can't control and those which we do control.

The good news is that you can only do so much about things that are really out of your control. It's not your fault. Do you feel better? The other good news is that most things that you think are out of your control aren't. And you don't even have to change your character. Just exercise your independence and free will. After all, you are a home officer.

For example, even though some of us may be slobs, we've been learning how to get our paper organized. We discover that we can use systems that worked for others and still be ourselves. Getting our papers straight is a big step toward time management. If you only handle a piece of paper once, then you're not doomed to handle it each time you're looking for something else. Okay, if you're really incorrigible, so you handle a piece of paper only twice.

Two basic irrefutable truths fuel time management tactics: The longer it takes you to do what you have to do, the longer it takes you to get done what you have to get done. Time spent on what you don't have to do is time not being spent on what you do have to do.

When time management experts talk about those things we have to do, they always top the list with our life goals. Do these tasks, chores, and projects that we've placed on center stage help us move toward our goals? If so, how do we make them better? If not, why are we doing them?

At various spots in this book, we've referred to "to do" lists. Perhaps you are in the habit of maintaining one. It can help, but in order for it to work really well the "to do" list needs one particular ingredient—analysis.

Lakein has urged his clients, readers, and seminar attendees to analyze all tasks in terms of their priority ratings: A, B, and C. A is top priority and C is low priority. Such cubbyholing does not demand that all A's get done first. It simply allows you to identify what really has to be done, as well as what is of passing consequence.

In his book *Time Power* (Harper & Row), management consultant Charles Hobbs likes to point out the difference between urgent and vital: "Urgent simply means calling for immediate action, but it has nothing to do with priorities." The fact that somebody wants something done now, doesn't mean that the aforementioned something is important. Only the priorities are vital. Hobbs says that we should know the difference between "an urgent triviality" and a "vital matter."

Many people who play the A, B, C ratings game discover that it's a license for legerdemain. Some of those C chores just disappear.

When you've committed your priorities to paper, you can focus on them daily, warding off sudden attention shifts caused by phone calls, correspondence, or even bright ideas. The prime attitude of time management is to keep your eye on the donut and not on the hole. The prioritized "to do" list quietly but effectively nags. It whines that this thing you don't want to do really has to be done. It wearily suggests that this other task that western civilization really craves doesn't have to be done now, or tomorrow, or next week.

Are you obliged to plow into huge, forbidding, complex projects that you've taken on even though they are too big for you? I'm afraid so. Lakein and other time management consultants advise that when confronted with a massive undertaking, don't get daunted. Break it down into little pieces. (We talked about this in Chapter Three.) Get the work done a portion at a time.

Once in a while I still have to reteach myself this piece of advice. When faced with a big project, or even one that has some unpleasant features, I might let my mind play Rollerball. I fear that if I start I'll get stuck in the hedges and never make it to the finish line. My ever-so-shrewd mind concludes that the best way to avoid getting stymied is not to start. (Heh heh, I'll show them.)

My brain, which has had some experience in dealing with my mind, knows that I'll feel more hopeful when I allow myself to experience accomplishment. I work on one small area, and there's now less to do, a significant fact that doesn't escape me. The system works.

Another category of controllable time-sucker is, in a sense, more insidious. It has to do with demands made upon us by the world—the phone, neighbors, errands, and so on. (Again, we examined this a bit in Chapter Three.)

When we look at a situation, we can't just groan about the injustice of it all. We have to identify what the true source of pain really is. Too often, we will find it's a decision we made without even realizing we had a choice. For example, it's too easy to say I can't get anything done because the phone keeps ringing. It's true that you have no control over who is going to call you. You have lots of control over how you respond. The problem isn't that the phone is ringing. The problem is that you're answering it when it rings. In Chapter Three, I suggested that you might want to put an answering machine on your home line. If you have an electronic phone, you probably can turn off the ringer. You also can do that with your business phone when you need a slab of undisturbed time.

Corporate executives and middle managers who attend time management seminars learn the potent mantra: "Find ways to delegate." It's a good lesson that even home officers can learn. When we delegate, however, we need not succumb to hierarchical power games. We can be a bit more flexible and creative in how we free up our time. For example, using a telephone answering machine in the manner we described is a form of delegation.

I know a writer who solved an agonizing temporal conflict in an unexpected way. Facing a series of deadlines, he needed nine-day weeks if he had any hope of getting the work in on time. He looked for ways to snatch time from home or work responsibilities. He realized that he missed the most obvious. Because he worked at home, he had assumed responsibility for cooking and shopping. Upon further examination, he realized that the cooking took even more time than he realized. Each day, as he glanced at the clock to see how close gourmet hour was, he would concentrate less and less on his work. He did not get back to work until after he and his family dined.

He sighed. It was too bad his wife was so tired when she came home from work. Then, for some reason, he thought of hiring a cook. He asked a neighbor's cleaning lady if she would come one day a week to shop and cook. Clearly, it's a middle-class solution, but his use of delegation rewarded him with an additional twelve hours of productive time a week.

Delegate assignments to your computer. For example, develop a series of form letters that answer the kinds of questions that most commonly fall upon your desk. You may also want to develop a collection of mix-and-match paragraphs so that you can pull together the right combination at will for really excellent personalized responses.

Another major delegation area would be the hiring of outside professionals. Yes, you've seen it all and done it all, and if you want something done right then you've got to do it by yourself. But who's got the time? Giving a task to an outside professional gets you closer to the payoff. It also transforms your nonproductive hours into billable hours.

I've hired typing services to transcribe interviews I've taped. A lawyer who bought a mega-memory hard disk drive hired a consultant to install the drive. Identify an activity that probably will consume too much of your time, and you'll find a trained professional who can do it faster and, most likely, better.

Some people fortify their "to do" lists with tickler files. They keep thirty-one folders labeled "one" to "thirty-one." Each folder represents a day of the month. You insert into the appropriate folder those materials and information you will need on that day. For example, a client might tell you that she'll be out of town for two weeks; she'll be back on the fifth and she wants you to send your bid to her at that time. If your bid is available, you put it into the folder marked "five." If you haven't yet prepared it, you might put a bid form into the folder marked "three." The folders keep rotating. On the morning of the fifteenth, you take the folder marked fourteen and put it in the back. Anything in the folder should get filed in the appropriate place(s). A tickler file should be kept nearby. A deep desk drawer is one logical site.

CATALOG

Lateral File Cabinets (Oxford). Available in two-, three-, four-, or five-drawer sizes, the cabinets are 18″ deep and come in 36″ or 42″ widths. They have built-in rails on which to place hanging folders. (Oxford hopes you'll use sister brand, Pendaflex.) The 42″-wide cabinets have cross rails that accommodate front-to-back filing. The suspension drawers glide smoothly on ball-bearing slides. You can't open more than one drawer at a time. It is a safety feature that prevents the loss of balance that leads to tipping over. You can adjust the back panels to hold either letter-size or legal-size files. The standard colors are beige, black, and putty. Custom colors also are available for a higher price. Contact: Esselte Pendaflex, 71 Clinton Rd., Garden City NY 11530.

Foamworks Desk Organizer (Design Ideas). These are modular foam-rubber pieces that fit in center or side desk drawers. They have neatly cut recesses to accommodate various standard desk familiars, such as pencils, memo pads, paper clips, and postage stamp rolls. Contact: Design Ideas, 6 Fair Oaks, Springfield IL 62704; (217) 546-6454.

Magazine File (Fellowes). A gray on putty varnished corrugated fiberboard box, the file is designed specifically for holding *Time*-size and smaller periodicals. The diagonally cut sides and minimal front make it easy to see the magazines. The file width is 4″, so a little less than

Oxford Lateral File Cabinets

that can be crammed inside. Contact: Fellowes Manufacturing Company, 1789 Norwood Ave., Itasca IL 60143; (708) 893-1600.

Hot File Filing Pocket (Eldon, $41.99, box of four). These are hanging receptacles, usually occupied by files. They have at least two noteworthy attributes. Depending on where you hang the Hot Files, their contents are visible and in easy reach. Also, since they mount on the wall, they're useful appetite appeasers for the space-hungry. Add-on pockets can be added on to form a system. You can mount your Hot Files in a variety of ways. They can be screwed to the wall. Magnetic mounts attach the pockets to file cabinets and other metal surfaces. With hangers, the Hot Files can be attached to panel tops or shelving. There also are Hot File II pockets that have rounded edges rather than straight edges. Colors include jet black, putty, solar yellow, and walnut. Contact: Eldon Office Products, P.O. Box 22667, Long Beach CA 90801-5667.

Pencil Palace (Eldon). It looks like a weird abstract sculpture titled "Hunger," or perhaps "Mother." The different-size clustered compartments hold such items as pens, rulers, rubber bands, paper clips,

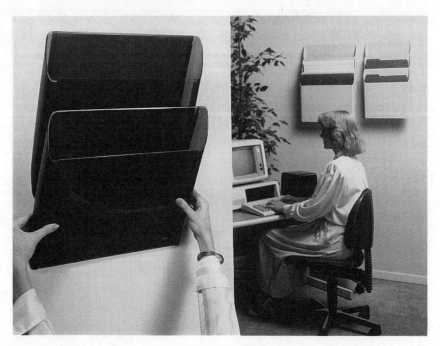

Hot File Filing Pockets

push pins, and pencils. It's made of plastic and is 4⅞″ wide and 5⅞⁄₁₆″ deep. The tallest of the five compartments is 8¹⁵⁄₁₆″ high. The colors are ebony, smoke, putty, lilac, green, pink, and blue. Contact: Eldon Office Products, P.O. Box 22667, Long Beach CA 90801-5667.

Diagonal Files (Eldon). This file brings a sorted virtue to the pile of papers and projects that can camp on a desk. The diagonal arrangement of the file's six compartments makes it easier to see what's where. The panels can be angled to the left or the right. The ribbed floor encourages the contents to stand up straight. The smooth, flat panels can be labeled. The file's cushioned feet protect the desktop. The diagonal file is 19¹¹⁄₁₆″ long, 6⅞″ wide, and 7¹⁄₁₆″ deep. Available in ebony, smoke, and putty. Contact: Eldon Office Products, P.O. Box 22667, Long Beach CA 90801-5667.

Eldonwal System (Eldon Products, assorted prices). Although designed primarily for the big-time office's modular panels that provide solitude without autonomy, this system can be used quite successfully with what the manufacturer calls "permanent walls." You mount plastic slotted bars onto your wall. Various organizing accessories snap onto brackets that in turn slip into the slots. It is a most stylish approach to coaxing working space out of your walls.

A full range of items work with this system. For example, hanging file arms hold hanging files. Utility shelves are 12″ deep and come in two-foot, three-foot and four-foot lengths. These are good for bulky items. Stackable letter trays also fit into the Eldonwal System. When

Pencil Palace

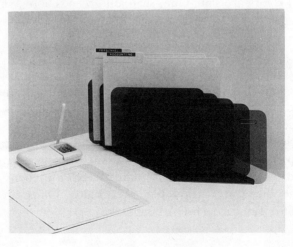

Eldon Diagonal Files

Eldonwal System

using the stackable letter trays, Eldon suggests that you also get chrome ladders that add stability to the stackables. The Eldonwal accessory shelf provides a home for those desktop chachkas such as stapler, paper clip holder, and tape dispenser.

Other system components include four-division sorter (the dividers tilt right or left), vertical file box, EDP tray for massive printouts, side load letter tray, Hot File starter set, hot tub, and message bar. Eldonwal colors are slate blue, seafoam green, ebony, smoke, taupe, putty, chocolate, and gray. Contact: Eldon Office Products, P.O. Box 22667, Long Beach CA 90801-5667.

Image 1500 Stapler (Eldon). It is a sleekly styled stapler with rounded corners. The head lifts up for easy reloading. Made of tough plastic and chrome-plated steel, it holds 210 chisel-point standard staples at a time. This desktop stapler is part of Eldon's Image series. Other items with the same styling include tape dispenser, calendar holder, pencil cup, letter trays, book ends, stamp dispenser, paper clip dispenser, and business card holder. Image colors are ebony, burgundy, putty, slate blue, and gray. Contact: Eldon Office Products, P.O. Box 22667, Long Beach CA 90801-5667.

Gold Fibre Writing Pad (Ampad). A high-quality 50-leaf pad (letter- or legal-size) with lots of little extras. The paper has a smooth, hard finish. The pinhole perforations allow you to tear the pages off neatly and easily. The extra heavy chipboard back provides a supportive writing surface. Its binding—made of Tyvek, the DuPont material used for those extra-strong parcel envelopes that you can't rip apart—has a leather look. The ruled lines are faint so that your writing can stand out. Contact: Ampad, Courthouse Plaza NE, Dayton OH 45463.

Reporter's Notebook (Ampad). A slimmed-down version (4″ by 8″) of the venerable steno pad, the reporter's notebook is an ideal size to cram into a coat pocket. The stiff covers give a helpful writing surface. Alternate ruled lines are faint. There are 70 sheets to a pad. Contact: Ampad, Courthouse Plaza NE, Dayton OH 45463.

Desk Pads (Efficiency). These 22″ by 17″ pads fit atop the work surface in much the same way as the comparably sized desk blotter. They are the perfect canvas upon which to scribble a short note, do a bit of math, or even improve one's doodlemanship. The perforated sheets are easy to rip off when you're ready for your next sheet. The pads are available in quadrille (four squares per inch) and plain (white, buff, and green tint). You express style through the bindings and corners (woodgrain and blue for quadrille; woodgrain, brown, and green). Contact: Efficiency, Courthouse Plaza, Dayton OH 45463.

Bulletin Bar (Eldon). This 6″, 12″, or 18″ strip gives a bulletin board perk to a limited space. The bar is a 1″ high length of cork in an attractive plastic frame (red, white, almond, or ebony). It can be mounted either by magnetic strip or by self-sticking tape. Sticking a pin in just one corner of an item maximizes the available space. Contact: Eldon Office Products, P.O. Box 22667, Long Beach CA 90801-5667.

Punchodex PB-29 (Rolodex, $9.50). It is a moderately priced three-hole paper punch that is appropriate for occasional hole-punching. It can do up to ten pages of 16-pound bond paper at a time. The punch heads are nickel-plated and the chips neatly fall into an easily emptied tray. Contact: Rolodex, 245 Secaucus Rd., Secaucus NJ 07094.

Heavy-Duty Three-Hole Punch (Maruzen International, $274.95). Punch holes for a three-ring binder. The Maruzen M-3000 can donutize a ⅝″ pile of papers (approximately 150 sheets) at one time. The manually operated punch is easy to use. The hollow punch mechanism captures the chips, which can be easily discarded. Contact: Maruzen International, 917D North Plum Grove Rd., Schaumburg IL 60173; (312) 240-1128.

Spectra-Dex (Cel-u-Dex, $1.75–$3.10). It helps organize your looseleaf book in a clear and colorful manner. It comes with color-coded tabs (5, 8, or 10) and a contents cover page. The contents page is divided into color-coded areas, each of which forms an arrow that points rightward. You write or type your title and/or description of a section; then you place a laminated colored tab at the beginning of the section. An arrow should be pointing straight at that tab and the tab should be the same color as the arrow. Contact: Celudex, P.O. Box 4084, New Windsor NY 12550.

Framed (Sassafras). These freestanding metal picture frames easily double as small bulletin boards. Items are affixed with magnets. Basic geometric shapes (circle, triangle, or square) and bright enamel paint colors (red, white, blue, yellow, and black) combine to make a cheerful presence. The size ranges are 4½″ to 8½″ (square), 6½″ to 10½″ per side (triangle), and 6½″ to 10½″ diameter (circle). Each board comes with four magnets. Contact: Sassafras Enterprises, 1622 West Carroll Ave., Chicago IL 60612; (312) 226-2000.

File-Trak (Cadence). You insert six tilting dividers into a 9½″-long base, and you've got an instant organizer. It can sit on top of all sorts of flat surfaces: desks, bookcases, file cabinets. For a longer File-Trak system, you can attach two or more bases with connector bars. File-Trak is made of high-impact plastic polymer and is available in white, putty, or black. Contact: Cadence, 1520 Pratt Blvd., Elk Grove IL 60007.

Tasket (Cadence, $16.95). It is definitely a member of the milkbox species, but it performs a worthwhile trick. When it's empty, you can snap it flat and store it away. The Tasket is particularly useful for those whose work sporadically creates piles of files and papers. You can neatly arrange the newborn documents and folders in a Tasket. When the project is over, remove the contents to permanent storage, put the Tasket away, and pray for the next project. Included with the Tasket are rods that you can insert in the box and use for hanging files. An optional set of four casters ($8.95) allows for mobility and

Stick & Tie

works well with a stack of two boxes. Made of polypropylene and stainless steel pin hinges, the Taskets measure (outside) 10¾" by 20¾" by 13¾" and are available in white, red, blue, beige, and gray. Contact: Cadence, 1520 Pratt Blvd., Elk Grove IL 60007.

Monthly Planner (Visual Organizer's $1.95–$7.95). It is a calendar with a mission. It presents one month per page with large spaces for each day. In addition, each page has sections for top-priority list, important phone calls, and meetings/reminders. It's available in five sizes from desktop 17" by 22" down to 5½" by 8¼" for big pockets. Contact: Visual Organizers, 355 Beinoris, Wood Dale IL 60191.

Home Office Box (Cadence). A desktop organizing system, the box holds three or four drawers. A large drawer holds a removable organizer tray. The two smaller drawers can contain stationery, note pads, and forms. The four-drawer model has a second large drawer. The design prevents the drawers from slipping out altogether, but the drawer fronts can be removed for storage. Contact: Cadence, 1520 Pratt Blvd., Elk Grove IL 60007.

Wire Baskets (Sassafras Enterprises). Wire baskets represent one way to organize shelves, drawers, and desktops. You put stuff in the basket, which you can then see. The colors are red, white, blue, yellow, and black; and the five sizes range from mini (6¼" by 7¾") to extra large (10¾" by 13½"). Extra large easily holds 8½" by 11" paper. Contact: Sassafras Enterprises, 1622 W. Carroll Ave., Chicago IL 60612; (312) 226-2000.

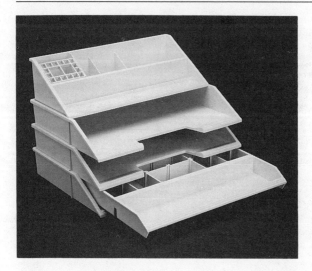

Rubbermaid Modular Desk
Organizer Set

Stick & Tie (Itoya). The old two-circle string fasteners on manila envelopes have been set free. The fasteners can be used to secure such items as binders, storage cartons, overstuffed folders, and yes, manila envelopes. They attach to any smooth-surface (plastic, glass, paper, etc.) item, thanks to their adhesive backings. There are four fasteners to a pack. Contact: Itoya, 4729 Alla Rd., Marina Del Rey CA 90292.

Modular Desk Organizer Set (Rubbermaid). The set consists of seven pieces (five 3″ by 3″, one 3″ by 9″, and one 3″ by 12″). They interlock and can be configured in a bunch of different ways. The resulting "a place for everything" assemblage can fit within a standard desk drawer or on the work surface. The desk organizer sets come in almond, red, and slate blue. Additional pieces can be purchased in packages of three. Contact: Rubbermaid, 3124 Valley Ave., Winchester VA 22601.

Post-it Notes, etc. (3M). These little pieces of paper that you can attach, remove, and restick to surfaces represent a revolutionary product. Looking a little like cheerful yellow petals, Post-it notes cluster on computer monitors, stand out on telephones and lamps, and pop up on books, memos, contracts, and other communicable pieces of paper. Learning from the different applications devised by customers, 3M has created a populous family of Post-it products. The pads come in a variety of sizes (1″ by 2″ up to 4″ by 6″) and colors (pink, cream, blue, green, white, light gray, and, of course, yellow). The larger sizes are lined. Vividly colored Post-it tape flags resemble and are akin to acetate index tabs such as you find marking off the sections of a loose-leaf binder. The flag can mark off sections of a book, contract, or report. The colors are red, blue, green, yellow, and white. You can

Post-it Pads

get custom-printed Post-its that, for example, bear your name or logo. The Post-it-spawned industry includes attractive plastic trays that are receptacles for Post-it pads. Contact: 3M Commercial Office Supply Division, Building 223-3S-03, 3M Center, St. Paul MN 55144-1000.

Workmates (Velcro). Really stick it to your office with a range of organizational problem solvers that do it the Velcro way. Attach the Sta Put pen holder (and your pen) to a telephone, lamp, or desk calendar. There's also a Sta Put pen. The Note Clips hold memos and other pieces of paper that you wish to keep in front of your eyes. The Velcro part can stick to a wall, computer monitor, or bookend. With the drawer organizer, you can stick such items as keys, tape, correction fluid, rulers, and other light odds and ends on the inner sides of the wall. Cord Controls keep electric cords and computer cables untangled and safe. Strap It is the Velcro version of the book belt. It's elasticized and opens and closes easily. The 20″ Strap It is recommended for books, binders, and small piles of files. The 32″ version is suggested for large pieces such as computer printouts and notebooks. Hold Its allow you to use vertical spaces (walls, sides of desks, file cabinets, etc.). The Light Duty Hold It can carry up to one pound. It's also good for keeping objects in place on your desk. The Heavy Duty Hold It can hang up to three pounds worth of something. Other Velcro

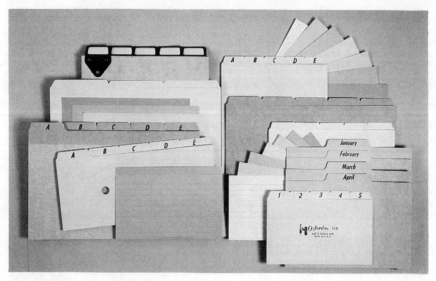

Oxford Index Cards and Guides

WorkMates are Picture Hanger, Poster Hanger, Cord Cover, Chair Mate Anchor, Carpet Anchor, Binder Lok, and Plant Tie. Contact: Velcro USA, 406 Brown Ave., Manchester NH 03108.

Softiles (Velcro). After removing the paper backing, you stick the adhesive side of the 10″ by 12″ tile onto the wall, door, file cabinet, or other such space. The Velcro surface lends an official fabric bulletin board look. You then attach note clips and hooks, both with Velcro backing, to the tile. Use the hooks and clips to hang what you wish (e.g., note pads, calendars, memos, scissors). For heavier items—such as clocks, plants, and pictures—Velcro suggests the use of Hold-Its. A Softile will hold up to five pounds. Two tiles are in a package and the available colors are sterling, sea foam, plum, desert sand, dusty rose, and ice blue. Contact: Velcro USA, 406 Brown Ave., Manchester NH 03108.

Index Cards (Oxford, $8/1,000). Lined white 3″ by 5″ cards form the information bank backbone that keeps many businesses going very well. They are easy to work with (for those reasonably skilled in alphabetical and/or numerical order). Index cards are portable and probably make great pets. Oxford's index cards are precisely cut and made of heavy card stock. The company says that the cards are vertically grained, which keeps them upright for filing. Oxford also makes index cards in colors (blue, buff, canary, cherry, green, and salmon) and other sizes (4″ by 6″ and 5″ by 8″). Contact: Esselte Pendaflex, 71 Clinton Rd., Garden City NY 11530.

Index Card Guides (Oxford, $2.07–$3.08). Use these serenely light blue pressboard tabbed cards to organize your index cards. The guides, which have high tabs for easy identification, come in three versions: monthly (the fewest and cheapest), alphabetical, and daily. Contact: Esselte Pendaflex, 71 Clinton Rd., Garden City NY 11530.

Index Card Cabinets (Rubbermaid, $22.95). The solid plastic cabinet holds up to 1,600 cards. The drawer moves easily, and contains a "follow block" so that cards always are upright. Rubbermaid designs its card file cabinets so that one can interlock with another, either vertically or horizontally. Contact: Rubbermaid, 3124 Valley Ave., Winchester VA 22601.

RESOURCES

PUBLICATIONS/VIDEOS

Records Management Handbook with Retention Schedule (Fellowes Manufacturing, $2). This book, created by a major manufacturer of storage products, can be very useful, as long as you understand one crucial truth. Its contents have nothing to do with the needs of a home office. It talks to large corporations whose major function in this world seems to be to generate miles of paper and rivers of digital data on floppy disks. It presumes rooms devoted just to record storage, and staff whose sole task is to minister to those records. Even so, a stroll through the handbook should suggest some ideas to you about retaining records for current reference, transferring inactive records to storage, and disposing of those records no longer needed. It also contains a "suggested retention schedule for business records"—a thorough listing of how many years a business should retain its various records. Contact: Fellowes Manufacturing, 1789 Norwood Ave., Itasca IL 60143; (708) 893-1600.

How to Be Organized in Spite of Yourself by Sunny Schlenger and Roberta Roesch (NAL Books, $17.95). Professional organizer Schlenger and established journalist Roesch combine to present an effective approach to organizing your space (as in home office) and time. The key to organizing, they say, is to understand your personal approach to the process. The book describes five styles of organizing time—hopper, perfectionist plus, allergic to detail, fence-sitter and cliff-hanger—and five styles of organizing space—everything out, nothing out, right angular, pack rat, and total slob. None of these categories should be considered negative, explain the authors. When you know your style, you stop fighting yourself. Instead, you maximize your strengths and minimize your weaknesses. The authors show us how. Contact: New American Library, 1633 Broadway, New York NY 10019.

How to Get Control of Your Time and Your Life by Alan Lakein (NAL Books). Lakein combines incisive instruction with down-to-earth examples. The book has helped many people turn every minute of their lives into prime time. I think the book is out of print. Don't wait for it to be republished. It's worth the time and trip to your library.

Time Power by Dr. Charles R. Hobbs (Harper & Row, $16.95; $7.95, paperback). *Business Week* called this "one of the best books on [strategic time planning]." Hobbs helps readers identify their priorities with a series of questions and exercises. Contact: Harper & Row, 10 E. 53rd St., New York NY 10022.

ORGANIZATIONS/SERVICES

Organizer (Carol Kropnick). A place for everything and everything in its place. Carol Kropnick's place is the New York metropolitan area. She organizes offices and projects. Contact: Carol Kropnick, 135 Eastern Parkway, Brooklyn NY 11238; (718) 638-4909.

Finding an Organizer (NAPO). There is a National Association of Professional Organizers. You can contact it to find someone who'll put things in order for you. Although currently limited to four chapters (three on the West Coast, one in New York), its members can be found all over the country. The New York chapter office happily provides referrals. If you need an organizer, regardless of where you live, give the New York folks a jingle. Contact: NAPO; (914) 666-6414.

I Hate Filing Club (Pendaflex, free). Secretaries customarily wreak order on the wilderness of paper, and this "club" is intended for them. But you and I can join. (Membership standards are lax.) The major benefit is an occasional newsletter that gives an informed insight into the intricacies of filing. (Esselte Pendaflex is a major manufacturer of office products.) Other benefits include free samples of Pendaflex products and rebate offers. You also can get *How to File,* an informative thirty-six-page book, by sending either $4.95 or five flaps from Pendaflex folder boxes. Club members can get cuter items (mugs, umbrellas, teddy bears, etc.) emblazoned with the "I Hate Filing" logo for some dollars and a flap or two or three. Contact: I Hate Filing Club, Esselte Pendaflex Corporation, 71 Clinton Rd., Garden City NY 11530.

The Art Department

It may not be nice or fair or even smart, but people do make judgments on the basis of appearances. In a sense, home officers are lucky. A lot of people with whom we work don't see us. We can be stark naked when we telephone them, and they'll never know. We can even wear double-knit polyester. Our secret is safe. We may be invisible to the world, but our pieces of paper—business cards, letterheads, flyers, brochures, advertisements—shouldn't be. Each of these items has a design. It's both vital and urgent that the designs are attractive, professionally appropriate, and present the best possible image for the way we position ourselves.

Thus, we turn to the Art Department. Your art director has only two responsibilities: thinking and doing. First let's look at doing because it's easier.

To make anything that is going to be printed, you start with a paste-up board. It is a piece of paper upon which the layout is drawn and the copy is pasted. You put the elements of the design exactly where you want them on the page. Design elements include illustrations, photographs, blocks of text, and headlines. Tools help you define the lines that form the structure of your design. Your printer might supply you with paste-up boards. If not, you can buy them. Sometimes elements are pasted onto transparent paper that is taped to the board or placed in envelopes that accompany the board. Their positioning always is indicated on the board. The layout and elements are photographed to create a plate from which copies are made.

THE LEVEL

"As a minimum," says Susan Davis, author of *59 More Studio Secrets for the Studio Artist* (North Light Publishing, $29.95), "you need a clean level surface—such as a drawing board—on which to work. You need a flat edge—usually a T-square because you know it's absolutely straight. With a ruler, you're never really sure. You need a triangle to put against the T-square to make sure something is really square."

The flat edge and the triangle aid the eye in lining up the elements exactly. Most designers use rubber cement to paste down elements. It's cheap and tacky. It dries relatively quickly, but the cemented elements can be moved around, if necessary, until you find just the right spot. Davis says that graphic artists use gum erasers to remove excess rubber cement from the mechanical. Otherwise, the cement will pick up dirt, and an image of the dirt will show up on the plate.

Another design tool is a "nonrepro" blue pencil. For some reason, it does not register when the mechanical is photographed, so designers use it to make notations on their layouts. (Not every blue pencil has this stealth bomber quality.) "For example," says Susan Davis, who also writes a column for *Step by Step Graphics* magazine, "you mark the layout with a blue pencil to show where you want text copy or headlines."

Usually the actual illustration or photograph will be larger or smaller than you want it to appear in the final design. The final size is indicated in two ways. You use a nonrepro blue pencil to outline the space the art will occupy. You figure out the percentage by which the picture will be enlarged or reduced, and you note the result on the layout. For example, you'd say, "reduce 40 percent." Some designers use calculators to discover the desired proportion. Some use copiers that reduce and enlarge. A venerable tool is the proportion wheel. It operates like a pie-shaped slide rule. The inner circle has calibrations representing the original size. The outer circle measurements are for the size on the page. A window reveals the percentage of change.

Two constant guardians of artwork are precision and cleanliness. When items need to be cut (for example, to remove two lines of type from a copy block), the cuts must be made precisely. Let your scissors sleep. "Use a single-edged blade for cutting," says Susan Davis, "or the more sophisticated X-Acto knife. Hold the razor or knife on the edge of your T-square or triangle and cut along the edge to make sure you have a perfectly straight edge."

Chances are that you'll have words somewhere on the page you create. The words will fall into one of two categories: text or headlines.

(A little common sense is in order here. If you're making a letterhead, technically speaking you won't have text or headlines. But the operative suggestions for headlines will work well. Similarly, if you're doing a photo caption, it would be appropriate to think of it as text.)

WISE TO THE WORDS

The best thing you can do with your words—text or headlines—is have them set in type by a professional typesetter. They will look better and make a clearer impression and last longer (an important feature for those who will place the same ad over and over again).

Some people will use computer printout or even typing for their text. Purists say that it's impossible to get printer-generated type to look good enough. I would argue with this. I think it's perfectly appropriate when there's no effort to conceal the computer origin and when the low-rent look doesn't undercut the message you're sending out. A couple of computer programs make the printer produce better-looking than normal characters.

You also might create headlines with the computer. Headlines are easier to see than text, which means that flaws in the headlines are easier to see. Be very critical when you view the computer output.

Again, typesetting is the best approach. Still, you'll find several opportunities for excellence and hard work in the making of headlines. A number of companies make transfer type in sheets. With these, you make words in much the same way that you'd apply a decal. You rub the individual letters onto a piece of transparent paper. There is a wonderfully vast variety of type styles available in transfer letters. You'll find not only every conceivable style but you'll be able to pick from uppercase and lowercase, many different point sizes, and the additional options of bold, semibold, and italic. Symbols and different thicknesses of line also are available in transfer type format. It definitely is a one-step-at-a-time process. The best tool to use when applying letters is a burnisher. Many patient people have made letterheads with transfer type.

There also are electronic lettering machines. They work with either a typewriter-like keyboard or with a wheel. You turn the wheel and stop at the letter of choice until you have spelled out the word. Both wheel and keyboard lettering machines yield your words on an adhesive-backed tape. The letters are evenly spaced and ready to be placed. The more sophisticated machines offer more variety in type style and size.

The most sophisticated machine you can use in the design-it-yourself world may be the computer, particularly when it's driven by a desktop publishing (DTP) program. DTP users experience joy as they blend text and graphics, make headlines, and explore all the intricacies of type.

Unfortunately, most nondesigners who use DTP programs do not understand DTP's strengths and their own weaknesses.

A desktop publishing program really excels at processing pages, making a design by eliminating such mechanical steps as moving elements around and pasting them down. It'll make a master format or template and instantly fit designated material into this template. Consequently, every page of a newsletter will have the same look and feel with a minimum effort.

A word processor does not an author make. I can't become an accountant by using a spreadsheet. One certainly can't become a designer by using a desktop publishing program. Should we wistfully wave goodbye to DTP? Not at all. If we use it as a maker of clean, attractive pages, we're fine. If we follow the simple templates provided by the software developers, we've got ourselves one heck of a productivity tool.

Publicist Wes Thomas offers an excellent suggestion: "If you want your template for a document—newsletter, brochure, whatever—don't try to design your own. Most people don't have the eye for it and don't realize they're putting out garbage. It'll end up looking like junk. People have really screwed up their corporate image—particularly smaller companies that don't know any better. Get a graphic designer initially to help you set it up and make sure it looks good. The designer should create a template in consultation with you and put that on your software. Preferably it would be someone with the same setup as you have. Get the designer to select the fonts, the layout, the sizes, everything. I would keep that format and not fool around with it."

SPACE AND LOGIC

These basic tools—manual and electronic—will help you make your design concrete so that it can be printed. Making it concrete is one thing. Making it have a concrete soul is something else. Art directors like to describe design as a type of logic that presents the client's message and fulfills the client's goals. The page has a premise. The elements are building blocks that voice a coherent statement. Thinking, or at least planning, is the best tool you can hope to use when you design.

"The first design element," says Charles Goslin, adjunct professor of design at Pratt Institute and the owner of his own Brooklyn-based firm, Charles Goslin Design, "is the rectangle." The seemingly blank page, the arena on which you make the design, is more than just a set of borders. It helps define the value of the other elements and has a value of its own.

"I think some people who are not professional designers," says Goslin, "look at the rectangle just as a space to be filled. They look at the page the way one looks at the town dump. But if, for example, you're doing an advertisement that's on a page with other advertisements, some of the rectangle's space (also known as countershape) should be used for isolation. Isolate your message from this jumble on the page. Err on the side of too much countershape, rather than too little—not for the beauty of the design but for the projection of the message."

Ed Gold, executive vice-president and creative director of Barton-Gillet, a Baltimore-based institutional marketing firm, agrees with Goslin about the importance of space: "Nondesigners think of space as something that's left out rather than something that's put in. They don't see space as working for them. For example, if you wanted to put emphasis on a heading, you can make it bigger or put more space around it. Both accomplish the same thing, but if you put more space around it, you'll probably do it more attractively."

Goslin praises the virtues of directness and simplicity: "In heaven's name, avoid being verbose with images or words. Don't collaborate with the clutter all around by burying your message. A good, serious part of design is editing. If it's not important, dump it. If it can be covered elsewhere, dump it."

DESIGN ERRORS

Ed Gold, author of *The Business of Graphic Design* (Watson Guptill, $24.95), describes a series of conceptual errors made by people who are not professional graphic designers: "They don't recognize that contrasts add drama to a page. The drama doesn't exist if the contrasts aren't clear. They'll shove a number of photographs on a spread and make them all the same size. They'll use typefaces that are too close in size. The heading might be in fourteen point and the text might be in twelve. You can't see the difference too clearly. There should be no ambiguity, whatsoever. Bend over backwards. Go smaller than you have to go; go bigger than you have to go. This will get you drama.

"They don't have a clear focal point on the page. The eye wants to go somewhere. They put too many elements on the page and the eye doesn't know where to go."

How do you know, I wondered, what the most important element on the page is. I got the answer I dreaded: "It's whatever you want it to be." Logic again. After all, design is all about making a statement visible. And it's your statement.

"A clear focal point usually is the most important thing," Gold adds. "Usually it's the thing that will grab them most first. Make it big.

"They don't recognize that photographs are not just boxes. Photos are active. They have information. They have lines of direction. They have tones."

Nonthinking can lead to some unfortunate situations. For example, someone might design a page, complete with a square space for a photo that he or she hasn't yet seen or thought about.

"They put the photograph in," says Gold, "and it doesn't work because it's conflicting with the design of the page. They should start with the photographs. Select the photographs, and weed out all those you don't really need. Get it down to the fewest that you can possibly use to make your point. Crop in as closely as you can to get as much drama as you can, but do not give up any information.

"A lot of nondesigners don't plan very well in advance. They don't plan to accommodate every single element in advance. They don't plan the number of photographs they're going to have, the length of their copy, their headings. If, on the other hand, the structure is well planned in advance, it accommodates all your information. When you clearly identify the elements and are very selective about why you're using things or how many you're using, it drives everything else. You're going to have something that looks organized and disciplined, and the reader will get a sense of the logic.

"Don't try to be creative, because you just get yourself fouled up. It's very rare that you have to do something that's never been seen before.

"It's much easier to be successful using a few elements than by using many elements. You have fewer decisions to make. If all you're dealing with is one full-page photograph facing a page of text, you don't have an awful lot of things to put in balance. Start adding photographs and elements. Every time you add one more element you complicate the process. You get to where you have an awful lot of things to bring into balance and have in proper proportion to each other."

The keep-it-simple credo also rules the use of type styles. "A lot of people just try to use too many typefaces," says Gold. "You shouldn't have to use more than two or three type styles at the very most. The goal should be to set the type so that it's readable. That involves a lot of things—the amount of spacing, the length of paragraphs, the number of paragraphs, the size of the type. So many things make the page readable. The first objective is to ask what personality you want to communicate. You could choose from a very limited number of typefaces for that personality. Certain typefaces have a slightly older, more traditional, appearance. You might want to communicate a very conservative personality. You might want something that is rather contemporary.

"I think you can get by with a very, very limited vocabulary of typefaces very well. You're far better off than trying to constantly find new faces. If you can get a handle on one good old style Roman typeface like Garamond; one or two good transitional typefaces like Baskerville or Caslon; one or two good bookfaces—Times Roman, Century; one good modern face like Bodoni; a couple of sans serifs like Helvetica, Franklin Gothic, Univers, any of those; you'll not have to worry about any other type. There's no reason to go to anything new except boredom—and that's one thing nondesigners ought not concern themselves with."

Gold points out that design professionals and nondesigners operate in different environments. It doesn't mean they have license to clutter and we don't. Design is their business, and therefore their efforts must support their drive to market designers. It is important that they refine and assert their professional identity and distinctive style. Nondesigners have no such need. We just have to get our message across. Producing a lucid statement is an achievement all by itself.

HIRING A PRO

Whenever possible, it's advisable to hire a professional designer. It is the safer, easier, and better choice. Designers have the experience of working with illustrations and type styles. They know what they're doing and why. They have the manual skills to do the work faster, better, cleaner, smarter. They have the art knowledge to make a design that presents a clear, powerful, visual statement. They'll explain that since graphic design is so important, hiring a professional is the best money you'll ever spend. (If you can't act on it, at least remember it as a good line to use.)

Professor Goslin of Pratt Institute says don't be certain that you can't afford a good designer. It may be that your timetable and the nature of your project fit in well with a designer's plans or schedule.

"If it's true, don't be afraid to say, 'I need something special; I want something special, and I can't pay you much.' Even if there's very little money in it, there can be rewards."

It's possible that the designer might see your project as an entrance to another segment of the marketplace, or as a way to showcase his or her style, or as an interlude for joy. I don't think you should count on any of those carrots to be significant incentives, as such opportunities also can appear with jobs that pay well. Still, remember that you shouldn't be blind to the chance of working with a professional designer. Even if you're charged "full price," you'll get effective, attractive work from someone that you pay fairly.

When interviewing prospective designers, explain everything that is needed for a decision: the nature of your project, your goals, where their work will be used, and the budget. You'll probably look through their portfolios—the collected examples of their work that they want people to see. Concentrate on their portfolios and not on how well they talk or whether you get "good vibes" from them. (This is not to suggest that being articulate and personable should stigmatize anyone.)

"The most important thing you should pay attention to," says Gold, "is the style of the designer. They all have a style. You don't have to be able to characterize the style. You just have to feel that what you see is in synch with your taste."

When you hire a designer, tell him or her everything. "Being a graphic designer," says Charles Goslin, "is a very good source of a liberal education. You immerse yourself in the client's information and problems."

"You tell the designer every solitary thing that can be said," agrees Gold. "What's the audience? What do you really want to achieve? What are the problems? What does your product do? You should try to get all your information in advance and have it ready when the designer starts talking with you."

"Don't tell the designer how to accomplish things," says Goslin. "Tell the designer what you want accomplished."

When evaluating the work the designer has done for you, it's necessary to be specific and to provide reasons, especially if your goal is to emerge with a winning design. For example, saying, "The type is too small" means nothing. It's an expression of personal taste that may have no relation to the design's intended function. However, saying, "The audience for this is over fifty-five, and I think the type is too small for them to read" is helpful. If you feel something's wrong and you don't know what it is, explore your concerns with the designer. You may be right. You may be wrong. When we're the vendors, we know how wise it is to assume the customer is always right. But when we're buying services, it's downright stupid to simply dismiss the informed opinion of the professional we've hired.

DESIGN AS A SECOND LANGUAGE

There's a good rule to use when dealing with graphics people (designers, paste-up artists, printers, photographers). Do not try to speak their language unless you've taken a pretty good Berlitz course and/or you can speak the tongue idiomatically. (This dictum also has value when dealing with other outside consultants.) We engage these people because of their specialized expertise, so nothing in the contract says we have to look smart when talking with them. In fact, indiscriminate lingo-slinging might encourage us to agree to something that we think we understand, but really don't, or to think we want something we really don't.

A simpler rule to follow is to know what effect you want as specifically as possible. If there's a concept that you have difficulty in explaining, find an example of it and show it to the graphics professional. Make sure they explain to you what the process to achieve the desired effect would be, what it entails, how close to the mark you really can get, how much it will cost, and what compromises you might be able to make for reduced costs. Rather than imply understanding of the process, make sure you find out its various steps and the timetable the professional and you each must follow to get the job done on time.

CATALOG

PXB Portable Drawing Board (Alvin). This board gives you an instant art studio. Its plastic legs afford just the right angle. So-called "grip-track" tractor feet keep the board stable and still. It's got a professional quality white melamine surface. The board's lock system holds the built-in straightedge in place. Its tuck-away handle makes it easy to move the drawing board between its storage area and your desk. The board comes in five sizes, ranging from 16″ by 21″ to 31″ by 42″. Contact: Alvin & Co., 1335 Bluehills Ave. Ext., Bloomfield CT 06002; (800) 444-ALVIN; in CT (203) 243-8991.

Instant Photography (Polaroid Spectra System). Sometimes you need a photo of something—a product, a house for sale, a person—right away. The Spectra system offers two advantages. There's the tradi-

PXB Portable Drawing Board

tional Polaroid value of instant gratification. You'll immediately know whether or not the picture can be used. If not, you'll have a chance to do it over. Second, the Spectra is a fairly hassle-free experience. It uses sonar focusing and electronics to automatically determine and set shutter speed, aperture opening, and amount of flash. The Spectra yields a 3.6" by 2.9" image. Contact: Polaroid Corporation, 575 Technology Sq., Cambridge MA 02139; (800) 343-5000.

Accu-Line (American Commerce Connections, $30–$50). This surface enables you to draw straight lines freehand. It's good for making charts, schematics, floor plans, precise designs, and other such types of geometric joys. The surface is embossed with more than 2,500 pyramids per square inch. These provide precise channels through which your pen point can glide. You can draw horizontal, vertical, and diagonal lines. The Accu-Line is imprinted with a protractor and a scale to facilitate even greater accuracy of design. Some people have used it to draw schematics right before the very eyes of their thoroughly impressed clients. Available in 8½" by 11" or 17" by 11". Contact: American Commerce Connections, P.O. Box 2595, Anderson IN 46018.

Accu-Line

Artist's Materials Catalog (Arthur Brown & Co., free). In its 230 pages, this venerable (since 1924) catalog lists and describes all the specialized art products you ever would need. These include brushes, markers, lettering transfer sheets, cutting tools, drawing tables, drawing accessories, and all sorts of highly evolved products. Arthur Brown & Co. is both a distributor and a retailer. Contact: Your local art supply store or Arthur Brown & Co., P.O. Box 7820, Maspeth NY 11378; (800) 237-0619; in NY (718) 779-6464.

National Association of Desktop Publishers (NADTP, $60–$95/yr). This nonprofit trade association is for people with an interest in desktop publishing. Essentially, membership buys you information, discounts on books and products, and the opportunity to network with others who use computers to design and typeset published material. Members range from the one-person newsletter publishing company to the corporate graphics and publishing services departments. Vendors of desktop publishing hardware and software also are NADTP members. Most perks go to the "professional" category of membership (translation: those willing to spend $95 a year). These include the following: a subscription to the quarterly *National Association of Desktop Publishers Journal*— the journal, 140 or so pages, provides a neat balance of material for those just getting their feet wet (with ink?) and those who wish to be further on the cutting edge; *Desktop Publishers Forum,* an eight-page bimonthly newsletter that mixes DTP news with NADTP news; the *Desktop Publishers Book Catalog* (books you can buy at a discount); the *Desktop Publishers Source Book,* which tells what desktop publishing is and where to find it plus some evaluations; and membership in the Desktop Publishers GEnie Roundtable, a bulletin board with public domain DTP software, clip art, fonts, and news and interchange among members. The GEnie registration fee is waived for professional NADTP members.

Basic membership, at $60 a year, provides all the stated benefits except for the journal subscription. The third type of membership, also at $60 a year, is for those who just want the journal. Contact: NADTP, P.O. Box 508, Kenmore Station, Boston MA 02215; (617) 437-6472.

Publish-It! (Timeworks Platinum, $199.95). "When I say," writes a *PC Resource* magazine reviewer, " 'Publish-It! is the best desktop publishing program you can buy,' I mean that literally." The reviewer went on to explain that the two benchmark programs, Pagemaker and Ventura Publisher, are considerably more expensive. Furthermore, Publish-It has most if not all of the graphics and text-handling features that many users really need. It also has a built-in word processor. In addition, it's easy to learn. Contact: Timeworks Platinum, 444 Lake Cooke Rd., Deerfield IL 60015; (312) 948-9200.

Off-the-Shelf DTP Illustrations (Micrografx, different prices). Sequestered in almost every American commercial art studio is a collection of books known as "clip art." The idea is simple. When you don't have the time or the need to create a new illustration for some project, go use one of the public domain drawings collected within the covers of a clip art book. The clip art approach is a natural for desktop publishing. The art is on the software. Micrografx offers a good variety of general and special-interest illustrations, symbols, and decorations. Also, Micrografx offers three respected graphics programs: "Designer," "Graph Plus," and "Draw Plus." The company's catalog also offers T-shirts and sweatshirts. Contact: Micrografx, 1303 Arapaho, Richardson TX 75081-2444.

Art Gum Eraser (Faber-Castell, $6.55/dozen). The 2″-wide eraser is a classic. It doesn't leave any grease behind. It doesn't harm ink and it's gentle. Graphic artists use the gum eraser to pick up unsightly extra rubber cement. Contact: Faber-Castell, 4 Century Dr., Parsippany NJ 07054; (201) 539-4537.

Proportion Wheel (C-Thru Ruler Company). Round and round it goes. Aligning the two circular scales will tell you by what percentage an illustration must be enlarged or reduced to reach the desired size. Contact: The C-Thru Ruler Company, Box 256, Bloomfield CT 06002; (203) 243-0303.

T-Square (Fairgate, $18.35). This 24″ aluminum instrument was born to be precise. The head and blade are exactly aligned. The blade is scored in inches (¹/₁₆″ calibrations). Also available in 12″ to 48″ lengths. Contact: Fairgate Rule Co., 22 Adams Ave., Cold Spring NY 10516; (914) 265-3677.

Type-Set-It (Good Ideas, $395). A low-budget approach to typesetting, this computer program improves the look of any printer's output, whether you have a 9-pin dot matrix or laser printer. It also makes a number of fonts available. It's best used for announcements, infrequent flyers, circulars, and forms, and for those low-volume items where the typesetting fees would eat up too much of the costs. (Conversely, Type-Set-It is really underkill when professional typesetting charges are a relatively minimal part of the overall budget.) As should be expected, when this program is in use, the printer operates at a slower speed. Contact: Good Ideas (508) 475-7238.

Transfer Lettering (Letraset). The New Jersey-based company is the leader among letterers. I'm sure that one of its hundreds of type styles will suit you. There's more to choice than style. Do you need capitals, lowercase letters, and/or numerals? What size (measured in points) do you want? (This book has been set in eleven point.) Know the answers to these two questions before you buy your lettering sheets. (Don't short-sheet yourself.) For more informed results, get a copy of the *Letraset Graphic Materials Handbook* ($5.95). The guide's main attraction is its index of type styles. It also contains a glossary and a "Designing Ideas" section. You're likely to find it in an art or office supplies store. Contact: Letraset USA, 40 Eisenhower Dr., Paramus NJ 07653; (201) 845-6100.

Burnisher (Letraset, $3.95). It is the basic tool especially designed for working with transfer lettering. You can get a spoontip burnisher for use with larger type, or a teflon tip for smaller point sizes. Contact: Letraset USA, 40 Eisenhower Dr., Paramus NJ 07653; (201) 845-6100.

Max Lettering Machine

Lettering Machine (Max Business Machines Corp., $1,495). Max's Letrex LM-500 is an easy-to-use, versatile lettering machine. You use either a ribbon cassette for printing directly onto paper or a cassette of adhesive-backed tape when you want to place the lettering just so on a different surface. The LCD shows 16 characters. The memory stores 8,000 characters. Working with a typewriter-style keyboard, you can vary the height and width of the characters. You can make them slant. By simply pressing the keys, you can have reverse print, outlined, mirror image, sideways, underlined, and bordered characters. Change fonts just by slipping a card in a slot. Contact: Max Business Machines, 585 Commercial Ave., Garden City NY 11530; (516) 222-2184.

"Nonrepro" Blue Pencils (Berol, $4.50–$7.75/dozen). You can get Berol's thick-leaded Prismacolor nonprint blue pencil or its Verithin fine-leaded nonphoto blue pencil. Contact: Berol USA, P.O. Box 2248, Brentwood TN 37024-2248; (615) 371-1199.

Paste-Up Board (Pro Board, $21.95 and up). This is where you paste your camera-ready copy. The coated board is just right for mechanicals and simple artwork. It's premarked to indicate page borders, and it's got a nonrepro blue grid to help with exact placement. Contact: Arthur Brown & Co., P.O. Box 7820, Maspeth NY 11378; (800) 237-0619; in NY (718) 779-6464.

X-Acto Knife (Hunt Manufacturing, $3.40). Artists can pick through a range of knives and blades. Probably, it's a good idea to start with the X-Press knife. With this, you don't handle the blade when removing it. You just twist a knob on top of the handle. The X-Press comes with a number 11 blade, which is good for paper. Contact: Hunt Manufacturing Company, 230 South Broad St., Philadelphia PA 19102.

Rubber Cement Dispenser (Arthur Brown, $4.25 and up). When you buy rubber cement in bulk (and you can), it's good to keep your working batch in one of these dispensers. They have airtight caps that do not rust. The caps hold built-in brushes that have adjustable handles. You can raise or lower the brush portion that's under the lid. The brush itself will stay in the cement and not dry out. Contact: Arthur Brown & Co., P.O. Box 7820, Maspeth NY 11378; (800) 237-0619; in NY (718) 779-6464.

RESOURCES

The Business of Graphic Design by Ed Gold (Watson-Guptill, $24.95). This book also fits in the "Professional Help" chapter, especially for those of you who happen to be graphic designers. It offers some tangible advice about how people in the visual creative professions can run their businesses. If you anticipate using graphic designers regularly, this book might give you some insight into what they need and expect. Contact: Watson-Guptill, 1 Astor Plaza, 1515 Broadway, New York NY 10036.

59 More Studio Secrets for the Studio Artist by Susan Davis (North Light Books, $29.95). Although intended for professionals, this book can help do-it-yourselfers who have design ability and some familiarity with the tools. Davis contacted leading design firms and asked for their favorite tips for getting the job done. The book has some good advice on doing layouts and using the copier to good effect (about a third of the book's tips involve copiers) as well as techniques for such activities as airbrushing, using markers, and lettering. Contact: North Light Books, 1307 Dena Ave., Cincinnati OH 45207.

CHAPTER 12

The Personnel Department

All the "stop your sniveling and pull yourself together right now" books written for corporate managers stress the value of delegation. They mean delegation to a secretary and/or other corporate vassal. We home officers tend not to have vassals even when we're in the middle of the ocean. This can be lethal.

As if our solitude weren't enough, we're also afflicted with independence. The if-you-want-the-job-done-right-then-do-it-yourself attitude may be counterproductive and even hasten a certain rendezvous with the bone farm. You may know more about your business than anybody, and you especially may know and be adept at the exact way to handle certain chores. But so what? What could you be doing instead? Then, of course, there are those tasks that bore us, as well as those little routines we so ably screw up.

Angelo Valenti asks his clients to look at the different activities they do. "How much time do they take," he asks, "and what are the different skill levels? Identify the low skill levels and start delegating." Who do you turn to?

"There are people in your neighborhood," says Valenti. "High school and college students, the mother who has her kids in school for six hours a day, the retired person who can come in for three hours a day and do the bookkeeping, envelope stuffing, the collating, the simple phone calls so you can expand and leverage your time. By looking at how to delegate you can figure out who you can hire. Then you can come up with a job description that accurately states what this person can and should do for you."

NOT A CRASS ACT

Getting help does not necessarily require the crass act of paying out money. There is what I call the Mary O'Connor principle. A cousin of mine (who will not be identified) in a service business (which will not be specified) was reaching new hysterical peaks one sunny afternoon. Too many clients owed her too much money. In desperation she donned an authentic-sounding Irish brogue and called many of the errant clients. She explained that she was Mary O'Connor, the firm's bookkeeper, and the account was in arrears. The tactic worked. The accent was convincing. Nobody recognized my cousin's voice. Enough clients paid up enough money. One customer invited Mary O'Connor to lunch. Another, seeing a solution to his own cash flow problems, tried to hire Mary O'Connor away from my cousin.

Although this particular Mary O'Connor is a mythical being, the principle itself is a gem. To the outside world secretaries and accounts receivable bookkeepers serve as neutral dedicated figures. They have no authority to give anybody clemency. They don't want to hear any irrelevant information. They will not be satisfied until rows of numbers match. They don't want to get off the phone until they've completed their task. I know several people who have friends who make strategic phone calls as a favor.

A Manhattan therapist occasionally has a neighbor do phone work for her. The neighbor, who identifies herself as the secretary, schedules appointments and inquires into the whereabouts of overdue payments. Previously, the therapist, when attempting to schedule, found herself listening to protracted monologues of the patients' problems. It ate up her time without really helping the patients. The therapist's own requests for payment proved to be embarrassing and (even worse) nonproductive. On the other hand, the neighbor's I'm-here-for-business posture lent her an air of nonnegotiable authority that the therapist did not have in these contexts.

A photographer who specializes in wildlife and travel work has a friend babysit his business whenever he's on the road. The friend checks the answering machine and the mail. She returns phone calls and explains that the photographer is on assignment and will be back at such and such a date. Checks that come in get deposited in the bank. Simple queries get answered. The photographer is helped because his business is cared for while he's away. The friend enjoys it because it's a change of pace for her.

We can't always invoke the Mary O'Connor principle. For one

thing, not everybody has friends; or at least not everybody has friends with the time or temperament to help with these phone calls.

Brooklyn-based Ira Mayer of Entertainment Promotion Marketing is blessed with what he calls an "off-premise office manager." His assistant, who had worked with Mayer previously, holds a nearly full-time job in another part of the city. She has the flexibility to provide administrative services for Mayer and, in fact, a couple of other clients.

"She is paid on a retainer," says Mayer, "to just take care of day-to-day stuff that needs to be done. Her office is based in Manhattan, so when we have things that need to be done immediately in Manhattan, she can get them done. For example, she keeps extra copies of the newsletter in her office so if somebody needs something messengered, she can get it to them quickly. If I have a fight with a utility company over something, she does the battle."

If the phones need to be covered, she can check the answering machine from afar, and also make necessary phone calls. She makes regular visits to EPM to ride herd on the filing.

Actually Ira Mayer and his wife Riva Bennett (his business and life partner) bring another creative approach to personnel matters. They have two children, including an infant. Their 9 to 5 babysitter works for them four days a week.

"She helps us with office chores between one and three when the baby sleeps," says Ira Mayer. "For example, she does a lot of our labeling and postage. That includes her in our business, which might give a little extra oomph to her day and a break from taking care of a three-year-old. We can compensate her a little more because she is also contributing to a source of income for us."

When Tony Stewart, developer of the Home Office program, was doing well enough he hired a part-time assistant to work ten hours a week. He hired a family friend who also happened to know a lot about computers. Her duties include filing, fielding phone calls and phone messages, and when possible, answering technical questions regarding the Home Office program.

"When I finally could afford someone who could do those ten hours a week of work—those things that took me away from what I really liked doing—it was like lifting a weight off my shoulders. It was the best money I spent from an emotional point of view. In the long run it enables me to improve the product, design a better marketing plan, and get more sleep."

Publicist Dan Janal hires his mother and a few of her friends. They come in once or twice a week, sit around the table, stuff envelopes, and have a great old time. On the other hand, a West Coast publicist hired someone she knew, and thereby entered the Twilight Zone.

"I was at a point," she says, "where I felt the work load was overwhelming. I needed to concentrate my efforts on more productive things than filing. I hired a next-door neighbor who was retiring from her job."

It seemed like a perfect match. Here was someone the publicist could trust to be in her home. If the publicist were away from the house, packages could be accepted by the neighbor. There was a little problem with chemistry.

"She'd throw open the windows," says the publicist, "and throw open the doors and put on the radio and drink coffee all day. I couldn't handle the behavior. Moreover, she worked at her previous job for thirty years and she had an attitude. She was screwing up with the clients, and she was screwing up with the press.

"I ran into a real problem. She was a next-door neighbor and a friend. I realized almost immediately that it wasn't going to work out, and that I needed to do something. The worst part was that I had to fire her. It was painful to me and painful to her and we're not talking to each other."

Through the magic of hindsight, we can see a couple of fatal errors by the publicist. She had never worked on any kind of project with her neighbor. She selected the neighbor on the basis of proximity, rather than for any skills appropriate for public relations. Those who had success in hiring people they knew share a method that differs from the publicist's approach.

They either had previous experience of working with the person they hired, or they saw that person in action. They usually selected someone who had the requisite skills plus some extra attitude, training, or inclination that was right for their industries or professions.

WHAT TO DO

In hiring for the home office, there are two ways to go. You can hire a person or you can fill a position. The net results can be the same. Your criteria can be the same, and in both cases the idea is to ease your load. The difference simply is at the starting point.

Mary Pekas of the Telemarketing Institute explains how she came to hire her first staffer: "We'd been playing 'what if' games for a lot of years. What if I really do start my business—will you come and work for me. I hired her as soon as I could."

The first outsider Bull & Bear Marketing Group hired was a friend of Bob Beaudoin. The two originally met at the bank where they both had worked.

"When I first had this idea," says Beaudoin, "I bounced ideas off him. In that process, he got really enthused, and his corporate environment seemed less exciting. I knew that his customers might become my customers. But I also trusted his judgment. He just gave his notice. I think we'll name him CFO."

The "hire a person" rule gets invoked when you want the strengths of a particular individual added to your organization. One of the strengths can be the way your performance improves in that person's presence. Once you're convinced you need this person, you're obliged to create the right job for him or her. Together the two of you can analyze the business and where it needs to go, and the strengths and vulnerabilities that each of you display. What could your friend do better than you? What time-consuming task can this particular individual take off your shoulders? Does this person have any talents, skill, or qualities that will help you expand your markets? Are you ready (as in do you have the do re mi) to hire this person now?

As the two of you bat these questions around, the appropriate job (if any) will take shape. Whether a "support" or "executive" position, the person's extras will help the company. The extras could be anything: fluency in Japanese, three summers as a caddy, a degree in clinical psychology, a background in dance, previous employment as a medical receptionist, the ownership of a business, and so on.

Filling a position is the other and more classic approach. Here, you start out with a sense of what you want somebody else to do. If a candidate does not come to mind immediately out of your own network you may have to work at getting the right person. The first chore is to think through what you need.

"People really should spend some time thinking about what they're looking for," says Lin Grensing, author of *A Small Business Guide to Employee Selection* (Self-Counsel Press, 1986). "A lot of times that won't happen. Then you'll have these people coming in and going out and you're comparing them all against each other, rather than comparing them against certain requirements for the job."

All jobs are divided into three parts. The first component is made up of the desperately desired skills and responsibilities. What are the tasks that you wish to dump on some unsuspecting individual? How much of the job is devoted to each of these responsibilities?

If you're looking for a support person, how much phone work, filing, and/or keyboard work do you require? Answers to these questions suggest the degree to which certain skills are necessary.

Let's say the demands are such that the telephones would have to be surgically removed from your assistant's ear each day. You would then require someone with good phone skills or at least someone comfortable with the telephone. Minimal phone use puts phone savvy lower on the list of required subjects. Filing requires good organizing abilities, and the ability to work in a systematic fashion, and perhaps a strong stomach. Neatness helps.

Do you have a lot of letters to get out, or presentations to prepare? If you're using a typewriter, you want the person to be a competent typist. The more paper you cast upon the water, the more efficiency in typing you should require. If you're blessed with a computer, do the applicants know the particular word processing program you use? Could they learn? Have they ever worked with computers before?

If you need to bring a professional or technical person on board, other requirements may come into play. Do the applicants have the proper licensing or degrees? If they are to deal with clients, do they have the proper personality or temperament? Are they familiar with your corner of the industry and/or marketplace? Conversely, do they have more experience with a corner of the industry and/or marketplace that you would like to enter? Do they have skills you don't have?

The second part of the job was hinted at above. It is the industry in which the job takes place, as well as the industry in which the employee has the most experience. Can your prospective employee work effectively in your business? Are the clients and vendors too laid-back, too aggressive, too crude, too refined? Is the jargon too difficult to learn? Are the areas requiring judgment and knowledge of product and services too much to learn on your time? On the other hand, could the fact that the applicant comes from a totally different background add strength to your organization? For example, if you sell computer software and you want to sell to school districts, a salesperson who was an educator could help a lot.

The job you are offering can represent an opportunity, the third factor in a job analysis. Let us count the ways:

- The chance to move up in one's chosen profession.
- The chance to learn about a whole new field.
- The chance to learn valuable or at least interesting skills.

- The chance to earn more money.
- The chance to stay involved in one's profession while working fewer hours.
- The chance to work fewer hours.
- The chance to have a more flexible schedule.

Now that you've analyzed the job, you know what the job really is all about.

WORKING CONDITIONS

It's time to look at the working conditions. How many days a week do you need, and how many hours a day? Is there room for flexibility in the schedule? Where in your office will this person work? What is the space like? Are there any employee benefits? (Any vacation time or personal days? Can you add this person to your health plan or set up a health plan for him or her?) Is your office chilly because you're conserving fuel? Is your office a hassle for people who have allergies? (Too much dust? Overlooking the garden?) Do you want it quiet? Do you insist on working with loud rock-and-roll in the background? Do you have a dress code (e.g., all employees must wear shorts, tee shirts, and sandals)?

The final ingredient in the working conditions is you. What kind of a boss are you? Are you the type of employer who feels people shouldn't have to be told what to do? Are you the sort who knows there are only two ways of doing things—the wrong way and your way? Do you lash out at the people around you when pressure mounts? Do you want to discourage employees from bothering you with questions? Do you insist on explaining every little detail?

The working conditions and job analysis are an inventory of what you need and what you can offer. Now all you have to do is fill the position.

If you're looking for a staff person, rather than someone on the same professional level, you might check into university-conducted programs such as co-op education and internships. The details differ from school to school and program to program. At its ideal, students expressing an interest and aptitude for your business are referred to you. Sometimes students get credit. When you talk with the program administrator, make sure you understand all the fail-safe mechanisms. Also, you still are exercising a choice intended to make your business work better. Be sure that you are comfortable with your prospective employee. By working with such a program, you have a good chance of getting a motivated, ambitious, and loyal assistant.

If you do place a classified ad, observe a number of principles. You have to use the ad to reach exactly the right person, and avoid expending your resources (particularly interviewing time) on the wrong people. Stress the skills, backgrounds, and attitudes you desire. Be positive, but realistic. If you make the job appear to be a form of recreation, you will attract those applicants who are looking for recreation.

At the interview, have the applicants fill out an employment application form. You can copy it from a book at the library, get a "standard" form from your local office supply shop, or design one yourself. Using the form is a message that although the setting is residential, the activity is business. Obvious items to include are employment history, references, education and special training, address and phone number, how long at address, previous address, hobbies and special interests, and Social Security number.

In their textbook, *Starting and Managing the Small Business* (McGraw-Hill, 1988), Arthur H. Kuriloff and John M. Hemphill, Jr., make an interesting point: "It's been found from careful study that most interviewers form an opinion about the candidate in the first four minutes. They then spend the rest of the interview hour seeking proof to justify that opinion."

The authors point out that this approach is not useful, especially since the first few minutes are when the job-seeker is most likely to be ill at ease. They argue for objectivity. At least wait until all or most of the interview is over before you pass judgment.

Essay questions (otherwise known as open-ended questions) definitely work better than multiple-choice queries. "When you're interviewing," says Lin Grensing, "and you want to get the interviewee to do most of the talking, open-ended questions typically help you get the kind of information you want. Don't ask someone, 'Do you enjoy working with numbers?' where they can answer yes or no and that's it. Instead you can ask them, 'What types of work do you find most enjoyable?' You get a longer response."

You're looking for someone who will work well with you. No matter how perfect you are, there lurks some impurity that makes you a special person. Whoever you hire will be obliged to deal with your lovable quirks. In the interests of equal time, I should note that prospective employees also have personalities and habits that could result in problems. It's fair to send away the person who always needs to be told what to do if you simply don't have time for that sort of supervision.

BOSS BASICS

Let's say that neither you nor your new colleague have any serious personality disorders. You'd really like this new situation to work at its very best. You might like to consider a number of helpful attitudes.

"Be really clear about what you expect to do," says author Grensing. "That's going to help both of you. Be clear about what they're going to be doing, what kind of quality you expect from them, and what's going to happen if they're not performing up to your expectations."

As a general rule, and in this period in particular, it helps to know what your company's mission and goals are. Share this vision with the people who work for you. If they understand your priorities and sense of purpose, it helps them help you in many ways. They have a better sense of what to say to clients with whom they talk. Instead of succumbing to rote, they will find it easier to prioritize when unexpected situations develop. They can bring more effectiveness to their work when they know how their responsibilities fit in.

Provide sufficient training and orientation. If nothing else, you have to train people for how you want things done. Take something as simple as answering the phone. Which do you prefer?

"Hello, G&L Widgit Works."

"Hello, this is Cheryl. How may I help you?"

"Hello, 5992."

"Hello, law office."

How do you want mail handled? When do you want paperwork processed? Are there certain hours when you do or don't want consultation offered to clients? Do you want people writing in pen or pencil? (Pen looks better; pencil is easier to correct.) Some of the issues may speak to the image you wish to present. Others may seem picayune, but they may reflect the way you are most comfortable.

In addition to office procedures, training deals with larger issues. How does your business work? What should you and your customers expect of each other? Then, of course, the employee might be taking on new responsibilities. The orientation period is nothing less than vocational training.

You may feel that you just don't have time to train anybody, and you may be right. Still, failure to adequately train your employees can lead to snafus and unscheduled wastes of your time at the worst possible moments. The amount of training time you can spare may affect the amount of experience a candidate must bring to the job.

Did you pick the right person, or is everything going bust? "I think," says Lin Grensing, "you can tell that it is working out a lot quicker than you can tell it isn't. You can get a feel right away for whether the person is doing things the way you like, is showing initiative, if there's a good rapport.

"Knowing it isn't working is a little harder because there's a learning curve you'll always be taking into consideration. If somebody has been working for you for a month and is still needing supervision, and is asking a lot of questions, and making a lot of mistakes, that would be a good signal that it wasn't a good idea."

How fair should you be, especially if you know you're difficult to work for? "As long as you've been up front," says Grensing, "as to what your expectations are, and this person isn't meeting them, I don't think it's unfair to tell them you don't need their services any longer."

It's my observation that people base their management of employees on their notions of how to be good parents. There's probably a ratio between the number of neurotic wage slaves and confused kids.

Respect the individuality of your employees. Respect their experience, knowledge, and personalities. Don't hesitate to give as much direction as the employees need. Let them know what you expect. Should they only come to you if they have a problem? Should they keep you posted every step of the way? Do they have any decision-making responsibility? If something you're supposed to do is part of the project, should they bug you about it? Should they wait to hear from you? What are the deadlines?

If your employee claims to have a better way to do something, you might actually learn from it. Even if the idea is all wrong, does it have some useful seed? If nothing else, thank them for the thought and tell them you're flattered by the interest they are bringing to the job. (It works better if you mean it.)

Lately business magazines have been reporting the startling news that employees respond to praise. A good boss doesn't hesitate to give strokes for a job well done, a thoughtful idea, or a loyal action. Allow employees to feel involved in the business. Be sensitive to their problems.

The above attributes aren't just noble; they also happen to be practical. When you respect people who work with you, they respect themselves, you, and the work they're doing. If you don't care about them, why should they care about you?

CATALOG

Working Hours (Power Up! Software, $99.95). Designed to schedule personnel, this computer program works well for anybody who has to send employees, contract laborers, or associates into the field on a regular basis. For example, those who operate house-cleaning agencies can determine (and double-check) whose house is being cleaned, on what day, during what hours, and by whom. The basic information you manipulate is weekly schedules, names, hours, shifts, tasks, or assignments. You can tinker with the schedule without erasing and rewriting. You can use last week's schedule as a model for next week's schedule, and again save some valuable chart construction time. The information you maintain about personnel can include name, address, phone number, birthdate, social security number, times not available, and appropriate personalized comments. There are six different formats. For example, you can look at a master schedule that shows what everybody is doing for a particular week, or you can look at an individual's schedule. Contact: Power Up! Software Corp., P.O. Box 7600, San Mateo CA 94403-7600; (800) 851-2917; in CA (800) 223-1479.

RESOURCES

A Small Business Guide to Employee Selection by Lin Grensing (Self-Counsel Press, 1986). Most of the work in knowing whom to hire is accomplished by knowing how to hire. Although not directed specifically at home-based businesses, this book can help you determine which stranger to take into your home. Information includes sample advertisements and application forms, interview questions, and role-playing exercises. Contact: Self-Counsel Press, 1704 North State St., Bellingham WA 98225; (206) 676-4530.

CHAPTER 13

Debt and Taxes

Somebody told me that she looked at the home office as "one of the last great tax shelters." I'm not comfortable with this view because it encourages the IRS to give us more scrutiny than we really deserve. Still, I want to present credible, useful tax information that will withstand the changes in code wrought by time. I decided to stress the thinking and methods that put you in the best possible position to deal with finances and taxes.

Consequently, I interviewed my accountant, Marvin Nyman, CPA, for some solid insights. I later learned that Marvin is a ringer. He has made a habit for some time of going on the radio and answering listeners' questions in a clear but authoritative manner. Here is the edited transcript of our conversations. "YHO" stands for *Your Home Office*, otherwise known as the interviewer.

A TRUE ACCOUNT

YHO: Why don't we begin with the notion that somebody is starting a home office. What should that person do?

NYMAN: From an accounting point of view, probably the best thing to do is open up a separate bank account for your business. You would deposit all of your receipts into it, and pay all of your bills from it. It really gives you an accounting of what your business is doing. There's no commingling it with the rest of your personal receipts and disbursements. Then, there's the tax audit possibility. If you were to be audited on your business, you would have a segregated account where you have things that are only business-related. Likewise the auditors wouldn't be looking at your personal documentation and drawing conclusions you don't want them to draw from what they are seeing.

YHO: If you're in a start-up position where you're putting money in rather than taking it out, does that confuse the issue?

NYMAN: No, because you also would set up a cash receipts ledger. You would show loans from yourself in that ledger. As you start to receive income from clients, that would be so stated. You would note the billing date, date received, maybe the invoice number, the amount received, and the client's name. So, there's no problem with transferring your own funds into your business account, as long as you account for them properly, from a bookkeeping point of view.

YHO: So, we've talked about setting up your account and your cash ledger.

NYMAN: Right! You really would have three ledgers. You would have a sales ledger. You would assign a number in the ledger to each invoice as it goes out. The register would also include customer name and invoice amount. When the money is collected and deposited in the bank, that payment would be entered in your cash receipt ledger. Your third ledger would be a cash disbursements ledger. This is going to be a numerical accounting of each check you're disbursing.

You're going to set that up with several columns. Of course, you're going to have check number, date disbursed, who it's paid out to, and the amount. Then, you're going to have additional columns for expense categories. The labeling for the other columns depends on your type of business. It could be merchandise purchases, office supplies, overhead expenses, possibly rent expenses.

You don't have to be real formal with the ledgers. You want to be able to have an accounting at any point in time. You want to have good records should you ever have a tax audit. You don't want to waste a lot of time and do overkill. Just do whatever works for you. Put the registers in a presentable form, so at the end of the period—whether that's the year, the quarter, or the month—you can make a presentation to your accountant and say, "This is what I did," without his having to go back and figure everything out.

YHO: Marvin, to say to somebody like me that, "you don't have to be too formal" could be dangerous. How unformal can we be? First of all, don't we have to keep three separate ledgers?

NYMAN: You should. I would say that a sales register is not absolutely required, but it does give you an idea of what your outstanding receivables are. Until the money is collected you have an entry in your register showing an outstanding receivable. If you're just starting up, and you only have a couple of invoices, and not too much is happening, that's fine. Still, I think it's a good idea to get into good bookkeeping habits before your business really grows.

YHO: In other words, the informality might be how frequently you make an entry. Do you make an entry as soon as the information comes in or every couple of days or . . .

NYMAN: Periodically. Don't drive yourself crazy. What's important is that as your business grows, you want to be able to rely on the record-keeping and not waste a lot of time having to redo things that could have been done simply to begin with. You want to sell. You want to market. You don't want to have to duplicate bookkeeping steps.

YHO: I assume a ledger is a ledger, but are any special features required or are there any brands you prefer?

NYMAN: I would not get a bound book. I would get accounting paper that has the two-hole punch at the top. You could remove sheets if they have to be photocopied or given to someone else. It's a lot easier than working with a bound book. When you start to take apart a bound book it's a hassle. If you rip a page out, the sheet connected to it on the other side of the binding gets loose. The other side of the coin is that with a bound book you can't lose a page unless you tear it out. Looseleaf books work also. You number the sheets and keep them in order.

YHO: What do you see clients forgetting to do as far as record-keeping is concerned?

NYMAN: The biggest problem comes from people who commingle their business and personal records. Also, some don't maintain a set of books as the year goes by. At the end of the year they have to remember what a check is for, or they haven't kept the receipted copy of a paid invoice.

Also, bear in mind that when you start a business you might be paying a lot of bills in cash because you can't get credit or you go to the store and buy six of this and one of that and four of this. It's important to hold onto bills for things that you pay for by cash. If any are above a certain amount—$10 or $20—then actually enter the item itself in the cash disbursement ledger. At the end of the year, you can have a record of all these petty cash items that otherwise can run away from you. It certainly would be a problem if a person got audited and had no documentation.

At a minimum they should put receipts paid in cash into an envelope during the year. At year's end, they should list the receipts out and categorize them. At least, they'll have them all in one place.

It's real easy to start losing parking receipts, toll receipts, and supply receipts. Before you know it, you can expect there to be a few hundred dollars you have no way to account for.

YHO: Would you recommend keeping records on the computer?

NYMAN: That's fine. There are very simple bookkeeping packages that can be used to do this. You can also set up your own on Lotus or some other spreadsheet program.

YHO: What about the person who already has started a business and set up the home office, but thinks now might be a good time to get financial records organized?

NYMAN: They should go through the personal checkbook, and segregate those checks drawn for the business. I would suggest that they list all cash receipts and disbursements that were business-related that were paid from their personal checkbook before a business account was opened. I would even recommend they photocopy these earlier business checks from the personal accounts. Hold onto these for at least three years and also have the actual check in the personal records.

YHO: Speaking of holding onto records, how long should one hold onto records?

NYMAN: An individual is subject to an IRS audit for the later of three years from the date of filing or the due date of the tax return. If you filed your 1989 taxes by April 15, 1990, the IRS can audit that return until April 15, 1993. If you took an extension, and filed by October 15, 1990, the IRS would have three years from that date.

YHO: Somehow this reminds me that I did do one smart thing. I designated a separate phone line for my business.

NYMAN: I agree. You certainly can prove that you have a dedicated line for your business. The IRS might question it as a business phone if you don't have it as a business listing. It depends on the examiner.

Let me also say there was a change in the tax law that went into effect in 1989. If, in your home office, you use your home phone for business, the IRS will no longer let you take a portion of the base charge as a business expense. You only can take specific toll calls as a business expense. Even if you can prove that 90 percent of the toll calls were for business, you can't take any of the base charges.

YHO: What about local calls over the base charges?

NYMAN: Only if you could prove those message units were for business. I don't see how you can do that. You can keep some sort of phone log, but that doesn't tell you very much about the message units.

YHO: Along those same lines are there any other things one should do?

NYMAN: To really legitimize the home office in the eyes of the IRS, the home office should have a separate business listing for that telephone line.

You see, the IRS examiner does an overview of your tax return, and then discusses the return with you or your representative. My experience is that examiners will scrutinize a lot more closely if they get a bad feeling initially about the return. It helps if you can lay things out for them and say, "Here's my business phone; here's my stationery; here's the listing in the phone book; here's the advertising I've done."

Right away the examiner is going to see this is a legitimate business. This is especially important if the business is showing a loss.

YHO: In addition to the second phone, are there trappings of a like nature?

NYMAN: For all home office expenses—rent, home depreciation, utilities, things of that nature—to be deductible, the tax law has a very definite requirement. The home office area must be used exclusively and continuously for business. There can't be anything of a personal nature, relative to nonbusiness in that area. It can't be your living room *and* your office.

YHO: Can it be a designated spot in your living room that only is your office?

NYMAN: The answer is no. The entire room must be used for business. Sometimes, people with smaller apartments fall into problems with this. I suggest they somehow break up a room—whether with work cabinets, a divider, or furniture. Break one room into two. I'm not saying it's all black and white. It certainly is gray and up to the examiner. If it sounds reasonable I think the auditor will go along with you.

Let's talk about the deductibility of home office rents and things like that. Number one, you cannot take home office expenses such as rent, utilities, or home depreciation to create a loss on a tax return. I'll give you an example. Let's say you have $5,000 of income, and you have $4,000 of direct expenses—supplies, advertising, phone bills, etc. And let's say the actual portion of your home office rent is $2,400. You now can deduct only $1,000 of this legitimate expense because you cannot create a loss by using home office rental expenses.

Let me also say that starting in 1988, the IRS made it a little more difficult to take home office losses. The IRS always likes to feel that you are running a hobby out of your home—not a business. The basic rule—and there certainly are some exceptions—is that you must show a profit in three out of five years. If you don't—if you have losses first year, second year, third year—the IRS can contend this is a hobby not entered into for profit, and therefore disallow any loss. This is certainly an important issue. It brings up again the importance of documenting, proving it really is a business with the possibility of showing a profit in the future.

YHO: What else do they look at in audits?

NYMAN: An area the IRS always looks at closely is expenses, such as automobile, transportation, and entertainment expenses. Relative to entertainment expenses, there are the five W's: who, what, when, where, and why.

The IRS wants to know who you entertained, what you discussed, when it happened, where it was, and why it was related to business. If you can't document these, you're very likely to get it disallowed. Some people who pay with a credit card, actually write on the back of the receipt who they went out with.

For entertainment expenses in excess of $25, some form of receipt is absolutely required, whether it's a credit card receipt or a restaurant receipt. Meals under $25 do not have to be documented by receipt, but rather by an entry in your diary as to what it is all about.

YHO: You used a word that you haven't used before—*diary.*

NYMAN: It is important to maintain a diary of business meetings, who you saw, entertainment expenses, travel costs, and things of that nature. It gives the IRS—if you're audited—a document they can rely on as documentation for deductions you're taking on your tax return.

YHO: What else should we keep in mind?

NYMAN: When you set up a home office, remember what you're now using for business that used to be personal. What is a desk or bookcase's value when you convert it to business use? Let's say you paid $500 for a desk two years ago. What would be its value now that you are using the desk for business? You can use the IRS depreciation guidelines. Under the current tax laws, office furniture would be depreciated over seven years.

YHO: Are these guidelines easy for the layperson to use?

NYMAN: Anyone reading the depreciation tables would be able to figure out the allowable deduction, or how much depreciation has been taken. Depreciation is calculated on IRS form 4562. Other valuable instruction booklets are available from the IRS. I guess the point is that if people are willing to read the publications, they really can educate themselves to running their businesses from a tax and accounting point of view.

YHO: Speaking of that personal desk that became part of the home office, when you set up do you pay yourself for it?

NYMAN: No. At the end of the year, you or your accountant would make a journal entry on your business books: "A desk for $500. I converted it to business. It's now worth $300." From a business point of view you can depreciate $300 worth of desk. There's no question that when you start your home office, you might have a lot of furniture, fixtures, equipment, possibly a computer, and things like that, that will now become business items.

YHO: What about Social Security?

NYMAN: As a self-employed person, you're subject to self-employment taxes which, in 1988, are at the rate of 13.02 percent. You would file a schedule C with your tax return. You would pay self-employment, Social Security taxes on the net—not gross—income of your schedule C. In other words, if you collected $50,000, and had $35,000 of expenses, you would pay self-employment and Social Security on $15,000, by completing form 1040 SE.

Let's say last year you were an employee and were paid on a W-2. Of course, you would have the withholding taken out for you. All of a sudden you became self-employed, and now no one's taking out your withholding. You should always check with your accountant as to whether or not you should start paying in estimated taxes to avoid any penalty due to the IRS when you file your end of the year tax return.

YHO: You mean there are some situations where you should and some where you shouldn't?

NYMAN: That's right. Let's say that last year you were employed and your total tax liability was $5,000. (Tax liability is not the amount you pay with your return, after figuring in your withholding. It's the total figure due that's based on your income—your total income tax expense for the year.) On January 1, you became self-employed. No one's withholding taxes for you. Let's say that your income as a self-employed is much, much more this year than it was on last year's W-2. During the course of the year, you should pay in $5,000 on your estimated taxes. (You base this year's estimated payment on last year's real expense.) Even if on the following April 15, you owe a million dollars in taxes, the IRS cannot penalize you for not paying enough estimated taxes. You paid in an amount equal to what your prior year tax liability was.

YHO: So, check with your accountant on the estimated taxes, but be prepared to pay something.

NYMAN: Correct! Don't think all that collected money is yours free and clear. I would suggest that people who start self-employment actually call their accountants and ask, "What percentage of my self-employment income should I put into a savings account to either pay estimated taxes during the year or pay the following April 15, so that when I owe the tax man the money isn't gone?"

RECORD SPINNING

The record-keeping-impaired may be interested in knowing about so-called pegboard or one-write systems. Instead of rewriting the same information in various places (e.g., check, checkbook stub, ledger, invoice, return envelope), you simply write out the check. The format uses carbon bands and/or NCR paper plus the careful arrangement of all the entry destinations. The information written on the check once is simultaneously entered in all the other right spots.

The one-write advocates point to the system's time-saving value. They also feel it eliminates the kind of error that can occur when information is copied from one place to another. There's an additional benefit for many. Manufacturers and distributors use vertical marketing. In addition to the all-purpose versions, one-write systems are designed for specific professions and industries. Essentially manufacturers of this product really are in the publishing business. They manufacture forms, binders, and, of course, customized checks and envelopes. They either sell direct to consumers or through distributors (very often office supply stores). If you have trouble locating a one-write source, contact the National One-Write Systems Association, P.O. Box 8187, Silver Spring, MD 20907-8187; (301) 589-8125.

Ira Mayer of Entertainment Promotion Marketing recently handed over his financial record-keeping to his computer. He is very pleased, particularly at the way raw information instantly can be used to provide very specific status information.

"I always wanted more information than my hand bookkeeping was going to give me," says Mayer. "I wanted things broken down differently. I wanted to know exactly how much of our postage was going toward the newsletter and how much was going toward special reports and how much was going toward conferences and seminars, etc. There was no practical way of doing that by hand. Using the computer gave me something that already is going to be programmed and is going to give my accountant the numbers he needs at the end of the year, so that I don't have to go back and reformat everything.

"The downside to it is that I had to learn how to use an accounting program and I screwed that up three times. In the long run, spending the extra three days that it took to rekey everything is okay. The information is in a uniform system that's readable. It gives me profit and loss information on every project we do, so that I know what to continue and what to discontinue. It's forcing me to treat it in a businesslike manner. Before I was going too much by the gut."

TAX AND TELECOMMUTING

There are no tax side effects to telecommuting. For example, you cannot deduct rent for the space you use. More important, do not fall into the "clever" trap. It may be tempting to make a deal with your employer to pretend you are an independent contractor. The company reduces your compensation package salary plus benefits, but you get more take-home because there are no deductions.

Forget it. "The IRS has been very careful to say," says Gil Gordon, "that the determination of status is not based on what the two parties say, or what they write on a piece of paper, but how the facts appear to an independent outsider.

"The examples I always give of independent contractors are plumbers," continues Gordon. "They work for a lot of people. They have their own tools. They set their own rates. They follow their own methods, and they're not supervised. Contrast this with a data entry clerk, a programmer, whatever—people who are employees no matter what you call them.

"Believe me, in this age of a high deficit, the IRS will classify the person as an employee when there is the least bit of doubt."

FLOW GENTLY

Remember this old joke?

"Business is just great. We're buying the blouse for $5 and we're selling it for $4."

"How can you make any money?"

"Simple. We're selling thousands of them."

Cash flow is the balance between income and outgo. Life gets a bit messy when cash flows out at a faster rate and volume than it flows in. Angelo Valenti, the small business coach, says that failure to understand cash flow can do you in. That departing dough has to come from somewhere. It's unfortunate to use savings just to stay in place when those savings were intended for growth. The interest expense that comes from borrowing worsens the cash flow pressure. You have to corral more income just to be static. Cash flow starts with having clients.

"A good idea," says Valenti, "lots of energy, a good attitude, money in the bank is all wonderful, but that doesn't give you a business. Having clients gives you a business."

To improve your cash flow picture, according to Valenti, there are some very definite questions you must ask yourself. And you must act on the answers. "Have I billed someone who owes me money? Can I collect it? Have I contracted with anybody for something that I could produce, so that I can bill them for it and collect? What needs to be produced this week so that I can bill on it?

"Suppose there are a number of things I can do but only one of them will turn into a check this week? That one is a priority. Let me make sure that gets done.

"The next thing I need to do to generate cash flow is to sell. Is there anybody I can close with? That's the first thing I look at. Who has proposals? Who have I talked to that I can close with and get a contract, a purchase order form? If nobody, are there any proposals or bids or estimates that need to go out? If not, are there any appointments I can set up? If not, how am I going to generate a lead? All of those things will impact my cash flow."

Having the invoices floating out there in the ether isn't enough. You've got to get the payments. Letting your customers pay with a charge card is one way to do an end run around the whole billing process. Those slips you deposit are treated as cash. Payment for the service is painless. You are charged a fee per transaction. In many cases, that's a sliding fee. You pay a percentage of the sale. The greater the purchase, the lower the percentage. The only hitch is that banks tend to hate the idea of allowing home-based businesses to set up *merchant accounts* (the official term for the arrangement whereby you get paid by plastic). Credit card processors are the only other possible grantors of merchant accounts. They are companies that act as intermediaries between banks and individual businesses. However, these organizations require linkage with banks, and therefore have great respect for bank policies.

"Over the last eighteen months," said credit card processor Irv Breschner late in 1989, "99.9 percent of the banks have gotten out of merchant banking unless the customer has a good account or is doing retail. There's virtually no place for the home-based business to go."

Home officers tend to think that this callous disregard for our economic betterment is blatant prejudice against the credibility of our businesses. To some extent, this may be true. There's a different kind of ignorance, based on a very real problem, according to Tim Litle of the New Hampshire–based credit card processor, Litle & Co. Litle feels that home-based businesspeople who understand the problems may have a better chance of successfully communicating with the banks.

"The merchant account grantor," explains Litle, "essentially is granting credit. That's the whole issue. The bank doesn't know exactly what amount of credit it is granting. It doesn't know the amount of liability it may be taking on."

The bank opens itself up to holding a very large bag. The opportunities for abuse can make grown bankers quiver. Even the shakiest of retail stores seems less perilous. The retailer can examine the credit card. Then the customer gets the merchandise and the retailer gets the payment.

It's different with mail and phone orders, the nearly universal intended use of a home office merchant account. "When a transaction occurs where the card isn't present," says Litle, "you have no way of looking at the signature, or the embossing on the card. You have no way of knowing if all that [credit card information you're given] is true.

"If the transaction isn't good because the cardholders say they never bought it, the rules are such that the customer won't pay the credit card bill and the bank will charge back to the merchant. Typically, the merchant continues to make deposits and the chargeback is offset against the deposits. But if the merchant goes out of business and can't pay, the bank has to pay and therefore there is a risk for losing money."

In addition, there are the businesses that know how to accept and deposit payments. They're just a bit shaky when it comes to sending out the goods to the customer. More than a breach of etiquette, it is a violation. Whether the merchants are hopelessly overburdened, or waiting for shipments from their suppliers, or just flat out venal it matters not. Chargebacks come charging in, and there's the bank with that bag, again.

"Small companies sometimes submit phony transactions," says Litle. "The bank doesn't understand there's a problem for several weeks.

Meanwhile, the company disappears. The bank will be paying for four months and up to six months.

"What a banker does understand is that a friend lost a job because he granted merchant status and all of a sudden got clobbered with a career-damaging big loss. Banks know how to make loans of $10,000, but are uncomfortable with granting credit when they don't know the extent of liability," Litle emphasizes.

Still, Litle feels that if you want a merchant account, you should knock on your local bank's door, especially if you have an account with the bank. The institution already will have some sense of your history and integrity. Don't chide the banker for not wanting to deal with people who work out of their homes. Instead, demonstrate that you've thought about the bank's concern with unspecified credit.

"Say," advises Tim Litle, " 'I understand what the bank's problem is, and here's how I hope to solve it.' " Litle suggests offering to keep a specified amount of money in an account strictly as a reserve against chargeback problems. The concept is not unlike a security deposit for a leased apartment.

"Tell them," continues Litle, " 'I don't know how much the deposit should be, but let's talk about it. I want you to feel comfortable.' " This approach should reduce the feeling of risk, and therefore might work. Very often credit card processors ask clients to post money in reserve.

DIAL A DEADBEAT

While waiting for your merchant account to come through, don't stop collecting on your unpaid invoices. George Walther of TelExcel feels the telephone, when properly used, helps nudge a client from being a problem to being a payer. "The most important point," says Walther, "is that the process of collections is a game. It consists of four quarters. The first is notification. That's when you let the people know they owe you money. It may be that you've mailed them an invoice.

"The second quarter is the reminder. That's when you send them a statement that says, 'Hey, we still haven't gotten your payment on the invoice. You still owe it to us. Please send it.' "

Walther says the third quarter is negotiation. You want the client to work out some kind of payment plan. Your voyage has taken you practically to the edge of the world. All that's left is compulsion, the fourth quarter.

"Compulsion is rarely effective," says Walther. "It may be effective in collecting money. But it's never effective in what we really want to do in business, which is foster a long-term positive relationship. The key to collection is playing the game faster. Get paid at step one instead of letting anything drag on to step two or step three.

"When you talk about somebody owing you money, you can visualize them as being in their home with a stack of bills and a paycheck. The stack of bills is bigger than the paycheck. Some people are going to get paid and some are not. Your objective is to be one of the people who gets paid. How do you do that?

"We know that if you have any leverage, you have an advantage. If you're the power company, you're going to turn off their lights if they don't pay the bill. Lacking that kind of advantage, personal contact gives you the biggest leverage."

By talking to them on the phone, you become real. They cannot avoid your palpable existence. They may still try to lie, as in "the check is in the mail."

"The key on the telephone," says Walther, "is to have an immediate reasoned response for a delaying situation that comes up. If they say 'the check is in the mail,' you never should respond by saying 'well gee that's nice.' You always respond with a question that's designed to give you more information, such as, 'You mailed the check? I'm glad to hear that. I'll be glad to hold on. Would you please get your checkbook. That way I can write the check number and the date here in my records. I won't have to bug you about it later if it should become lost in the mail. It would be easier to trace.'

"In other words, if you haven't really mailed the check I'm going to find out right now. If you have and you tell me the check number, fine. I know it's in the mail. Augment faceless mail contact with real direct personal contact by making voice contact."

CATALOG

Peachtree Complete III (Peachtree Software, $199). This program combines ease of use with heavy-duty accounting capability at a peach of a price. Everything is accomplished with windows and pop-up menus. Even if you're in the middle of making an entry or completing a form, you easily can double-check the information stored elsewhere in the program. As you might expect, it has modules for General Ledger, which accepts up to 35,000 transactions per month and provides sophisticated reporting; Accounts Receivable, which keeps track of up to 14,000 customers and 44,000 transactions per month; Invoicing, which produces up to 5,500 invoices, numbers automatically, allows inclusion of long narrative fields on the invoice, and produces reports of back-ordered items; Accounts Payable, which handles over 14,000 vendors, but only allows 20,000 transactions per month, as well as partial payment of invoices, forecasts of cash requirements by specified dates, and printing of checks. Other modules are Inventory, Purchase Order, Job Cost, Payroll, and Fixed Assets. The Payroll module, which can process up to 3,900 employees, probably provides a lot more service than most home officers really need. However, it does have built-in current tax tables, does withholding calculations automatically, and can be treated as a bonus module.

Peachtree Complete III would be of particular interest to mail-order merchants, independent contractors such as plumbers who customarily use and charge for materials, and enterprising sorts who actively operate two or more companies. It probably is of less use to the lone consultant whose record-keeping needs are more modest. Contact: Peachtree Software (800) 247-3224.

One-Write Plus (Great American Software, $299). A *Home Office Computing* reviewer called it "the only accounting program I reviewed that someone with no accounting background can easily use." By entering the information you would enter on a onc-write system check, you provide all that is needed to make the program work. The computer aspect is where the "Plus" in the title comes from. Among the many blessings bestowed by "One-Write Plus" are cash disbursements, cash receipts, and general journals; trial balance; general ledger; balance sheet; choice of three invoice formats (services, professional and inventory); calculation and application of discounts and finance charges; allowance of flexible aging and payment terms; information storage about customers and vendors (up to 2,000 each); and automatic recording of recurring monthly invoices.

The program creates all kinds of status reports. If you'd like, you can actually use it to write out checks. Unless you do a whole bunch at one time, or you have a printer that's dedicated to forms, it's probably an option worth ignoring. Frequent changing of paper in a printer can be a pain in the platen. It would be easier to use "One-Write Plus" as a two-write system (manual cutting of checks and computer entry). Do be assured that you can get continuous-form checks and other customized stationery (e.g., invoices, window envelopes) to use with "One-Write Plus." Contact: Great American Software, 9 Columbia Dr., P.O. Box 910, Amherst NH 03031-0910; (800)528-5015; in NH (603) 889-5400.

Service Industry Accounting (Brown-Wagh Publishing, $395). Targeted at professionals, manufacturers, and tradespeople, "Service Industry Accounting'' has the standard components that you would expect in an accounting program. These include general ledger, invoicing, accounts receivable, and accounts payable. They make possible intricately detailed reports. ''Job Card'' and ''Inventory'' features make this program particularly special. The job card stores information about the costs (material, labor, other purchases) attributed to each individual job. It also helps with estimates. Believe it or not, the inventory feature keeps track of your inventory. This section can be updated by entries elsewhere in the program. Contact: Brown-Wagh Publishing, 16795 Lark Ave., Suite 210, Los Gatos CA 95030; (800) 451-0900; in CA (408) 395-3838.

RESOURCES

PUBLICATIONS/VIDEOS

IRS Publications (Internal Revenue Service, free). The IRS offers a collection of printed materials that address specific questions and concerns, including number 463, ''Travel, Entertainment, and Gift Expenses''; number 917, ''Business Use of a Car''; number 534, ''Depreciation''; number 535, ''Business Expenses''; number 587, ''Business Use of Your Home''; and number 583, ''Information for Business Taxpayers.'' Contact: Internal Revenue Service. Check the local white pages for phone number, or a local library for forms and publications.

ORGANIZATIONS/SERVICES

Credit Card Processor Maybe (Litle & Co., fee varies). This New England–based firm handles 20 million credit card processing transactions a year. Although its roster includes some of America's largest mail-order catalog houses, Litle & Co. will take on some small, new businesses that they believe have potential for growth. They do not take all that apply. Tim Litle regrets that he cannot provide the kind of extensive hand-holding that a small company may want. Contact: Litle & Co., 54 Stiles Rd., Salem NH 03079; (603) 893-9333.

Another Credit Card Processor, Maybe (Targeted Marketing, Inc.). At the time of this writing, a respected direct marketing figure has been trying to construct a credit card processing service specifically for new, home-based mail-order businesses. He does not know what the future holds for this enterprise. He said you can contact him to learn how he makes out. Contact: Irv Brechner, P.O. Box 5125, Ridgewood NJ 07451; (201) 445-7196.

Marvin the Accountant (Gaber & Nyman). This reliable accounting firm practices in the New York area (since 1967). As indicated earlier in the chapter, Marvin Nyman is my accountant. He's a general practitioner specializing in small- and medium-sized businesses and individual tax preparation and planning. In my opinion, he gives good, prudent advice and has many clients who work at home. Contact Gaber & Nyman, 715 Rte. 304, Bardonia NY 10954.

CHAPTER 14

The Marketing Department

"Most people don't realize they're running two companies," says Angelo Valenti. "An interior designer runs an interior design company and a marketing company. A computer consultant runs a computer company and a marketing company."

Basically, Valenti is right. An approach to marketing should be integrated into what you do. It's a special way of thinking about your *business,* as opposed to your profession or occupation or product or service. You may be one of the fortunate ones who genuinely does not have to market. You may be such a major force in your field that it would be wasteful to allocate time, effort, and resources for marketing. I'm not being facetious. Some people operate in very specialized universes and are known by everyone who has to know them. Their clientele comes exclusively through referral.

Marketing is for people who want change or are affected by change. Who does that exclude? Change can be growth or shrinkage. It can be fueled by a drive toward more markets, better markets, and other markets, or a loss of good markets. To manage change in the marketplace, one has to understand marketing—whatever that is.

Trying to grasp marketing isn't easy. Casual bystanders confuse it with advertising, public relations, and/or sales.

At its simplest, marketing really starts out as a point of view, a filter through which you look at your world. You see targeted customers as well as what they want and relate to. Marketing decisions happen when you act on this vision.

For example, you may decide to raise your prices. It's a financial move so you ask yourself questions about your costs, skills, and plain old opportunity. It's also a marketing decision, because your market (including potential customers) will react. Now you ask yourself questions about what customers you might lose and keep based on various increases. You also might ask what clients you'll attract because of increased services that the new pricing makes possible. You also want to think about what your competition is doing. Are they raising their prices? Do they offer what you offer? Although all the answers affect the price, these questions are not based on the product. They are based on the market.

Let's look through the marketing filter and get a clearer glimpse of how it touches the various aspects of our business. Pretend we've come up with a recipe for a great grape jelly. Our grape jelly business tasks are straightforward. Manufacturing: Cook up a mess of grape jelly. Packaging: Pour the grape jelly into jars. Finance: Set a price. Sales: Get stores to stock our grape jelly. Distribution: Find the most effective way to get the grape jelly from our basement to store shelves.

Now we add marketing to the formula. The crucial step is deciding who our market is. Who's the most likely person to buy or use our grape jelly? Alternately we can ask to whom we would like to sell our grape jelly. Our actual customers may not be the people with whom we would like to curry favor. Not only do we ask these questions but we come up with answers.

When we cook the grape jelly, we might adjust the taste so that it appeals more to those people whom we have designated as our market. That deliberate fine-tuning of the flavor is a marketing decision. Cramming grape jelly into a jar and pasting a label that says, "yep, there's grape jelly in this jar" is packaging. We get into marketing when we decide the shape of the jar. Is it a reusable tumbler? Does it have an elegant design? And what about the label? Are balloon-bearing colorful clowns cavorting across the label? Chances are that it's destined for a household with children. Is there friendly information about natural ingredients and low-key words that tell the story of this grape jelly? The probable intended market is the thirtysomething crowd.

As noted above, we also can look at price. Sure, we consider all our direct and indirect costs. We come up with a markup that gives us a rewarding profit. Now we must consider our market. Does the price we want to charge seem right to them? Is it priced too high or too low? Are we selling grape jelly for the kiddies at a gourmet price? Are we selling gourmet grape jelly for such a low price that our market shuns it? Suppose our pricing is out of synch with our market, and we can't jiggle our pricing anymore. We might want to rethink who our market should be. We also can search for ways to present our grape jelly so that the price does make sense.

The sense of who is the market drives the marketing component of sales. What kind of stores are the best to carry our grape jellies? Supermarkets? If so, which supermarkets: upscale or mass market? Gourmet shops? Delicatessens? Health food stores? Ethnic stores? What would make the store owners feel it's a good idea to sell our grape jelly? Special displays and posters to set up in the stores? Free samples to customers? Free trips to store managers who sell the most grape jelly?

Another marketing aspect of sales involves encouraging people in our likely market to march into the stores and buy cases of our grape jelly. How about coupons? Recipe booklets? Sendaway offers? Quality? Publicity in food magazines, young-mother magazines, and health magazines? Even distribution has a marketing aspect. We know our market, and we know which stores serve that market. What kind of distribution network helps us reach those stores?

The same thinking works if you're a craftsperson, computer consultant, plumber, graphic designer, etc. Each of us has a market, a pool of current and potential customers. We simply should be alert to how our clients react to what we do in our businesses.

Marketing then is the trek that begins with your idea for a product or service and ends with the creation of customers—people who push their money into your hands. A marketing plan is a map of that journey. The map helps you get there sooner, safer, and more comfortably. You can draw that map on parchment, scribble it on the back of an envelope, or keep it in your head.

Successful marketing starts with a gigantic insight. Regardless of what inspires your business decisions, you must know that each move carries a marketing implication.

These marketing components should be reviewed. You can chuck them into the fire if you'd like, but look at them first. Know they are there and know what they are. Otherwise, you might get mugged by your own shadow.

The answers to five big questions construct a marketing plan:

1. Who is your market?
2. What does your market want?
3. Where does your product fit in the marketplace?
4. How do you want your market to perceive your product?
5. How do you reach your market?

WHO IS YOUR MARKET?

What do those who can, do, or should buy your product have in common? If you're a plumber your pool of customers is made up of people with indoor plumbing. That's just a start. Perhaps you specialize in landmark rowhouses, or high-rise commercial skyscrapers. Your market might be defined by the neighborhood in which you live. Each of those markets suggests a specific knowledge, experience, sensitivity, inventory, and, to some extent, business practice. Each requires its own marketing plan. It's kind of crucial to identify the market that's right for you. It reminds me of the time I met the world's most accomplished Armenian poet. His stature mattered little to people who could not understand his language. Sending your message to the market that's wrong for you is like speaking your poetry to ears that cannot understand.

When Tony Stewart first marketed his "Home Office" computer program, he picked the wrong professions to market to. He did it for the best of reasons. Stewart originally developed the program out of his desire to run his filmmaking business better. He shared his first efforts with friends and friends of friends. Not surprisingly, they too were in the film community. Most testers loved the program. When Stewart officially launched his new business, he knew that filmmakers had praise for the software.

"I went to film publications," says Stewart, "and I had a list of some members of a filmmakers union." It was all very logical, and he spent sorely needed dollars on professional journal ads, mailing lists, and direct mail advertising. He obtained negligible results. It only occurred to Tony Stewart later that the average film craftsperson turned out to be less likely to have a computer than someone in another profession. It's hard to convince computerless people that they really should buy a piece of computer software.

Stewart then realized that, at the very least, his market was made up of people who owned computers. He began to direct his efforts at computer owners, and found much more satisfying results.

When I was a magazine editor, my colleagues and I would leaf through every new magazine that swaggered onto the newsstands. We'd make note of the graphics, features, columns, and general editorial thrust, and ask the same question: "Who's going to buy this magazine?" Unbeknownst to us, those on the business side of publishing would flip through the very same pages, and give the very same scrutiny and ask an entirely different question: "Who's going to advertise in this magazine?" Both business and editorial people were asking, "Who is the market?" Of course, each was thinking of a different marketplace.

At first glance, it would seem that a market can be defined rigorously by the product. The parents of infants constitute the market for disposable diapers. Case closed. But you can find clear distinctions. Some diapers get carted home in Chevys and some in Volvos. Marketing takes advantage of this distinction.

We could define our market by citing one or two traits or we could apply the layered look. Use the answers to any or all of a group of questions.

- Are you a business-to-consumer marketer or a business-to-business marketer? (You can be both, but each might require different approaches.)
- What special interests does your market have?
- What are their occupations?
- What gender, if any, is more likely to use what you're selling?
- What is the average age of your most likely customer?
- What is the average level of education attained by your market?
- What percentage of your market is married, single, divorced?
- Where can they be found? Are they mostly urban or rural? Are they concentrated in particular localities, states, or regions?
- What are their zip codes?
- Do they live in private homes or apartments? Do they own or rent?
- What other purchases do they make?
- How much money a year do they spend on recreation?
- Do they own a car?
- Do they travel?
- Do they use credit cards?
- How much money a year do they spend on your industry?
- What are their values?
- If you are selling to other businesses, what businesses are you selling to?
- If you are selling to many kinds of businesses, who or what title in those businesses has the authority and responsibility to buy from you?
- Is the person who makes the purchase the same person who uses your product or service?

The right answers add up to who are the best customers for what you do. It has to be the given from which you proceed. Otherwise, "ideal" criteria such as who has or spends the most money or who has the most time are irrelevant. Venture capitalists tend to have more money than eleven-year-old boys. But if the product is bubble gum, then big deal; or rather no deal.

It's possible to use common sense and gut instinct to analyze the market. If you start a catering business, you know your customers will at some point in their lives feel a need to provide food for a bunch of people, and will not want to cook or serve at that event. You know that your customers will be adults. You may not know their average incomes or education, but you know they would not even talk with you unless they were willing to pay for the equivalent of taking twenty, fifty, or a hundred people out to eat. On the other hand, knowledge of the market's income and education may tell you something about what kind of menus to offer. If you're planning to do a lot of weddings and bar mitzvahs, then the locality you are marketing to had better not be a retirement community.

How targeted can marketing get? Media maven Tony Schwartz was hired by a group of retailers. Their desire to keep their stores open on Sunday was opposed by New York State's then-powerful legislative leader Stanley Steingut. Schwartz devised an advertising campaign aimed at a market of one—Steingut. The media man ran a radio advertisement on a station in Albany, New York's state capital and therefore Steingut's home while the legislature was in session.

In a crucial part of the ad, the announcer said, "You know what Stanley says? He says we can't buy a sofa on Sunday. Stanley says it's all right if we want to buy a sailboat. But the crib and the baby carriage? Out! Can't buy it. . . . You don't know who Stanley is? Stanley Steingut, the New York State Assembly Speaker. He's backing a law that will close the department stores and supermarkets on Sundays. You want to call Stanley? I'll give you his number: (518) 472-3100. If Stanley knows how you feel about it, maybe he'll change his mind."

Apparently, Steingut thought the commercials were running far and wide, and definitely too close to home. As political columnist Ken Auletta put it, "Steingut changed his vote and telephone number." According to Schwartz, the cost of radio time for the ads was $200.

Schwartz literally knew who his market was. The rest of us can turn to marketing research, a broad discipline used to find everything there is to know about a particular market. Marketing research can be expensive. It requires the gathering and analysis of information about a group of people (often in the millions) that constitute a market for a particular product. It often includes testing of the product. (Let's take it to Columbus, Ohio, and see how people react to our marketing tactics. Let's see what they think of the product. Let's see if we would be smarter to change any part of it, including the package.) General Foods has to spend millions on marketing research, but we probably don't. To learn more about who your market is, use one or more of the following inexpensive tactics:

- Study your customers to see what they have in common.
- Ask your customers questions.
- Provide a questionnaire for your customers to fill out and explain that the answers will help you serve them better. Electronics manufacturers add their marketing questions to their warranty registration cards.
- Share information with peers and vendors. They may confirm something you've suspected, or point out something you have not seen.
- Talk to retailers who might serve the same market you do. For example, if you run a word processing business, you might learn more about your market when you talk to the owner of a quick photocopy shop.
- Read publications that serve your profession or industry. The editors usually have a good seat from which they can see a lot of the action, and they always are alert to trends. They often print stories about research findings. Release of this info tends to be self-serving to the major corporation that commissioned the research. But the information still can help you.
- Carefully read newspapers and other publications for news that relates to your market. A story about something else may contain a nugget of information for you. A newspaper article about how young couples stay in rather than step out may interest a creator of board games or gourmet microwave popcorn or a furniture designer. It's not only what the article says but what implications it has for you that's important.
- Order a copy of an existing demographic study.
- Use your computer to ferret out information from data bases. The information would range from articles that help you define your market to census data.
- Contact appropriate U.S. government agencies for specific information that they may have gathered.
- Contact appropriate trade associations.

Even when you develop eminently usable, pinpoint information, there's always room for more fine-tuning. Bull & Bear has added a clever twist to its mailings. Their prime product, a silver coin with a bear on one side and a bull on the other, is a perfect gift for a corporation to present to valued customers. Based on experience and research, Bull & Bear has a good handle on who in the company generally is charged with buying gifts or premiums. Still, affixed to each direct mail enclosure is a custom-printed Post-it. The message reads, "If you can't use this unique offer, please route to Christmas file, corporate gift buyer, promotions director, or marketing manager."

"We found," says Bob Beaudoin, "that when we started using that device, we got a much better response. People apparently did pass it on to an appropriate party."

Beaudoin says that this sticky enhancement was "surprisingly cheap." An order of 100 pads, each containing 100 sheets, costs them $150, which comes to .015 per sheet.

WHAT DOES YOUR MARKET WANT?

Once upon a time Henry Ford could offer a car in any color, as long as it was black, which well preceded such elements of consumer choice as global competition and rich Corinthian leather. Knowing who your market is, is not the same as knowing your market. It helps to know what the people want.

Sometimes your market wants what you have, even when you don't realize you have it. Ira Mayer and Riva Bennett's business *Entertainment Promotion Marketing* (EPM) exemplifies this very well. EPM, an excellent newsletter, covers the very specialized and significant niche of marketing in the entertainment industry and with the entertainment industry. The newsletter started reporting great information about 900 numbers. It was a good wake-up call to the subscribers. Mayer and Bennett discovered that their readers appreciated this information and wanted more, but also wanted it to be presented in a more direct, concentrated manner.

"We got so many calls inviting me to lunch to pick my brains," Ira Mayer says. "I went to the first one, and then I realized that I just can't do this. I don't have the time. We asked how do we formalize this and give people information they need and also help them to meet people they need to meet.

"We came up with the idea of doing a half-day seminar. We did all the promotion material in-house. We promoted it exclusively through our own newsletter and we had about four thousand names that we had collected. We got some coverage in various magazines like *Billboard* and *Hollywood Reporter*. We thought we would get about thirty or forty people, and had arranged to have it in a particular hotel. We felt that if by some miracle we had more than that, the hotel would have more space for us. It turned out we had close to a hundred people. They didn't have space so we moved it to the Hilton, which at the last minute did have space.''

Because Riva Bennett and Ira Mayer listened to what their market said it wanted, EPM added a series of beneficial seminars. Ken Skier also listened.

Skier, a highly respected creator of word processing programs, started his own software publishing program a couple of years ago. His first product was an ingenious piece of software that enlarges the cursor on laptop screens. Satisfied customers who were visually impaired told him they now could see the cursor, but they still had great difficulty discerning characters on the screen. They asked if he knew of any word processing program that would help them. To Skier's own surprise, he could not locate any program that made the characters bigger. He drew upon the expertise afforded by his laptop program and his word processing eminence. He developed ''Eye Relief'' to do just that. Because he listened to what his customers wanted, he was able to add a valued product.

In creating a portrait of what your market wants, there are so many contributing factors to choose from:

- What can they use the product for?
- How does it help them?
- Will it help them in the future?
- When do they use it?
- Is size important?
- What design features matter?
- How important is ease of use?
- What prices make sense?
- What kind of service do you provide?
- How easy is it for customers to order and buy from you?
- What credit arrangements, if any, do you extend?
- How does your product help fulfill the customer's self-image?
- How knowledgeable are you about your product and your customer's needs?
- What important features or attributes does your customer associate with the product?

Market research uncovers the whole logical decision-making apparatus, as well as all the seething, circuitous, sub-rosa reasons that control a choice for or against. You get an array of buttons to push. The market measures your product against everything your customers feel about themselves and the world, and everything they want. Do they want their technology cutting edge, state of the art, or so easy even a child can operate it? Do they want lots of handholding service for which they'll pay, or do they want deep discounts and here's-your-hat-what's-your-hurry service?

At its crudest level, knowing what people want enables us to tell them what they want to hear. My soap makes you feel clean and fresh. It isn't good coffee unless it has a deep, rich aroma.

Knowing more about what people want and why can provide complex and enduring rewards. You can learn the questions they have about your product. You can learn what they look for in a vendor. You can learn new uses or more significant uses for your product. You learn what features are more important to the market.

For example, all the comparisons between VHS and Beta home video systems clearly revealed the technical superiority of Beta. VHS won the hearts, minds, and remote control fingers of the public because time was on its side. Specifically, the home video market wanted more hours of recording time on a videotape. VHS consistently delivered that and Beta didn't.

You also get clues about the kind of image your market feels your company has or should have. "One of the things that caught people's attention from the very beginning," says computer consultant John McMullen, "was the high-quality engraved ivory stationery we used. It was just a minor thing to do, but people would notice our plush stationery and say, 'You're doing well.'"

A business journalist who also sells his services to corporations told me about an annual report he had written. The corporation solicited proposals for this job from three writers. My friend later learned that he got the job because his bid stated a higher fee than the other two. The company, equating cost with quality, did not want to take any chances.

How do you learn what the market wants? Observe how people make use of your product. A landscape architect who specializes in playgrounds told me of a rude experience he had some years before. He noticed that kids had more fun in a playground when it was in mid-construction than when it was completed. He delved more deeply into the psychology of play. Incorporating what he learned, he made radical changes in his approach to playground design. He enjoyed the sight of kids playing happily in his new (quite completed) playgrounds.

WHERE DOES YOUR PRODUCT
FIT IN THE MARKETPLACE?

Now you know who your market is, and what your market wants. How will you do?

Positioning is the mantra we invoke here. Positioning is to marketing as location is to retailing. A fine editor I worked with for some months loved to repeat something he once saw in *Mad* magazine. A sign in one pizzeria's window said, "Best pizza in the world." Near it was another pizzeria. Its sign said, "Best pizza in the country." A few doors down was still another pizza shop with a sign, "Best pizza in the city." The busiest pizzeria of the bunch was right next door. Its sign? "Best pizza on the block."

Position, also known as niche, is the location your product occupies in the market's mind. What's special about what you do. Are you the best, the cheapest, the easiest to use, the closest, the first, the latest, the only? Do you have special features that make you attractive to a particular class of users? Are you service-oriented? Do you have a fresh outlook? Do you have years of specialized experience?

A stroll through the Hammacher-Schlemmer catalog will reveal product after product that either is "the best," "the first," or "the only." Each of these labels is seen as a virtue. Not only do we see a positioning of the products but we see Hammacher-Schlemmer championing itself as a purveyor of the best, the first, and the only.

To discover or at least verify a position, let's get what you do on the runway and ask the following questions. Try to answer them from your market's point of view, not your own.

- Who or what are your competitors?
- Do their product(s) cost more, the same, or less than yours?
- What technical advantages do you offer?
- What practical advantages do you offer?
- What other features might make your product or service desirable?
- What features solve the user's problems?
- How accessible are you?
- Is anything unique about any of these features?
- Does your market want or care about these features?
- Does your packaging attract or repel?
- Is your product or service easy or cumbersome to use?
- Can you associate your product with some larger trend or fad?
- What background or special assets does your company have that are important to the market?

What answers do you come up with? You may be enjoying a festival of special features. That's fine. But for the sake of positioning, and all the little people who depend on you and made this moment possible, you must distill all these strengths into one positive, coherent, memorable posture. That's the niche you occupy.

Suppose you probe and pull and poke, and come up empty. There's nothing special in what you do, how you do it, where you do it, who you do it for or to. There still are a few ways to stake out a position.

Go back over the questions, and see if you forgot anything. Maybe you take something so much for granted that it never popped into your head. Something in your background, or special training, or experience gained by working with a particular segment of your clientele. For example, a man who offers the same type of computer training as his competition may have forgotten that he's the only one with a teaching background.

Look for a desirable feature you and your competition offer that nobody has thought to capitalize on. Everybody may provide a money-back guarantee, but you can be the first on your block to announce it. That feature becomes associated with you.

The third choice probably is the most painful and the most necessary. Reexamine what you're doing in the context of your market. Then, either change your product or change your market. It may be that your product is as appropriate as it can be, but there's no room for you in the marketplace. Pick up your lily pad and hop over to a fresher, friendlier pond. Repackage what you do for a different market. If you are a real estate lawyer who mostly has worked with property owners, you may want to fish elsewhere—condo and co-op sponsors, co-op corporations and condo associations, condo and co-op unit buyers and sellers. Or there may be a need for a lawyer who specializes in zoning matters. If you provide your product to corporations, maybe it's worth prospecting universities or hospitals or trade associations. Be sure to apply the same positioning analysis with any new market you explore.

Changing the product may or may not require major surgery. Everybody may make the same widget for the same price with the same bells and whistles. Perhaps all the widgets are black. So make a blue widget. Look at the costs more carefully. Streamline your offering. Do you provide something your clients rarely need or use? Pluck it out of the basic package, make it an option with its own charge, and cut the cost of basic service. Is there some ''advanced'' technology (e.g., facsimile machine, computer, E-mail, telephone answering machine) that could make your service easier to work with?

The wisest approach usually is to listen to your customers. Do they clearly favor some parts of what you offer over others? (Maybe your clients use you more for training than consulting. Then a-training you can go.) What problems do they wish your product would solve that it doesn't? (Perhaps your catering service could use a more extensive low-cholesterol gourmet menu.) Is there a related service you don't provide that they can use? (If they keep asking you to recommend people to fill executive positions, maybe you should add head-hunting to your repertoire.)

HOW DO YOU WANT YOUR MARKET TO PERCEIVE YOUR PRODUCT?

Years ago, Phillip Leonian, a world-class virtuoso photographer, had a most unconventional mouse problem. He photographed a mouse for a pharmaceutical ad. The result was a gem. Leonian thought so highly of the picture that he put it in his portfolio. Photographers use the portfolio, a collection of their images, to show what they can do for prospective and established clients. Adding the picture to the collection worked too well.

Here a mouse assignment, there a mouse assignment, and pretty soon he had a multiple-mouse portfolio. He knew he had one Mickey too many when he was asked to photograph a mouse in a Santa Claus outfit. This job was not satisfying. Leonian did not choose to see himself as a documentor of rodents. The first mouse picture was supposed to make the statement, "I do scientific photography." Instead, the market interpreted the message as "I do mice!"

Not only did Phillip Leonian remove the offending rodents but he took a closer look at his portfolio. He rearranged and focused it so that it clearly demonstrated his strengths to advertising agencies, his market.

All the research you have done on your market and your product should lead to a very special moment. What specifically do you want your market to know and feel about what you do? How do you make this message as pure and potent as you possibly can?

Your main tool is the position you have claimed for yourself. The position explains what is special and important about what you do and how you do it.

One computer consultant might position himself as an expert on the system needs of the real estate management profession. Another computer consultant might explain that she can tell you everything there is to know about a data base system.

Both messages might be directed at realty firms, ostensibly the same market. Probably the man with the total real estate management package deals mostly with companies that have no computer experience at all or are very new to the infernal devices. His message is that with his knowledge of both real estate needs and computers, he can help his clients computerize so that they will have an edge over their competitors who do not have computers or are not using systems specifically designed for the real estate industry.

The second consultant might be dealing with firms that have had their PCs up and running for quite a while. Now that they're comfortable they want to do more. Her message to clients is that her overview of the data base field helps her design the best information-gathering system for their individual business and gives an edge over their competitors who use standard industry packages. The message explains why your position is important to the market.

HOW DO YOU REACH YOUR MARKET?

The communication is not complete until somebody receives your message. All of this activity is just one aspect of a public relations campaign. PR, you'll recall, sits with advertising and sales as a friend at marketing's table.

It seems as if there are miles of shelves devoted only to books that explain advertising, publicity, and sales. The discussion of the three here will be a very basic primer. We'll start with definitions.

Advertising: "All the activities involved in presenting to a group a non-personal, oral, or visual, openly sponsored message regarding a product, service, or idea; this message called an advertisement is disseminated through one or more media, and is paid for by the identified sponsor." (*Fundamentals of Marketing,* 2nd ed., by William Stanton, McGraw-Hill, 1967.)

Publicity: "The release of information by an organization through the various communications media." (*The Encyclopedia of Management,* 2nd ed., edited by Carl Heyel, Van Nostrand Reinhold, 1973.)

Selling: "A direct dialog wherein the application of persuasion and knowledge (of both product and prospect) causes a transaction to break out." (YHO.)

Advertising, public relations, and sales rely on communication skills. You're right on target when what you communicate is based on your marketing preparation. Still advertising, public relations, and sales are

separate disciplines that can be applied without the benefits of marketing smarts. (The results will be haphazard, to be sure.)

With both publicity and advertising you send your message to the
public via a third party. The differences between the two are crucial.
With advertising, you pay for the publication space or broadcasting
time, and you supply the ad. Because you're paying, you have total
control over the contents of the ad. As long as you have the money,
you can place your message wherever and whenever you want. Therefore, you also have control over what market segment is exposed to
your message and with what frequency.

With publicity, you supply information to the media. (Obviously,
this information reflects and reinforces your message.) If media people
want to, they may devote time or space to you or your product. They
may do a story solely about the subject that's nearest and dearest to
your heart, or they may include your information as part of a larger
story. Because the material is presented within a news or feature story,
it has a credibility that advertising does not. Furthermore, you don't
pay the publication or broadcaster a cent for the exposure you get.
(Some people simplistically refer to publicity as "free advertising,"
even though publicity incurs expenses, some of which can be quite
sizable.)

Publicity's "bargain rates" and attention-getting powers are offset
by the total unreliability of the results. The paper may run a wonderful
story about you and forget to tell people that you have a product, or
where they can order that product. The writer may spend three hours
with you, and quote you only once—a quote by the way that makes
you wish you weren't quoted at all. The TV talk show host may be
more interested in entertaining the audience than in letting you say
what's special about what you do. And on and on and on. For the
most part, people won't abuse you but your carefully honed message
is secondary to their news, feature, and career needs.

The total control advertising gives is formidable. The market gets
your undiluted message, unsullied by intermediaries who would dare
dispute or disregard the importance of what you have to say. You can
beam the message over the radio fifteen times a week while people
drive home from work. Unfortunately, each ad costs money, which
would be okay if each ad also drove your message home. Would you
believe there actually are people who work very hard at ignoring ads?
Their eyes will pass right over advertisements in magazines and newspapers. They'll even leave a room when an ad comes on television or
radio.

Advertising is best used for directing your message in its pure form to your market on a steady, planned basis. Publicity is best used to add believability and depth to the public's understanding of your message. Publicity and advertising support each other in giving you recognition.

Publicity's basic unit is the pitch, the organized statement that explains why now is the very best time to give your widget editorial coverage. Even though the ultimate goal is to get your story out to the public, aim the pitch directly at a media person. The pitch does not contain the whole story. The pitch conveys just enough of the story to indicate that something solid is available. The pitch emphasizes that it is a story worth doing. Built into the pitch is a sense of being current. The media is more likely to be interested in your widget if it's newsworthy. It's the newest. It's the best. It's the first. It's the only. It's the most expensive. It's the cheapest. It's the biggest. It's the smallest. It was made by Tibetan freedom fighters. It fights crime. It fights drugs. It fights zits. Stars use it. Rich people use it. Kids use it. It has some association, however tenuous, with something going on in the news. It went to the moon. It went to Camp David. It saved the lives in the recent disaster. Whatever.

The pitch, either a letter or a phone call, has to say something about the subject that explains why the magazine writer, the newscaster, the newspaper editor would serve their audiences well by covering it.

Many features originate with a public relations effort. Someone calls or writes the publication or broadcaster and says something along the lines of, "Have I got a story for you. My client has discovered that grape no longer is the jelly of choice among upwardly mobile preschoolers. They prefer kiwi fruit jelly."

Aha, a trend! The client has many wonderful stories to tell about how the jelly factory is getting orders for kiwi fruit jelly. The client will even supply tips for imaginative uses of the gourmet treat, as well as a brief discourse on the public's changing taste in jelly history.

There also may be a prepared response for those occasions when the media contacts you first. Many more stories start with the news-gathering organization. The writer seeks assistance (as in fast research) from a publicist. The writer calls the company or the PR person and asks for an interview so that she could learn many jelly gems.

"Wonderful," says the publicist, "my client has spoken out quite often about the need of the jelly industry to meet the challenges of the twenty-first century." "But," says the writer, "I'm just doing an article about popular flavors." "Perfect," says the publicist. "Come by on Wednesday for our monthly corporate jelly tasting. I'll also give you a package containing all the articles written about our jelly. We've gotten some fabulous reviews, and the CEO has written a small book about the history of jelly. I guess you need pictures—color or black-and-white?''

The publicity person may indeed have phone agility, but that is helped substantially by being prepared, by having at the ready the pitch angles and information that convey the company's message. The pitch also may be embedded in a press release. Whereas the pitch letter says, ''You ought to do a story about my company for these reasons,'' the press release plays a different role. It dresses up as a news story. (''New flavors are changing the jelly market, and kiwi fruit jelly sales have taken the lead. Local jelly processor Agar Pectin, president of That's My Jelly, Inc., says that orders for kiwi fruit jelly are up 20 percent. He attributes the trend to new values in the preschooler set.'')

Further down in the release, you can and probably should have a paragraph or two reflecting your market message. ''That's My Jelly was founded in 1982 in Agar Pectin's kitchen. It has gone on to become the leading gourmet jelly for toddlers.'' Avoid blatant hype. It's not believed and it erodes the credibility of the message that happens to be true. Instead of saying, ''I really think it's very good,'' quote a reviewer or an article or some satisfied customers.

Since the press release is a simulated news item, it's inappropriate to conclude by saying, ''so write about me.'' The convention is to state at the bottom of the stationery, ''For more information, contact . . .'' and then include a name and phone number. Despite the importance of the contact line, it's omitted from too many press releases. Even if you're a one-person shop, it wouldn't hurt to create stationery that has the big words PRESS RELEASE across the top and the contact line on the bottom. Some home officers think it's more impressive to have the press release come from another source, so they use the ploy of inserting a phony name as a contact. It can get even more complicated. When the call comes in for Mr. Nom-deplume, the home officer might say, ''This is he,'' or ''He's out of the office right now. Can I help you?''

Having a pitch ready is fine. It's effective only in a haphazard way if you think of it as the whole process and not just as a part. Getting publicity when you never had any before brings joy, and it's probably great for the complexion. Meaningful publicity—the right coverage in the right outlets at the right time—is superior. Publicity does not work in a vacuum. Successful publicists often avoid as clients businesses that do not have a business plan or a marketing plan.

The chanciness of the publicity process, especially when conducted by nonprofessionals, reinforces the need for planning. We bring some thought to the areas that are under our control—what we say, when, and to whom.

Judith S. Lederman and Wes Thomas are both public relations professionals. They do not know each other. They operate their businesses in different states. But they both have the knack of initially shocking some of their new clients with a simple truth: The publicity mill does not start churning tomorrow; efforts begin with silence. Or so it seems.

First it's necessary to understand the product, in relation to its market; then the publicist must sketch out the series of steps that fulfill the client's publicity needs and desires. (Note: What they need and what they want are not always the same. The client's idea of good publicity may be just, "Get me in the *New York Times*," or "Get me a *Newsweek* cover," not "Get me in the newsletter that goes to all the high rollers.")

Next, the publicist must prepare all the written materials that tell the story, explain the pitch, provide the background, and answer the kind of questions that get asked by the media. ("Is the company publicly held?" "What are the backgrounds of the key executives?" "Where does the company fit in the widget industry?" "What does your new widget do that others don't, and why is that important?" "What is the overall significance of your new technological breakthrough?" "Where are your factories?") Then the publicity "starts."

"The clients have to realize," says Wes Thomas, "there's a whole sequence they're going to go through. They have to build up credibility with the analysts and the knowledgeable technical writers first."

At press conferences, I've seen mainstream writers turn to the technical writers and say, "Is this product real?" A nod from a techie means a lot to the rest of us.

Now the message can go out to the greater public. Supporting materials might include reprints of the wise words of the unbiased industry analyst. The simple sequence Thomas describes is equally effective for many different kinds of publicity projects. There always are leading-edge or ahead-of-the-pack voices whose pronouncements are effective traffic lights, especially on busy streets. There may be differences in scale but not concept.

When Judith Lederman meets prospective clients, she asks them to fill out a questionnaire. Here are some of her questions:

- Describe your business/organization.
- Do you currently advertise in the media?
- If you do, or have in the past, where have you advertised?

- Are you interested primarily in trade or consumer publicity?
- Please list five publications or broadcast outlets that you would like to see profile your organization/products.
- Do you currently subscribe to any publications? If so, please list.
- Do you anticipate any major changes in your business/products within the next twelve months? If so, please describe.
- What would you like a public relations program to do for your business?

Her analysis of their answers helps her better understand the company, and its public relations needs and opportunities. The magazines in which they've advertised indicate their real beliefs about their market. The magazines they subscribe to also indicate market priorities, as well as points of view worth paying attention to. She weighs this information in the context of the company's self-description. (They can, after all, be advertising in the wrong places.) How might the company's envisioned changes affect its position in the marketplace?

Why exactly do they want publicity: To introduce a new product? To establish their eminence in a new category of consumer goods? Do they want to reach new markets? If so, which ones? Are they planning to go public next year? Do they have to be nice to dealers who are suddenly refusing to stock the product?

"More sales" or "increased recognition" are okay answers as far as they go. But "more sales to the gourmet market" or "increased recognition in the construction industry" are examples of more illuminating answers.

Home officers can use the same questions when we plan or review our own PR programs. We have to be specific and accurate when addressing such questions. The same kind of thinking can go into advertising plans, although there are many more options for hunting down and enticing the market.

National television ads for Dominatrix Pizza may give America a warm feeling for the product. (Mmm, just look at that pepperoni and that bubbling mozzarella cheese.) Newspaper ads may tell the locals that there's a Dominatrix in their town, and feature a dollar coupon to get the old juices going. If you're reading the paper on the way to work, you might tear out the coupon. Every time you see the coupon it reminds you of Dominatrix (and the bubbling cheese). The buying decision won't happen until you get hungry and crave a pizza delivery. Then, you're likely to turn to the yellow pages. You'll look under "pizza" and feel a certain sense of fulfillment upon spotting the Dominatrix ad.

The television, newspaper, and phone book ad each played a special role in spreading a part of the Dominatrix message. Actually each ad was placed by a different entity and to satisfy different market concerns. The national ad was placed by the parent company. It reaches the whole American pizza-loving market, and tells them that Dominatrix whips the competition. If the ad helps the franchisees sell more pizza, then the parent company makes more money. The ad also helps the parent company sell franchises. It's a demonstration of support to local fast food investors, and it shows that the parent company is for real.

The newspaper ad was placed by a group of local franchise holders. They pooled their pennies to purchase an ad that would reach a large slice of the city's total population. Moreover, that ad would be more likely to reach more people in their respective territories than would ads in neighborhood newspapers. By sharing, they paid a fair price for reaching the market, even though a large portion of the readership is of negligible value to the individual advertisers. The yellow pages ad closes the sale.

What about the pizzeria that can't afford to advertise on national TV or even the daily newspaper? The phone directory can help even the odds. In his book *Guerilla Marketing* (Houghton Mifflin, $8.95), Jay Conrad Levinson says, "A prime advantage of listing in the yellow pages is that you can appear as big as your biggest competitor, as large as the largest business of your type in town, as well established as the oldest business of your type in town." He explains that this parity occurs because most yellow-page directories limit advertisers to no more than one-quarter page.

The question of where to advertise also can be asked as, "Where is your market most receptive to your message?" "Transit advertising works well for beverages, food, and 'get away from it all' products like travel," say Kenneth Roman and Jane Maas in their book, *How to Advertise* (St. Martin's Press, 1976). "You are talking to people who may be thirsty, hungry, or tired."

Your understanding of the market plus your available budget should assist you in finding the right advertising medium. How much bang do you get for the buck? How many of the right people does the medium deliver? How many of the wrong people does it deliver? What is the cost per thousand of the right people? (The more wrong people delivered, the higher the cost per thousand for the right people. Even so, it still might be a bargain.)

For example, home officer Doe created computer software that helps doctors run their offices. Doe can advertise in computer magazines or controlled circulation publications just for doctors. Two questions arise. Do enough doctors who own computers subscribe to computer magazines (and if so, which ones)? Do enough doctors who receive these controlled circulation magazines own computers? Software publisher Doe may want to focus on publications aimed at businesses that serve doctors, such as medical supply houses. Perhaps too few doctors subscribe to computer magazines to justify the space rates. Too much of Doe's dough would be spent on people who aren't doctors. It also may be that not enough doctors who read the available advertising choices have computers. If the software is all that wonderful, then Doe should seriously think of selling a computer with the program. The message should be, "At last, the right reason to computerize your office."

Unlike the publicity that goes to the media, where it is processed and repackaged, the advertisement goes directly to your market. The advertisement's essential element is the fanfare. Some aspect, feature, or innate quality of the ad has got to attract and keep your market's attention. It could be a powerful photograph, a provocative headline, a captivating design, or an offer the target cannot refuse. You are competing with the other ads, the "meaty" part of the publication or broadcast, and everything else going on while your target presumably is being exposed to your ad.

A few simple rules will help you out, regardless of what advertising medium you choose. The first has been repeated so often that people don't pay attention.

1. Sell the sizzle—not the steak. We condition ourselves to react positively to certain perceptions. It's the bell that makes us salivate, not the good nutrition.

2. Sell the benefits—not the features. Your market is more likely to get excited when you tell them what the widget does for them than when you tell them what they'll find in this year's widget. "Speak Swiss like a native" is more enticing than "learn to speak Swiss."

3. Keep your ad focused. You should have a main idea (distilled from your marketing message) and everything in the ad should support that idea.

4. Keep your ad simple, which is certainly a good way to keep it focused. Let the headline, text, and illustrations be direct and definite.

5. Distrust originality. I can't believe I just said that, but I'm reporting what I've learned. Some of the most creative advertising professionals regularly denounce homages to creativity and originality. The function of advertising is to sell goods, they explain. A worthwhile ad sells product. A worthless ad doesn't. Uniqueness of expression is

a side issue. That unique expression may powerfully carry the message to your market in a way that makes a positive impression, which is fine and wonderful. All too often creativity for the sake of creativity sacrifices the power and importance of the message. That's bad advertising.

6. Know what you're talking about and why you say what you say. In some respects, this rule is the most important. Knowledge begins with an understanding of your product and its value. But that's not enough. You also should know what the market wants from your product. You also should know how the market uses your product. If you've gone to the trouble of conducting research—and I hope you have—even in an informal way, you should let that research help you make your ads. For example, should you appeal to their emotion or their reason? Are they looking for a bargain or a status symbol?

The laws of sizzle, benefits, focus, simplicity, nonoriginality, and knowledge should help you with any advertising medium. (In *Guerilla Marketing,* Jay Conrad Levinson's list of media includes "circulars and brochures . . . , classified ads, outdoor signs, advertisements in the yellow pages, newspapers and magazines, radio, television, billboards . . . , advertising specialties such as imprinted ballpoint pens . . . , demonstrations . . . , exhibiting at trade shows . . . , and T-shirts.")

Also, the various media do have their own particular needs. Roman and Maas, in their book *How to Advertise,* reveal many specialized tips. Here are some:

For print: "Get your message in the headline," "photographs are better than drawings," and "always put a caption under the photograph."

For radio: "Stretch the listener's imagination," "present one idea," "mention your brand name and your promise early," and "capitalize on events."

For television: "Look for a 'key visual,' . . . one frame that visually sums up the whole message," "grab the viewer's attention," and "register the name of your product."

Advertising and publicity deal with the market on a group level. It's the salesperson who brings the message to the individual consumers.

Carol Kropnick, the organizer, has a clientele that largely is made up of professional photographers. She knows that photographic pros get their films processed at custom photo-developing labs. She posts signs that announce her service on photo lab bulletin boards. The fact that the sign is in a custom lab tells professional photographers that her service is directed toward them. Moreover, her copy points out that she specializes in organizing tax-related records. She sends a clear message directly to her market. She even knows which bulletin boards have brought her the most business.

There are other ways that people find us. They clipped out an article we wrote for a trade journal and tracked us down. They saw us on that great TV show *Wake Up Hometown* and wondered if we would mind taking a look at a situation they face. They saw us speak at a seminar, and they liked what we said about how to deal with special problems. They sat next to us at a trade association dinner. They were enthralled by our overview and the way we used the right fork. In each case, it took effort on our part to lay out the trail of breadcrumbs they so smartly followed. It takes artful application of effort to make the right contacts for publication, public speaking, and broadcast appearances. In fact, this campaign also is a marketing challenge. This market consists of the people who decide.

It is your marketing position and the message based on that position that lends you unique authority when first announcing yourself to editors, broadcast producers, and conference planners. By the way, publications often sponsor or at least play a major role at conferences and trade shows. Getting published in the trade or specialized press is a prime path to the podium at industry events.

Somewhere along the way your message will get through. At that point the courier who picks up the baton and your message is a salesperson. We know who wears that hat in most home offices. Some people grit their teeth when they think about selling. They explain they don't have the personality to sell. They're right—and they're wrong.

They're right to the extent that dealing with other humans jangles their nerves. They don't like being hypocritically pleasant while people bother them with stupid questions. Perhaps they're more visually oriented or happiest when working with their hands and are uncomfortable when they have to express themselves verbally. Perhaps they dread being taken advantage of. And so on. I respect these reasons. I suspect such people are informed by some degree of self-awareness. Besides therapy costs too much and takes too long and there's a business to run.

I also resubmit that they are wrong. It might help to expand their notion of what selling is, and know that they need not sacrifice their principles at the altar of expedience. Selling need not be a persuasive, manipulative art. You need not try to "Joe Isuzu" your way to the bank.

Sales and marketing consultant B. Robert Anderson says, "Those of us who are sales professionals are in the field because we believe we have a service or product which will be useful to the prospect. . . . We are here to bring you something you need, something you can use. We're going to present it to you in as professional a way as we can. The reason we call it selling is that I know you need it before you know you need it. If Edison ran up and down the street saying to people would you like to buy an electric lightbulb, they would have laughed at him. 'Why get an electric lightbulb,' they'd say. 'I have kerosene.' "

Anderson's ethic is intended to describe the professional salesperson. Interestingly enough, the same clothes fit those of us who are obliged to sell in order to do what we most enjoy doing. Harness your affection for what you do to the professor within you. Let your market see the beauty and intricacy of the world you have created.

Some years ago I met William Sears, a consultant who trained people to sell. Corporations around the country hired this talented Californian to come and teach. I watched him work as he focused on engineers and other nonmarketing personnel.

They were bona fide members of the sales team, Sears pointed out, and they didn't think of themselves as salespeople. Yet they were the ones who, because of expertise, had the most credibility and therefore were vital to the process. He gave them an understanding of that process. He wasn't hired to alter personalities, consciousness, or job titles. He was there to show them how to use what they knew to help make sales possible.

Similarly, the most credible person to deliver your message is you. At the moment you and the prospect have come in contact with each other, negotiation has begun. Salespeople have been trained and trained themselves to think of sales as a discipline involving communication, persuasion, and perhaps a bit of missionary work. There are such laws as "help the buyers evaluate their needs," "learn their concerns," and "meet their objections."

An interesting trend has developed over the last fifteen years. Negotiating smarts have trickled down. For this reason, anything-but-salespeople might help themselves by reading a book about negotiation. I prefer books by Chester Karass. It's interesting and probably useful to commit surefire negotiating techniques to memory. But that's not why I recommend the radical tactic of reading. I find that ingesting a book on the subject simply helps one absorb a negotiating attitude, and that's what sustains us. Read a second book, *Selling Through Negotiation* by Homer B. Smith (Marketing Education Associates). His book is a good resource for selling to people who have been to negotiation seminars. My negotiation attitude has three components:

1. Understand that you have genuine power. You would not be in this negotiation if you did not have something the other party wanted.
2. Know that negotiation is an obligatory ceremony. In this ritual, the conflict is really between two visions of inevitability. Let me help both of us feel comfortable with the resulting vision.
3. Keep fixed in mind what you will and will not accept. Everything else—bad faith; good faith; appeals to guilt, shame, pride, or honor; threats; pleas; crudity; charm—means absolutely nothing.

I find this attitude keeps me focused on the issues and real importance of the particular negotiation. Instead of my ego being a hostage, it is a support. Of course, when dealing with someone real crazy or real mean, this wonderful enlightenment has been known to turn tail and run. But generally, the attitude helps.

Most home officers seem to accept or even welcome the sales process, which is true even if they never will totally master selling as a second language. Although the game-playing, social amenities and even the time spent may be bothersome, they find pleasure in the affirmations. It's usually a joy to know that people want, use, and approve of what you offer. If they feel their lives have been helped, that's even better. And the money isn't bad.

The chances are one way or another, for one reason or another, you are going to try to sell something to somebody. B. Robert Anderson, the sales and marketing consultant, has an important tip for you: "If you're in selling you are there to try to get an order. You're not there just to spread goodwill."

At a family barbecue, a cousin told us of his adventures in the world of sales. He dutifully called on a particular prospect every month. It always was a good meeting. My cousin ardently detailed the benefits of his products. The prospect listened respectfully, and even, it seemed, appreciatively. But there was no sale. My cousin always walked out a bit confused. Finally, after five months, he asked the big question: "Every time I'm here you treat me very well, but you never buy anything. What's wrong?" "Oh," said the man, "you want me to buy something. Why didn't you say so? Okay."

Sometimes people get so hung up on the process or minutiae of selling that they ignore the old story of "keeping your eye on the donut and not on the hole." It's a pathetic picture: the seller relentlessly hitting every single one of the important points, dragging out graphs and charts and slides; and the possible buyer shifting from leg to leg, drawing crude, erotic doodles, wondering if this hell will ever end.

B. Robert Anderson, who wrote the textbook *Professional Selling* (McGraw-Hill, 3rd ed.), advises that a little focus goes a long way.

"Remember," says Anderson, "the ABCs of selling—Always Be Closing! When I am trying to sell you something I am always trying to close the sale." We're not talking impatience, intolerance, or hysteria here. We're just meditating on why you came to be talking with this person at this time.

"You do it in a very nice way," continues Anderson. "Every time you lay out a piece of information, you say to the prospect in effect, 'Can I have the order?' The customer or prospect says 'No,' and you say, 'Here are three other things to consider.' You explain the three other things and then you say, 'May I have the order?' "

One other area that all home officers must look at is direct marketing. It can be a wonderfully effective form that is something of a mutant. It combines the advertising approach of directing a message toward a large part of the market at one time with the sales approach of talking to individuals one at a time. I'll use the dirty words that the Direct Marketing Association prefers not to hear: junk mail and junk phone calls.

I scathingly sling those terms around like anybody else. But you better believe that, at the moment I write these words, I'm looking forward to a direct mail campaign for this book. Furthermore, I have enjoyed the convenience of ordering all sorts of things from catalogs and having them shipped directly to my home and home office. I'm getting a newspaper delivered because the paper's telemarketing department called me. Direct mail and telemarketing give me the chance to order useful products and services. They acquaint me with opportunities I had not thought about. They inform me about products and services I had not known enough about. Ultimately, when confronted with the unscheduled opportunity, I make a decision. Either I buy, I set aside for another day, or I chuck it out with the other junk.

Salespeople talk about making cold calls: phoning somebody they don't know to get something from them (usually an appointment or money). Although the scope of the operation differs radically from that of the newspaper that called for a subscription or the local orchestra that wanted a donation, the principles are the same. I guess cold calls become telemarketing when a sense of system joins the party.

You start with a list of likely prospects for your message. Telemarketing demands brevity. You're taking up their time. They want you off the phone. Therefore, you must plan the expression of your message. If I say this, they'll say that. Then I can counter with this.

"You must use an outline to structure your phone presentation," says Jay Conrad Levinson in *Guerilla Marketing.* "If your outline is longer than one page, there is probably too much in it and you should try to streamline it. An outline not only creates a structure for your thoughts and ideas but also helps keep the call on track when the person at the other end redirects it."

Following an outline often is referred to as using a script. Telemarketing lets you talk with individuals in a personal manner. Using the telephone provides a genuine two-way communication. Not only do you hear each other's voice (and whatever feelings and attitudes the voices convey) but the caller gets to answer the other person's objections and concerns.

For more on fancy phoning, I'd suggest you review Chapter Seven, "Switchboard Central."

There are two essentials in direct marketing: your marketing message and the list. The beauty of direct mail is that you're sending a letter to a likely prospect. It's a personal communication. It just so happens that this communication may be in four-color, and computer-assisted every step of the way from the gathering of the name to the addressing of the envelope. Furthermore, the same personal message may have gone out to 20 million other people.

Once the recipients open their envelopes, your task is simplified. They are willing to listen to you, if only for a moment. (People in the business of direct marketing work very hard at making what you see on the envelope and through the envelope's window as enticing as possible. There is a reason, after all, that you already might be a winner.)

You can keep their attention as long as what you are saying relates to them, their wants, their identities, and their emotions. Herschell Gordon Lewis, in his book *Direct Mail Copy That Sells* (Prentice-Hall, $12.95), says that today's four great motivators are fear, guilt, greed, and exclusivity. He says that fear is the greatest and that the first rule of fear is that "the reader always must know that you have the solution to his problem." You are not just describing something they might want to buy. You are giving them the chance to get access to something that will make their lives better.

In a sense, a direct mail solicitation really is a short story, and the main character is the person who's reading it. It even has a structure. Roman and Maas in *How to Advertise* say that, "Every beginning copywriter in direct mail learns the AIDA formula. The acronym stands for the ideal structure of a sales letter: attention, interest, desire, action." You grab the readers' attention. You excite their interest. You speak to their desires and you spur them to action.

Take time to tell your story. Explore those details that are important to your market. It helps to write clearly and crisply. Do the words you use have tangibility? Do they have taste, sound, color, smell, and touch? You don't have to be a poet. You do have to be a storyteller. You do have to be convincing.

You need one more asset: the right mailing list. The list is one of the most fascinating inventions of modern times. At its best, it is a compilation of names of selected people who have demonstrated through their past buying actions that they absolutely would love to pay money for what you are offering.

One of the best and yet most basic lists you could hope to have is the list of your own customers. These are the people who already bought from you. There's a good chance they'll buy again if the product is replaceable or updateable, or if you are adding accessories or kindred products.

The leading mailing list sources are membership organizations, mail-order catalog houses, book clubs, and publications. Each of these has a list of people who are linked by some sort of commonality. The direct marketing discipline has been so refined that you can get very specific mailing lists. You can get a list of names sorted by gender, marital status, amount of children in the household (don't forget the kids' ages), hobby, profession, type of car driven, political philosophy, income bracket, zip code, and so on.

If you want to sell your gourmet jelly through direct mail, get a list from one of the food magazines or one of the mail-order purveyors of fancy foods. If you're packaging the jelly in specially crafted ceramic crocks designed by one of Italy's leading designers, then you reach for the collectibles mailing list (preferably the one with the names of people who collect ceramic items).

What people would have a passion for your product? What magazines or catalogs do they subscribe to? What book clubs or organizations might they join? The answers to these questions tell you whose mailing list might help you. Compilers are the originators of the lists. Usually the compiler's primary energy is devoted to another business. They call on list managers to manage the list. List brokers get permission from compilers or managers to rent the lists to direct marketers. If you don't know who the broker is, contact the compiler. Similarly, if you know who to market to, but don't know what list or lists to use, contact a broker. Brokers will have or get the right lists for you. (There should be no surcharges on lists when you use a broker.)

Lists are not sold. They're rented, usually for a one-time use. Often, as a condition of renting a list, you have to show what it is you're planning to mail. Lists are provided in many forms from floppy disks to stick-on labels. Usually the list broker requires a minimum order. A 30,000-name list may go for $70/1,000 with a minimum order of 5,000. And yes, there are telephone lists also.

RESOURCES

Totall Manager (Bartel Media, $395). This contact management program is built around the special requirements of a sales department. Working with your data base of contacts, you can filter in the people you want to call today (e.g., all those in California, all those who haven't ordered in five months, all those whose first name is Kevin) and keep track of what happens in the phone calls. The word processor is powerful enough and especially designed to allow you to move boiler-plate paragraphs around. The software has a market plan component. You also use the word processor to write "scripts." A script is the programmed flow of questions and comments used by telemarketers. Built into the scripts is what you say at any point when the person on the other end says "yes" or "no" to you. In creating the script, you just have to supply your questions and your appropriate responses to the prospect's answers. The software does all the programming. You devise a sequence of up to ten steps and objectives, typically starting with "send letter" and ending with "close sale." You follow this plan with as many or as few contacts as you'd like. It helps you keep track of where you are with the prospect, as well as what should happen next. The software also automates order-taking and expense-tracking. Contact: Bartel Software, 942 E. 7145 South, Suite A-101, Midvale UT 84047; (800) 777-6368.

PUBLICATIONS/VIDEOS

American Demographics Magazine (Dow Jones & Co., $58/year). If you'd like to keep up with some market research information, but prefer not to spend $15,000 on a study, this magazine might please you. Each issue presents articles about identifiable groups and markets (e.g., college-age group, health-care market), "how to" articles (e.g., "How to Use Income Statistics"), and news tidbits. The articles, often based on expensive studies, combine good information about attitudes with telling statistics, and are written in a lucid fashion. *American Demographics* has an interesting approach to reprints. The magazine assembles a package of articles that pertain to one general subject. For example, the "How to Tap the 50 + Market" contains the following titles: "Is Florida Our Future?" "Retirement's Life-style Pioneers," "The Nursing Home Dilemma," "The Comfortably Retired and the Pension Elite," "Inside the Mature Market," and "How Older Americans Spend Their Money." These packages cost from $15 to $22. Contact: American Demographics, 108 N. Cayuga St., Ithaca NY 14850; (800) 828-1133.

Direct Marketing (Hoke Communications Inc., $45/yr). A monthly publication, DM presents a constant flow of information for those who vend by phone and mail. Clearly, the emphasis is on the megacampaign, for example, the sweepstakes mailing that goes out to 20 million likely prospects. Still, plenty of applicable nuts and bolts material fills the pages. Columnists are likely to give hints on how to write headlines or classified ads. Moreover, the stories that deal specifically with the heavy hitters and mighty mailers contain useful nuggets. *Direct Marketing*'s how-to-do-it and, more interestingly, ways-to-think-about-it content might inspire you to refine the ways you market your products or services. Contact: Hoke Communications Inc., 224 Seventh St., Garden City NY 11530-5771; (800) 645-6132; in NY (516) 746-6700.

Telemarketing Yes-how (Paradigm Press). Intended as a college text, *Basic Telemarketing* by Mary Pekas can benefit home officers. Writing in a clear, pleasant voice, Pekas outlines phone fluency and delivery skills, and shows the importance of word selection. She also gives some insights into her conversational soft sell approach. A lot of the information also can be found in Pekas's *Telephone Mastery*. This book, however, focuses on using these skills specifically. Contact: Telemarketing Institute, P.O. Box 1632, Sioux Falls SD 57101; (605) 335-3970.

How to Advertise by Kenneth Roman and Jane Maas (St. Martin's Press, 1977, $10.95). Two advertising pros give it to you straight. In 156 pages and thirteen chapters, the authors present 204 rules. Each rule has a brief explanation and a concise example, and altogether they form a workable education. Topics covered include positioning a product or service; what works best in television, print, radio, outdoor and transit, and direct mail; media plans; and how to be a better client. Best of all, the authors talk to the advertiser (i.e., the client). This book will help whether you hire an advertising agency or you do your own advertising. Contact: St. Martin's Press, 175 Fifth Ave., New York NY 10010; (212) 674-5151.

Selling Through Negotiation by Homer B. Smith (Marketing Education Associates, $12.95). "Negotiation enters . . . where persuasion has stalled," says Smith. The author, past president of the National

Society of Sales Training Executives, believes that more people involved in selling should learn the role negotiation plays in facilitating
the close of a sale. It is especially wise, he notes, since you're likely
to deal with a buyer who's been through a how-to-negotiate seminar
or has studied one or more books on the subject. Part I is devoted
to "Developing Your Sales Negotiations Skills." This section has
earned a lot of attention for its material on how to deal with buyers
who have been trained to negotiate. Part II covers bringing your
negotiation and sales skills together to close. Part III provides some
depth to those two important negotiation skills: asking questions and
listening. Both *Selling Through Negotiation* and a previous Smith book,
A Salesman's Guide to More Effective Selling (MEA, $7.95), have been
praised as classics. Both are available by mail. Contact: Marketing
Education Association, 4004 Rosemary St., Chevy Chase MD
20015; (301) 656-5550.

The Only Mailing List Catalog You Need (American List Council, free)
The ALC is a list compiler, manager, and broker. In over fifty
pages, its catalog details the more than 10,000 lists it rents. It's
broken into high-interest categories (from accountants to zoos),
data bases (names from a number of different mailing lists with at
least one variable in common), state lists, and Standard Industrial
Classification (also known as yellow pages list). The American List
Council issues catalogs once or twice a year. The minimum order
the ALC accepts is for $150, with the exception of lists printed in
red. (For these lists you must buy a minimum amount of names,
and the fee usually exceeds $150.) Contact: ALC, 88 Orchard Rd.,
CN-5219, Princeton NJ 08543; (800) 822-LIST; in NJ (201) 874-
4300.

The Clustering of America by Michael J. Weiss (Harper & Row, $22.50).
A journalistic work that looks at how Americans identify ourselves,
and how that information gets used, this book has become required
reading for many who study demographics. As such, the book is a
painless introduction to a very provocative way of thinking about
demographics. It looks at the PRIZM (Potential Rating Index by
Zip Markets) method. This approach starts with sorting people into
all the standard categories (i.e., gender, marital status, material pos-
sessions, neighborhoods, etc.) as well as into social attitudes and
values and family. Groups of people in different areas display significant similarities. Each of the groups is identified by its zip code.
Those discrete zip codes, when bundled together, form a cluster with
clearly identifiable tastes, characteristics, and values. Geographical
boundaries mean less than cluster boundaries. So, the Jackson

Heights (NY) and Little River (FL) communities have more in common with each other than they do with their surrounding communities. It may be a very efficient way to target markets. A few of the clusters are "Money & Brains," "Gray Power," and "New Melting Pot." Contact: Harper & Row, 10 E. 53rd St., New York NY 10022.

Guerilla Marketing by Jay Conrad Levinson (Houghton Mifflin Company, $8.95). The subtitle is "Secrets for Making Big Profits from Your Small Business." Although I don't recall seeing "guerilla marketing" officially defined in this book, the notion is amply demonstrated. It's about being quick, clever, resourceful, and alert (a much nicer word than opportunistic). Levinson gives the lowdown on the best way to use every marketing message delivery system from bulletin boards to television. He proves that no matter how little you have to spend, you can get positive results. Contact: Houghton Mifflin Company, 2 Park St., Boston MA 02108.

PC Yellow Pages (Electric Bookshelf Inc., $26–$52/1,000 names). Use your computer and modem to call (900) 860-9210 and you will get a downloaded mailing list of fairly current businesses, according to specific locale and business categories. The charge goes onto your phone bill. The information includes name of firm, correct address, city, state, zip plus four, and the carrier route code. The program will tell you if you have enough names for carrier sort discount. At least 200 are necessary. Electric Bookshelf updates the list every month. Contact: Electric Bookshelf Inc., 3066 Mercer University Dr., Atlanta GA 30341; (404) 455-8763.

PC Press Assistant (Electric Bookshelf Inc., $295 and up). What we have here is clearly the ability to communicate. Electric Bookshelf has compiled a data base of 5,000 names, addresses, and fax numbers of magazines, newspapers, radio stations, television stations, and syndicated columnists. The software not only contains the contact information but when used in conjunction with a JT Fax Board can send your press releases to the fax machines of the selected media contact. The software comes packaged with a JT Fax Board for $495. (The cost, sans board, is $295.) Contact: Electric Bookshelf Inc., 3066 Mercer University Dr., Atlanta GA 30341; (404) 455-8763.

Direct Mail Copy that Sells by Hershell Gordon Lewis (Prentice-Hall, $12.95). The author lets the title demonstrate that he knows what he's talking about. Better than that, the book delivers the title's promise. Contact: Prentice-Hall, Route 9W, Englewood Cliffs NJ 07632.

Entertainment Marketing Newsletter (EPM Communications, $275/yr). The eight-page monthly *epm REPORT* covers the bridge between entertainment and marketing. (Publisher Ira Mayer feels that the tie between entertainment and marketing is the hot arena of the 1990s.) The newsletter talks both to entertainment companies that market and nonentertainment companies that use links to entertainment for marketing. It covers the entertainment media—everything from consumer electronics to film, video, cable, broadcast TV, and radio. It covers what's going on in such areas as the use of videocassettes to sell automobiles; mall tours by celebrities; sponsorship of entertainment events; placement of products in films; rebates, premiums, and coupons (as they relate to the entertainment industry); interactive 900 telephone numbers. Contact: EPM Communications, 488 E. 18th St., Brooklyn NY 11226-6702; (718) 469-9330.

Secrets from a Media Master (Films for the Humanities, $249–$699). Here are three tutorial videotapes: "Guerilla Media," "Media in Politics," and "Secrets of Effective Radio Advertising" by Tony Schwartz. They are drawn from Schwartz's thirty years of media experience. Each tape stands alone, but the collection definitely equals a postgraduate degree. In "Guerilla Media," he shows how to use unorthodox methods and thinking to overcome media indifference. "Media in Politics" obviously focuses on the political arena. He presents an understanding of how electronic media works. He shows, using a casebook approach, how to work with this understanding for the benefit of a candidate or a cause. In his radio advertising tape he shares his discoveries about how to make the most of this economical and effective medium. The tapes ($249 each) are sold as a set for $699. Organizations may be able to rent the individual tapes for $75 each. Contact: Films for the Humanities (800) 257-5126; in NJ (609) 452-1128.

Getting on the Air (Broadcast Interview Source, $225). Did you ever wonder how every radio talk show and every daily newspaper across America can round up just the right expert to give background on a suddenly breaking news story or special event? Well, neither did I. Nevertheless, it's good to know that you might be that expert. The *Directory of Experts, Authorities and Spokespersons* lists profiles of people who have something to share. The carefully controlled circulation book goes out twice a year to more than 5,000 selected media people. (Most are with newspapers or broadcast outlets.) Currently, each 480-page edition holds listings from 869 entities: Fortune 500 companies and public interest groups, as well as independent experts. A number of organizations have more than one spokesperson listed. In all, the directory lists about 2,000 experts. To be listed for one year, you pay $225. This buys a 50-word profile. (You can buy as much as a full-page ad for $768.) Being listed only makes sense if your entry attracts newspaper editors and broadcast producers. They look for topics tied to news, trends, and topical features. If you have to explain why what you do is important, the chances are that this investment would not be good for you. Contact: Broadcast Interview Source, 2233 Wisconsin Ave. NW Suite 406, Washington DC 20007-4104; (202) 333-4904.

Power Media Selects by Alan Caruba (Broadcast Interview Source, $166.50). This is a listing of media names and addresses (print and broadcast) to whom you can direct your public relations efforts. It is a special list because it spotlights the print and electronic journalists other media people often turn to for inspiration. Caruba used as his standard those media outlets that "actually influence other media in spotting and setting trends." For example, he lists those columnists who regularly get picked up by national syndicates. He also cites certain influential trade magazines and newsletters that tend to be invisible to the general public. In the case of large news-gathering organizations, such as the *New York Times,* he pinpoints to whom different types of stories should go. Thus, no press release need be buried in the potter's field of interoffice mail. It is a broad-based directory in that it includes leading newspapers, regional magazines, newswires and syndicates, columnists, and syndicated talk shows. The objectives of *Power Media Selects,* according to Caruba, "are to let you know who has clout, and to allow you to create a national PR campaign out of one book." Updates will be available throughout the year. Contact: Broadcast Interview Source, 2233 Wisconsin Ave. NW Suite 406, Washington DC 20007-4104; (202) 333-4904.

Professional Selling, 3rd ed., by B. Robert Anderson (Prentice-Hall). Written as a textbook, *Professional Selling* talks to the true student in each of us. Anderson's skills and experience as a marketing and management consultant shine through. He gives a thorough grounding in situations, attitudes, and philosophy, and the accent always is on the word *professional.*

ORGANIZATIONS/SERVICES

Direct Marketing Association (DMA). The DMA is the trade association for businesses involved in the selling of products and services by telephone and/or mail. The DMA is a good resource, even if you're not a member. If you need access to a direct marketing specialist in such areas as mailing lists, advertising agencies, and printing, the DMA will refer you to appropriate members. The advantages of membership can make joining a wise business decision, but the dues are hefty for the average home officer. The least expensive membership fee is $650/year. The prime benefit is information. You can get access to up-to-date insights and techniques used by the big guys. There's the full complement of seminars and publications. DMA has a marvelous research library that includes examples of award-winning campaigns, which can be lent to members. There are special-interest groups called councils that are devoted to the concerns of specific segments of the direct marketing industry. DMA runs an extensive lobbying effort. Contact: Direct Marketing Association, 6 E. 43rd St., New York NY; (212) 689-4977.

Marketing/Public Relations Consultant (JSL). Judith S. Lederman brings a solid background to her enterprise. Although she is a knowledgeable generalist, she is considered a specialist in electronic and health food products. Contact: Judith S. Lederman, 100 Cedar St., Dobbs Ferry NY 10522; (914) 693-4103.

Public Relations Consultant (Wes Thomas). As has been documented in other chapters, Wes Thomas specializes in public relations for leading-edge companies in the computer industry. He is smart and funny and an experienced guide who can take new technology enterprises through the media mine field. Contact: Wes Thomas Public Relations, P.O. Box 598, East Northport NY 11731; (516) 266-1652.

INDEX

Page numbers in *italics* refer to illustrations.